AGRARIAN QUESTIONS

OXFORD IN INDIA READINGS

Themes in Economics

GENERAL EDITORS
- Kaushik Basu
- Prabhat Patnaik

AGRARIAN QUESTIONS

Edited by
KAUSHIK BASU

OXFORD
UNIVERSITY PRESS

OXFORD
UNIVERSITY PRESS

YMCA Library Building, Jai Singh Road, New Delhi 110 001

Oxford University Press is a department of the University of Oxford. It furthers the
University's objective of excellence in research, scholarship, and education
by publishing worldwide in

Oxford New York

Auckland Cape Town Dar es Salaam Hong Kong Karachi Kuala Lumpur
Madrid Melbourne Mexico City Nairobi New Delhi Shanghai Taipei Toronto

With offices in

Argentina Austria Brazil Chile Czech Republic France Greece Guatemala
Hungary Italy Japan Poland Portugal Singapore South Korea Switzerland
Thailand Turkey Ukraine Vietnam

Oxford is a registered trademark of Oxford University Press
in the UK and in certain other countries

Published in India
by Oxford University Press, New Delhi

First published 1994
Oxford India Paperbacks 1997
Second impression 2010

ISBN-13: 978-019-564192-9
ISBN-10: 0-19-564192-2

Published by Oxford University Press
YMCA Library Building, Jai Singh Road, New Delhi 110001

Note from the General Editors

As economics advances rapidly and becomes both more mathematical and statistically founded, the need arises to interpret its general principles in the context of specific economies. In India, students are taught the latest models but it is usually left to them or the rare teacher to relate the models to the Indian context. The present series is an attempt to rectify this lacuna. Each book in this series presents the latest developments in a field and enunciates these in the context of the Indian economy.

The series was conceived with senior undergraduate and postgraduate students in mind. The aim is to provide accurate and interesting books with contributions from leading economists. While each book has a volume editor, we—the general editors—work with the volume editors in order to try and maintain some common norms and standards for the series as a whole.

Initially there was a third general editor, the late Sukhamoy Chakravarty. He was actively involved in the planning of the first few books in this series; and was a great source of inspiration to us till the last days of his life.

Kaushik Basu
Prabhat Patnaik

Contents

Contributors

KAUSHIK BASU
   Chief Economic Adviser, Government of India, and Cornell University, Ithaca

A. VAIDYANATHAN
   Madras Institute of Development Studies, Madras

ASHOK RUDRA
   (formerly at) Viswa Bharati University, Shantiniketan

NIRVIKAR SINGH
   University of California, Santa Cruz

SHUBHASHIS GANGOPADHYAY
   India Development Foundation, Gurgaon

UTSA PATNAIK
   (formerly at) Jawaharlal Nehru University, Delhi

J. MOHAN RAO
   University of Massachusetts, Amherst

Agrarian Economic Relations: Theory and Experience

KAUSHIK BASU

1. INTRODUCTION

Though interest in the analysis of agrarian economic relations goes back to the classic doctrines of political economy of the eighteenth and nineteenth centuries, it is arguable that it is in the last two decades that some of the most rapid advances in this field occurred. If Adam Smith came to life in the 1960s, he would find that he could follow most of the writings on agrarian structure. He may have needed a little bit of brushing up here and there (depending on how we presume he had been spending his time since 1790) in order to read some of the papers appearing in journals but, by and large, I believe my claim would be valid. If, on the other hand, he came to life only a little later, say in 1990, the same would not be true. He would have great difficulty with the literature, which has moved on rapidly in these last years, creating new insights into share tenancy, rural credit institutions, and technological progress.

There are two reasons for this. The advances in pure economic theory in recent years have been such as to be applicable to down-to-earth areas, such as agrarian economics. Secondly, detailed empirical research by both economists and anthropologists have brought to light a variety of institutional and factual details of rural life in less developed economies. Explaining these has created intellectual challenges and these, in turn, have provoked research. One of the most striking features of the earlier writings in this field is the extent to which these were 'fact-proof'. This was especially true when it came to Third World rural economies. Alfred Marshall, who was usually very well-versed in the facts of economic life in industrialized nations, never fussed too much when it came to making observations on economic life in the Third World. This was true of many others, including writers based in less developed economies.

This has changed sharply in the last one or two decades. In providing an empirical base for the theoretical research, Indian economists have played a major role. For instance, among the earliest studies on factor-market interlinkage in backward agrarian markets are the papers by Bharadwaj and Das (1975) and Bardhan and Rudra (1978).

Before that, Bharadwaj in 1974 and Bhaduri in 1973 had talked about interlinkage. But I am disinclined to treat these two references as contributions to interlinkage theory. In Bharadwaj (1974) interlinkage is simply mentioned without any supporting empirical evidence or theory. Likewise in Bhaduri (1973) interlinkage is a 'given'. Its empirical or theoretical basis is not discussed because Bhaduri's focus lay elsewhere: to use the assumption of interlinkage to derive an explanation of technological stagnation in certain agrarian economies.[1] The real precursor of Bharadwaj and Das (1975) and Bardhan and Rudra (1978) is the research in anthropology which held that it is the *multiplex* relation between agents which is the hallmark of primitive economies.[2] The theoretical literature on interlinkage emerged in response to these empirical findings and kept growing through the eighties and after: Braverman and Stiglitz (1982), Basu (1983, 1987), Bardhan (1984), Braverman and Guasch (1984), Gupta (1987), Ray and Sengupta (1989), Madan (1989), Basu and Bell (1991), Anant and Mukherji (1992), and Gangopadhyay (1994), to mention just a few.

The modern study of agrarian relations is one area where theoretical and empirical work have blended extremely well. In response to the theoretical research of the eighties began a second round of empirical research (Janakarajan, 1986; Sarap, 1990, 1991; Swaminathan, 1991), which was now more focused because it had a theoretical base which the work of the seventies did not have. This second wave of empirical research has given us plenty of micro insights into institutions and mores of agrarian economic relations.[3]

On sharecropping, credit markets, labour markets including bondage,

---

[1]Bhaduri's theory, briefly, and more recent work on technological stagnation, in detail, are critically examined in Singh (1994). For a different approach to this problem see Basu (1989b).

[2]The relevant anthropological writings are surveyed in Bardhan (1980).

[3]For a discussion of some of these, see Platteau and Abraham (1987) and Raj (1988).

a large literature has emerged from India. In what follows I shall recount some of these, selecting topics somewhat idiosyncratically reflecting my own interests and concentrating on themes where new *theoretical* insights have occurred.

This literature, though significant, would not have been as important as it is, if it had continued creating little models within its boundaries and having these empirically tested. The reason why this literature is exciting is that in recent years it seems to have stumbled upon some deep questions which lie at the boundary of economics, politics, and anthropology. Issues like power, coercion, and freedom are unavoidable in this terrain. But these topics are extremely difficult to formalize and theorize about. Yet in the recent literature on agrarian economic relations one sees some initial attempt to grapple with these. In this essay I wish to address some of these open-ended questions.

I want to however begin by treading upon more conventional grounds. So let me take up a subject which is theoretically very interesting, to wit, share tenancy.

2. SHARE TENANCY

If dispassionate discourse is the hallmark of science, the writings of political economists on share tenancy would have to be treated as a far cry from science. For reasons which I find difficult to comprehend, this subject seems to have touched an emotional chord in many, giving rise to both compassion and fury. John Stuart Mill (1848) and Higgs (1894) wrote admiringly of the system. On the other hand the Marquis de Mirabeau's observation (quoted in Higgs, 1894) that share tenancy is a 'deplorable method of cultivation, the daughter of necessity and mother of misery', sounds like the first line of a street fight.

The early wisdom on share tenancy, based on the writings of Smith (1776) and Marshall (1920), was that share tenancy is an inefficient system. The argument is easy to recapture. A share tenancy or sharecropping contract is by definition one in which the tenant promises to give the landlord a *fraction*, r, of the total output. The fraction is decided in advance and, it has been seen empirically, that it tends to be around 0.5.

Now assume, as is often the case, that it is the tenant who has to decide what input, like fertilizer, pesticides, etc., to use and he is the one who incurs the input costs. Assuming that r is 0.5, note that if through some new input the output increases by more than the cost of the input, it may still not be in the interest of the tenant to apply the input since, under share tenancy, the tenant does not get the *full* additional output but only half of it. Hence, unless the value of the additional output is at least double the cost of the new input, the input will be rejected by the tenant. Hence, on land given to share tenancy, the application of inputs—labour, fertilizer and other things—will tend to be sub-optimal. This was the essence of the Marshallian critique.

The charge of inefficiency is however not the only one against share tenancy. It has a corollary according to which it is irrational for a landlord to lease out his land on *share* contract instead of a *fixed-rent* contract or wage contract. The argument is this. Suppose a landlord switches to a fixed-rent contract, that is, one where the tenant pays a fixed amount of rent—this may be in cash or kind. Now since the tenant will get the full benefits of additional inputs used, he will apply more inputs. Hence, under fixed rent the total output from the same amount of land will be higher. If the landlord sets the fixed rent at a level such that the tenant earns whatever he used to earn (on average) under share tenancy, clearly the landlord will be better off. To sum up the argument: note that under a fixed-rental contract the total output is greater than under sharecropping. If the tenant's income is the same under both systems, the landlord's income, which is total output minus tenant's earning, must be greater under the fixed-rental arrangement.

QED.

Following this argument, the economists of the earlier part of this century set out to urge landlords to be rational and to switch over to the fixed-rental system. But by the seventies doubts began to arise. Instead of being committed to the Marshallian model of tenancy or its variants and treating rural landlords as irrational, perhaps we should rethink our model. Perhaps rural landlords are not foolish or irrational but it is our model which is missing out on some essential feature of reality and thereby wrongly showing up the landlord who gives his land to a *share* tenant as irrational. This is indeed the current view of share tenancy. And from the mid-seventies the focus of the share tenancy literature has shifted over to showing why sharecropping may indeed be the dominant tenurial arrangement where it occurs.

This has however turned out to be a hard area of research. The economist's ingenuity seems to have found its match in the rural landlord's alleged 'low cunning'. Some of the difficulties of theorizing on this I have described in Basu (1984, 1990) and I shall not dwell on them here. Let me instead explain a somewhat unusual line of theorizing I have attempted in Basu (1992) to explain the prevalence of share tenancy. The model I built is based on some casual empirical material gathered by me during field work in the village of Nawadih in the Giridih District of Bihar.

3. LIMITED LIABILITY IN AGRARIAN RELATIONS

The model requires one critical assumption, namely the *limited liability axiom*. The limited liability axiom (in this context) says that if after a landlord and a tenant agree to a contract there is a natural disaster which renders the crop yield sufficiently low, the tenant will have the right not to pay the full amount of the rent that he was supposed to pay.

Whereas the limited liability axiom has been extensively used in other areas (see, among others, Stiglitz and Weiss, 1981; Brealey and Myers, 1988) including, though more rarely, in the study of agrarian relations (see Kotwal, 1985; Shetty, 1988), its importance as an explanation of the existence of share tenancy seems to have gone unrecognized. But before turning to that I wish to dwell on its empirical validity.

Systematic data on this is difficult to find but casual empiricism—primarily by talking to individual farmers and also on some occasions to sons of farmers who have abandoned the paternal profession to become academics—suggests that the axiom is true. There are reasons to believe this axiom has also been historically valid. Recent research by Atchi Reddy (1990) has unearthed a large number of tenancy contracts from Nellore district dating back to the first half of the nineteenth century. This rich data source lends support to the belief that limited liability and bankruptcy clauses are not primarily the preserve of twentieth century industrialized nations but were often formally written into tenancy contracts in rural India.

Let me quote two examples from Atchi Reddy's rich data source. On 21 November 1834, Konderaju Parvathamma signed a tenancy agreement, *maktha kaul*, to lease her land to Bandela Pitchivadu. After specifying little details like 'you should cart the paddy to my residence in Nellore town for which the hire charges are Rs 1.00', the landlady goes on to state: 'In case of total failure of the crops due to lack of rains or floods, the tenant need not pay the rent but only the land revenue Rs 9.00'. Likewise when in 1868, Mula Anki Reddy leased out his 20.5 acres to Malireddy Ramireddy, the tenancy agreement said that 'He [the tenant] need not pay us anything in years of severe famines . . . '.

Now assume that the limited liability clause underlies all contracts. That is, no matter what contract is used, the tenant has the right to renege on making payment if the harvest fails totally.[4] Notice that, given such an assumption, the tenant will have a tendency to select riskier projects because the failure of a project does not hurt the tenant as much as it would in the absence of the limited liability axiom. Since such risk-taking will go against the landlord's interest, the landlord will try to devise a contract which steers the tenant to choose less risky projects and thereby minimizes the tension between the landlord's and the tenant's interests. If we consider the spectrum of contracts from share tenancy to fixed-rent tenancy, via all mixtures of the two, it can be shown that it is share tenancy that minimizes this tension.

From this explanation of share tenancy some testable propositions emerge.

1. Share tenancy is more likely in areas where output is weather-dependent.

2. It will also be more likely in areas where technology is relatively fixed in coefficients, that is, there is not much scope for substitution between land and other factors.

3. Share tenancy will tend to wither away as a region becomes well off because the limited liability clause will then not have much bite since everybody will have enough buffer wealth not to be able to invoke the bankruptcy cover in the event of harvest failures.

4.   CREDIT MARKETS

Closely related to the subject of land tenure is that of rural credit

---

[4]Strictly speaking the assumption could be more catholic requiring that *everybody*—that is, the tenant or the landlord—is allowed to forego his part of the contract if his wealth drops below a certain level. This assumption coupled with the assumption that the landlord is wealthy and has a sufficient buffer against natural disasters leads to my limited liability axiom.

markets. In Bhaduri's (1973) model of semi-feudalism it was the landlord who was also the moneylender. The theorist's initial intrigue with rural credit markets arose because of the high interest rates. On the face of it, this seemed to defy conventional logic. The initial attempts to understand this were in terms of the *lender's risk hypothesis*. According to this the high interest rate was essentially a compensation to the lender for the risk of default in markets where the hand of law is weak (for discussion see Bottomley, 1975; Basu, 1990). However, empirical studies revealed that default is not sufficiently high to explain interest rates as high as 120% per annum which is commonplace in rural India. Moreover, attention was drawn to the fact that not only can interest rates be very high in many backward areas but they can vary a lot.

To meet these empirical challenges more theories emerged (Bhaduri, 1977; Basu, 1983, 1984; Gangopadhyay and Sengupta, 1987) some of which tried to model the determination of interest rates and collateral prices simultaneously. However, in the study of rural credit some of the most instructive work has been in the empirical field, in particular, the micro-empirical studies like those of Nagaraj (1985), Sarap (1991), and Swaminathan (1991).

This vast empirical literature has thrown into disuse many standard analytical constructs. A legacy of a practice in advanced countries which we had happily borrowed is to report interest rates in annualized terms. Thus if someone said that he borrowed one hundred rupees with the promise to return Rs 150 after six months we would typically report this as a case of 100 per cent or 125 per cent interest rate (depending on whether we do, respectively, a simple or a compound interest computation) meaning that that is the effective annual interest rate. What recent evidence, especially the work of Nagaraj and Sarap, has revealed is what Rudra (1982) had warned long ago—that an annualized rate may be quite meaningless in the rural context. Here what matters is *not* the length of time for which credit is borrowed but other things like whether harvest occurs between the time of borrowing and the time of repayment. This is most clearly highlighted in the case of what in Karnataka is called a *holi* loan. For such a loan the amount of interest does not depend on when the money was borrowed as long as it is repaid immediately after the harvest.

Though there have been theoretical attempts to model the role of time (see Basu, 1989a) in credit transactions, there is considerable scope here for theory to catch up with the empirical findings. What we need to do is to model the relationship between rural seasonality and credit market institutions and rates.

Another complex problem is the relation between a person's political clout and credit terms and conditions. This comes out very clearly in the emergent literature on formal credit and the relation between formal and informal credit (for a recent theoretical model, see Gupta, Saha, and Sen, 1991). This also raises the question: How effective has government intervention been? On the face of it the impact of government seems impressive. The percentage of rural credit that comes from the formal sector, that is, from cooperatives and banks as opposed to the moneylender, has grown from 7.2 per cent in 1951 to 61.2 per cent in 1981.

However, once we scrape beneath these macro statistics, the scenario does not look quite as encouraging. Who gets the formal-sector credit? Do the rich and the poor get it on equal terms? Who are the major defaulters?

It is now well known that a bulk of the institutional or formal credit goes to the larger farmers. This was quite evident during my visits to the village of Nawadih in Bihar and it shows up in virtually all studies. One reason for this is the banker's legitimate need to ensure that the borrower has a fixed address, can demonstrate the need for production loan as opposed to consumption loan, and possesses marketable assets. Since it will be the rich farmers who can ensure these conditions, they corner much of the formal credit. But in addition to these reasons, there is the issue of nexus between the banker and influential large farmer. The farmer uses his contacts and influence to corner the bulk of the institutional credit. Moreover, given his power he gets it on better terms. This comes out very clearly from Sarap's study of villages in Orissa's Sambalpur district. He finds, for instance, that the bureaucratic delay that a borrower has to face in getting a formal loan is inversely related to the size of the borrower's landholding and that the transactions cost for a small loan is greater than that for a large loan.

Who are the defaulters? It is widely believed that it is the small farmers who default most because they live on the borderline and are frequently too poor to repay. Sarap's study confirms what Lipton

(1976) reports from other parts of the world, that the largest borrowers are the largest defaulters. Let me present here a detail (with figures rounded to integers) of Sarap's (1991) Table 3.6.

TABLE 1

Size of borrower's holding in acres	Overdues as % of total loan outstanding by the group	% of loan defaulted by the group of total loan defaulted
Up to 2.5	76	11
2.5–5.0	54	16
5.0–10.0	19	11
10.0 and above	81	62

As column 1 of Table 1 shows, default behaviour seems to be U-shaped with the smallest and largest farmers being the big defaulters. This seems to confirm Bhaduri's (1973) view of compulsory behaviour for the poor and voluntary for the rich. It is difficult to see the large farmers as being *compelled* to default because of poverty. Moreover, even if this happens in one or two years, surely a big farmer should recover his equilibrium and pay off his dues soon. But what does the data show? It shows that 42 per cent of the total loan outstanding against large farmers, that is those with more than 10 acres of land, was oustanding for more than 5 years.

Column 2 shows that a large proportion of the total default is that incurred by the large farmer.

The consequence of all this is easy to see. Since formal credit commands a much lower interest rate than informal credit—indeed the difference can be as much as 100 per cent—and the bulk of the formal credit is cornered by the richer farmers and the bulk of the default is also by them, it is very likely that far from contributing to equity, the large increase in formal credit has actually exacerbated the inequalities of rural economies.

This raises a rather tricky question regarding government intervention and markets. That markets often fail is beyond question. But is it axiomatic that where markets fail, the government ought to step in? The answer to this seems to me to be no. Much depends on the causes of market failure and the manner in which the government intervention occurs. It is possible that the large landlords will be able to twist the government machinery to their advantage. And in some situations they may be able to do it to the extent where they are actually better off in the presence of government than in the absence.

This is *not* an argument for government *non*-intervention, but a reminder that *any* government intervention need not be a cure for a market failure. In designing an intervention it is not enough to think of the economics of an ideally implemented plan but also to take account of its possible loopholes and political malleability of the scheme since there will invariably be powerful agents who will try to bend policies to their advantage.

A study of formal credit institutions suggests that large landlords bend schemes to their advantage. Economic power translates into political influence and this can, in turn, aid the further amassing of economic power. This brings me to one of the most vexing issues in economics: the interface between economics and politics and the role of power.

5. VIOLENCE, TRIADS AND POWER

The relentless pursuit of self-interest by individuals cannot in itself explain the functioning of markets and society. This is a simple enough truth which is widely misunderstood primarily by economists but also by sociologists and other social scientists. The misunderstanding has frequently led them into erroneous arguments. Let me illustrate this with an example.

Why do peasants return borrowed money to the moneylenders? Several reasons have been discussed in the literature but one which is intriguing to me is the 'threat of violence'. It has been argued by many that powerful landlords and moneylenders often use the threat of physical violence to ensure repayments from borrowers. My contention is not with this fact but with the presumption that such an interaction is explained in terms of individual rationality or self-seeking behaviour. The landlord or moneylender knows that by threatening violence he can get back his money and the poor borrower pays back because he knows that the violence is more painful than the satisfaction of holding on to the money. On the face of it, all action appears to be inspired by self-interest. But there is a serious flaw in this argument. If it is true that the borrower repays the money only because the cost of the threatened violence is too much, a serious question arises about the rationality of the moneylender. The question is: Why does he lend money? He should simply threaten violence and collect the 'repayment' without having lent in the first place. Hence, if there are no norms and social custom guiding human behaviour, it is not clear that violence in itself can be used to explain why certain kinds of transactions can take place.

An essential element in understanding why one agent is able to control another and exercise power is the triad (see Basu, 1986, 1990). An interaction is *triadic* if the transaction between *i* and *j* can influence and get influenced by an uninvolved third party. In a rural set-up if one peasant, call him P, turns down the landlord's offer, it is entirely possible that the cost to peasant P will not only be that of having no transactions with the landlord but his transactions with other agents can also get disrupted. If the landlord threatens other peasants that if they transact with P the landlord will not transact with them then it is quite possible that in the event of P rebuffing the landlord, P will face ostracism from not just the landlord but other agents as well. In the face of such a large threat he may prefer to take up the landlord's offer even if it is very unattractive from his point of view. Such interpersonal fears among poor peasants can be used by a landlord to exercise extortion and prolong his control over the local economy.

This viewpoint has an interesting implication for the notion of free and unfree labour. One of the clearest definitions of this was given by Daniel Thorner. I quote Thorner from Rudra (1994):

A free labourer is one who is able to accept or reject the conditions and wages offered by the employer . . . Once having taken a job he can decide to give notice and quit . . .

An unfree, or bond labourer, by contrast, is one whose bargaining power is virtually non-existent, or has been surrendered. Such a labourer does not possess the right or has yielded the right to refuse to work under the terms set by his master . . .

Though Rudra (1994) fully recognizes the problems of a dichotomous definition and goes on to discuss 'different *kinds* of unfree labour', I wish to draw attention to the same difficulty from a different angle.

Suppose when a labourer quits a landlord's job the landlord clarifies to the labourer that he (that is, the landlord) will never again employ the labourer. Is the labourer free? The answer in terms of Thorner's definition seems to be a clear yes.

Next suppose when the labourer quits the landlord's job, he tells the labourer that he will never again employ the labourer and he tells the village merchant that he will not buy merchandise from his shop if the merchant sells goods to this labourer. In other words we have a case of triadic power discussed above. In such a case, is the labourer free? The answer is no longer obvious.

Moreover, I can go on creating more and more extreme examples where the landlord makes the cost of quitting more and more onerous to the labourer by ensuring that he will not be able to find jobs with other small employers, will not be able to rent a place to stay, etc. What makes this conceptually difficult is that the landlord achieves this not through any extra-legal means but by simply exercising his own right not to trade with the merchant, not to deal with the small employers, not to transact with the house owners, etc.

Under such circumstances it is no longer clear what it means to say that a person is free to quit. Hence, Thorner's definitions seem to run into difficulty. But what this demonstrates most clearly is that we are on a terrain which is conceptually very hard. This is where the seemingly mundane empirical and theoretical exercises on land tenure, credit markets, interlinkage, and bonded labour of the last couple of decades have led us to. And I have no doubt that these open-ended questions will occupy a lot of our effort in the decades to come.

6. THIS BOOK

That there is a link between the structure of agrarian economic relations and agricultural productivity and growth has long been recognized: see Kalecki (1976). A fossilized agrarian structure can impede growth; a buoyant agriculture can facilitate it. Most arguments for land reform stem from a recognition of this. Yet the precise link between agrarian structure and actual agricultural growth has turned out to be elusive. Barring a few exceptions, such as Drazen and Eckstein (1988), there is no work which systematically analyses this link.

The present book tries to make amends for this lacuna in a small way. It covers some of the most important recent advances in the theory of agrarian relations, discusses these in the Indian context, and also discusses the performance of Indian agriculture. The links between these are not always fully spelt out—indeed at our current state of knowledge that would not be possible. But by bringing theory and experience between the same covers, it sets the ground for future research into this link.

In his comprehensive essay, Vaidyanathan (1994) provides an extremely valuable bird's-eye view of the actual experience of Indian agriculture since our freedom at midnight in 1947. This essay not only sets the ground for exploring the links between agricultural performance, agrarian relations, and actual economic progress, it also stands on its own as a 'reading' on or, for that matter, of the Indian agricultural experience. Vaidyanathan begins by summarizing some well-known macro-statistics concerning trends in Indian agricultural production since independence. The discussion is enriched by references to the differences between these and the pre-independence record. It is like a verbal regression analysis, complete with dummy variables. From these broad aggregates, he gradually unfolds little micro stories.

Since 1949, crop output has grown at the rate of 2.6 per cent per annum. But this figure hides an enormous diversity within. In Punjab the growth rate is over 6 per cent, in Tamil Nadu and Bihar less than one, and in many districts it is negative. What has happened to fluctuations in output? Have these increased or decreased over time? How much is the increase in output due to extensions in the area cultivated and how much is because of yield improvement? Vaidyanathan carefully examines these questions and then goes on to explore the role of technological and institutional changes as catalysts of growth.

Towards the end he goes on to discuss the role of agrarian relations, including the management of common property. This paves the way for the next four essays—by Ashok Rudra, Nirvikar Singh, Shubhashis Gangopadhyay, and Utsa Patnaik—which deal with a range of theoretical issues in agrarian economic relations. Some of the themes which Rudra, Singh, and Gangopadhyay discuss have been commented on in the earlier sections of this essay.

Utsa Patnaik (1994) begins by distinguishing between what she calls 'neo-classical' and 'Marxist' theories. She traces the fundamental differences to the *categories* of analysis, rather than the analysis itself.

She argues for the importance of locating the analysis of contracts within the relevant context of socio-economic relations. Though she couches this in the language of an outsider's critique of the mainstream, I feel that even among mainstream economists, some of the more innovative ones are aware of the importance of this venture. If there is not much evidence of this in the form of published papers and books it is because, as I tried to argue in the previous section, this is an exceedingly difficult area of research. Patnaik goes on to an interesting analysis of many of the topics, such as interlinkage, which arise elsewhere in the book, from a very different angle.

As noted at the outset of this section, the link between agriculture and our overall economic progress is important, yet not well understood. Mohan Rao's closing essay in this volume addresses this issue. It is an open-ended essay which picks up on many of the empirical and theoretical topics discussed by the other writers in this volume and leaves the reader with the provocation to think harder.

Galbraith, I seem to recall, said in the introduction to a collection of his essays that the only common thread that ran through the essays was that they were all by the same author. When I invited the six authors to contribute to this volume, I was apprehensive about giving up the possibility of even this last common thread. Agriculture is such a vast subject that it is possible for a group of authors to write a totally disparate set of papers. But, as I read through these essays, I could not help feeling that though they are disparate, they serve a very valuable purpose together which they could not have done each on its own.

REFERENCES

ANANT, T.C.A. and B. MUKHERJI (1992), Theories of interlinkage in agrarian markets: a critical appraisal, in K. Basu and P. Nayak, eds., *Development Policy and Economic Theory*, Oxford University Press, Delhi.

ATCHI REDDY, M. (1990), Tenancy in Nellore District 1833–1984, mimeo, Hyderabad.

BARDHAN, P.K. (1980), Interlocking factor markets and agrarian development: A review, *Oxford Economic Papers*, 32.

——— (1984), *Land, Labour and Rural Poverty*, Columbia University Press and Oxford University Press, Delhi.

BARDHAN, P.K., ed., (1989), *The Economic Theory of Agrarian Institutions*, Clarendon Press, Oxford.

BARDHAN, P.K. and A. RUDRA (1978), Interlinkage of land, labour and credit relations: An analysis of village survey data in East India, *Economic and Political Weekly*, Annual Number, 13.

BASU, K. (1983), The emergence of isolation and interlinkage in rural markets, *Oxford Economic Papers*, 35.

_____ (1984), *The Less Developed Economy: A Critique of Contemporary Theory*, Basil Blackwell, Oxford.

_____ (1986), One kind of power, *Oxford Economic Papers*, 38.

_____ (1987), Disneyland monopoly, interlinkage and usurious interest rates, *Journal of Public Economics*, 34.

_____ (1989a), Rural credit markets: The structure of interest rates, exploitation and efficiency, in Bardhan, ed., *Agrarian Institutions*.

_____ (1989b), Technological stagnation, tenurial laws and adverse selection, *American Economic Review*.

_____ (1990), *Agrarian Structure and Economic Underdevelopment*, Harwood Press.

_____ (1992), Limited liability and existence of share tenancy, *Journal of Development Economics*, 38.

BASU, K. and C. BELL (1991), Fragmented duopoly: theory and an illustration from agriculture, *Journal of Development Economics*, 36.

BHADURI, A. (1973), A study in agricultural backwardness under semi-feudalism, *Economic Journal*, 83 (reprinted in *Unconventional Economic Essays: Selected Papers of Amit Bhaduri*, OUP, Delhi, 1993).

_____ (1977), On the formation of usurious interest rates in backward agriculture, *Cambridge Journal of Economics*, 1 (reprinted in *Unconventional Economic Essays, Selected Papers of Amit Bhaduri*, OUP, Delhi,1993).

BHARADWAJ, K. (1974), *Production Conditions in Indian Agriculture*, Cambridge University Press, Cambridge.

BHARADWAJ, K. and P.K. DAS (1975), Tenurial conditions and mode of exploitation: A study of some villages in Orissa, *Economic and Political Weekly*, Annual Number, 10.

BOTTOMLEY, A. (1975), Interest rate determination in underdeveloped areas, *American Journal of Agricultural Economics*, 57.

BRAVERMAN, A. and L. GUASCH (1984), Capital requirements, screening and interlinked sharecropping and credit contracts, *Journal of Development Economics*, 14.

BRAVERMAN, A. and J. STIGLITZ (1982), Sharecropping and the interlinking of agrarian markets, *American Economic Review*, 72.

BREALEY, R.A. and S.C. MYERS (1988), *Principles of Corporate Finance*, 3rd edition, McGraw-Hill, New York.

DRAZEN, A. and Z. ECKSTEIN (1988), On the organization of rural markets and the process of economic development, *American Economic Review*, 78.

GANGOPADHYAY, S. (1994), Some issues in interlinked agrarian markets, this volume.

GANGOPADHYAY, S. and K. SENGUPTA (1987), Usury and collateral pricing: towards an alternative explanation, *Cambridge Journal of Economics*, 11.

GUPTA, M.R. (1987), A nutrition-based theory of interlinkage, *Journal of Quantitative Economics*, 3.

GUPTA, M.R., B. SAHA, and A. SEN (1991), Bribing and strategic delay: a theory of the interaction between formal and informal rural credit markets, mimeo, Indira Gandhi Institute of Development Research, Bombay.

HIGGS, A. (1894), Metayage in Western France, *Economic Journal*, 4.

JANAKARAJAN, S. (1986), Aspects of market inter-relationships in a changing agrarian economy: a case study from Tamil Nadu, Ph.D. dissertation, University of Madras.

KALECKI, M. (1976), *Essays on Developing Economies*, Harvester Press.

KOTWAL, A. (1985), Consumption credit and agricultural tenancy, *Journal of Development Economics*, 18.

LIPTON, M. (1976), Agricultural finance and rural credit in poor countries, *World Development*, 4.

MADAN, V. (1989), Efficiency wages and interlinked markets, *Journal of Quantitative Economics*, 5.

MARSHALL, A. (1920), *Principles of Economics*, 8th edition, Macmillan, London.

MILL, JOHN S. (1848), *Principles of Political Economy*, J.W. Parker.

NAGARAJ, K. (1985), Marketing structures for paddy and arecanut in South Kanara, in K.N. Raj, N. Bhattacharya, S. Guha, and S. Padhi, eds., *Essays on the Commercialization of Indian Agriculture*, Oxford University Press, Delhi.

PATNAIK, U. (1994), Tenancy and accumulation, this volume.

PLATTEAU, J.P. and A. ABRAHAM, (1987), An enquiry into quasi-credit systems in traditional fisherman communities, *Journal of Development Studies*, 23.

RAJ, K.N. (1988), Mobilization of the rural economy and the Indian experience, in G. Ranis and T.P. Schultz, eds., *The State of Development Economics*, Basil Blackwell, Oxford.

RAO, J.M. (1994), Agriculture in economic growth: handmaiden or equal partner?, this volume.

RAY, D. and K. SENGUPTA (1989), Interlinkages and the pattern of competition, in Bardhan, ed., *Agrarian Institutions*.

RUDRA, A. (1982), *Indian Agricultural Economics: Myths and Realities*, Allied Publishers, Delhi.

____ (1994), Unfree labour and Indian agriculture, this volume,

SARAP, K. (1990), Interest rate determination in backward agriculture: the role of economic and extra-economic control, *Cambridge Journal of Economics*, 14.

____ (1991), *Interlinked Agrarian Markets in Rural India*, Sage, New Delhi.

SHETTY, S. (1988), Limited liability, wealth differences and tenancy contracts in agrarian economics, *Journal of Development Economics*, 29.

SINGH, N. (1994), Some aspects of technological change and innovation in agriculture, this volume.

SMITH, A. (1776), *The Wealth of Nations*, Cadel and Strahan.

STIGLITZ, J. and A. WEISS (1981), Credit rationing with imperfect information, *American Economic Review*, 71.

SWAMINATHAN, M. (1991), Segmentation, collateral undervaluation and the rate of interest in agrarian credit markets, *Cambridge Journal of Economics*, 15.

VAIDYANATHAN, A. (1994), Performance of Indian agriculture since independence, this volume.

Performance of Indian Agriculture since Independence

A. VAIDYANATHAN*

The most striking feature of India's agricultural performance in the post-independence era is the sharp increase in the rate of output growth compared to earlier decades. During the first half of this century crop output is estimated to have grown at best around 1 per cent a year with some estimates placing it as low as 0.4 per cent a year (Blyn, 1966; Heston, 1977). Between 1949 and 1985, by contrast, the trend growth rate averaged around 2.6 per cent a year And despite the fact that since independence population has been growing more than twice as fast as in the previous decades, there was still a margin, though modest, for improvement in agricultural production per capita; in earlier decades agricultural growth fell short of population growth. Furthermore, while most of the growth prior to 1950 came from an extension of cultivated area, the major part of the growth since then has come from higher productivity per unit area.

The realized growth during the past four decades is, however, significantly below the target of around 4 per cent per annum visualized by successive five year plans. Statistical tests do not indicate any acceleration or deceleration in the growth of total crop output over this period. In particular, there is no evidence of a significant quickening in the pace of overall growth following the introduction of the high yielding varieties which is supposed to have heralded the 'Green Revolution' from the mid sixties. Taking the country as a whole, it would seem that the trend growth rate of crop output since inde-

*I am grateful to K. Nagaraj for his comments and suggestions. The usual caveat applies.

pendence has remained more or less constant at around 2.6 per cent a year.

The steady growth of aggregate output at the national level masks a great deal of variation in the performance of different crops and regions. One recent study covering the period 1949–50 to 1977–8 (Srinivasan, 1979) shows that the non-food crop output has grown slightly faster than that of foodgrains. Among individual crops the average rate of output growth ranged from less than 2 per cent a year for *bajra* to a maximum of 5.7 per cent a year for wheat. Out of the 13 major crops examined, only 5 (rice, wheat, groundnut, sugarcane, and cotton) recorded growth rates higher than the average for all crops; the rest (comprising all the so-called coarse grains, pulses, jute, tea, and tobacco) posted below average growth.

Wide regional variations in growth of output, both in the aggregate and in particular crops, is another significant feature of the post-independence phase: the latest study of this phenomenon (Bhalla and Tyagi, 1989) estimates that between the early sixties and the early eighties, the growth rate at the state level ranged from less than 1 per cent per annum (in Tamil Nadu and Bihar) to over 6 per cent a year (in Punjab). It also finds that, over the same period, out of the 281 districts covered, 17 reported an absolute decline in output; 82 districts recorded a growth rate of less than 1.5 per cent a year while 23 had more than 5 per cent per annum.[1]

This uneven growth means that the distribution of increments in production is highly skewed: thus the fast-growing states in north-west India which contributed around 25 per cent of the country's total crop output in the early 1960s account for more than half the increment in national output during the subsequent two decades. Since differences in the rate of rural population growth are much less than those in

[1]It needs noting that the Bhalla–Tyagi study like several others dealing with regional variations in growth (Minhas and Vaidyanathan, 1965; Bhalla and Alagh, 1979; Mahendra Dev, 1986) are based on comparisons of output levels at different points over a time span. Given that output fluctuates widely from year to year, the estimated growth rates as well as the rankings of different regions in terms of growth rates are not as reliable as those based on properly-fitted trend lines to the entire time series including the observations for all the years in that selected time span (see Vidya Sagar, 1980). This problem is naturally more acute for disaggregated district-level analyses, but also affects state-level analyses. Considering the importance of this, it is surprising to find so few systematic and rigorous analyses of trends in area, yield, and output using all the observations in a time series.

output, uneven output growth has aggravated regional disparities in per capita output whose coefficient of variation (across districts) is estimated to have risen progressively since the early 1960s (Mahendra Dev, 1985).

Finally, agricultural performance in the post-independence period is marked by considerable year-to-year fluctuations. This by itself is not particularly surprising, but what is significant is that fluctuations in output during the post-independence period are greater than in the first half of this century and that the fluctuations seem to be increasing over time. Sen (1967) first drew attention to the fact that during 1950–65, while output grew considerably faster than in the pre-independence decades, it was also marked by greater instability. Subsequent work (Mehra, 1981; Hazell, 1982; Rao et al., 1988) has shown that the degree of instability in the output of major crops individually and collectively during 1950–65 was markedly lower than subsequently. At the state level, however, this is not always the case. The degree of instability in foodgrains production growth is seen to be higher during 1971–85 than during the sixties only in 9 out of 17 states analysed (Rao et al., 1988).

This essay reviews the present state of our knowledge on the factors underlying the post-independence performance of Indian agriculture. The discussion is divided into three parts: We start, in the next section, with analyses aimed at assessing the contribution of area expansion, yield improvement, and crop-pattern shifts to observed changes in total crop output. The bases of these decomposition exercises, the relative importance of these elements in accounting for the growth of the total crop output actually experienced in different regions and different periods, and the insights they have to offer are discussed. This is followed by a discussion of the determinants—technological, economic, and institutional—of changes in each of the principal components of growth and, on a selective basis, the findings of available empirical studies on the subject. Systematic studies of growth experience embracing all these dimensions being rather rare, and also inherently complex, we focus in the concluding part on four strategic factors—namely irrigation, rainfed agriculture, biochemical technology, and state policy—which by any reckoning have a crucial bearing on the pace and pattern of agricultural growth.

SOURCES OF GROWTH AND FLUCTUATION

A common, and somewhat simplistic, approach to assessing the sources of growth in agricultural output is to view the latter as the product
of changes in area and changes in yield per unit area. Over the period
1950–83, while the overall crop output has grown at a more or less
constant trend rate, the area under cultivation, as well as the total
cropped area, shows a significant deceleration in growth, the pace of
deceleration in the former being more marked. Net sown area which
rose at a moderate rate during the fifties has practically levelled off in
the last decade or so. The tapering off in extension of cultivated area
is, however, compensated by an acceleration of the trends in the
average output per unit area (both net and gross). As a result while
area expansion contributed the major part of output growth in the early
fifties, yield improvement has become the more important source in
recent years.[2]

Crop-wise trends over the period 1949–77, as mentioned already,
show wide differences between crops in the relative contribution of
area and yield changes to output growth. Taking the period as a whole,
the relatively faster growth of non-food crops compared to foodgrains
was entirely due to the faster growth of the area sown of the former;
area growth also accounted for a higher proportion of output growth of
non-food crops (60 per cent) compared to foodgrains (35–40 per cent).
Crops experiencing high trend growth in output also show a tendency

---

[2]Two trend lines—one implying a constant growth rate and another to capture the
possibility of a varying growth rate—were fitted to production, area, and yield series. The
constant growth rate fitted the production series best while the quadratic form fitted the area
and the yield series better.

The parameters of the best-fitting functions for 1949–50 to 1983–4 were

Dependent Variable	Coefficient		
	$\log t$	$\log T^2$	$\bar{R}^2$
Production	0.02586		0.944
Net area sown	0.01187	-2.13^{-4}	0.959
Yield per net area sown	0.014	$+2.13^{-4}$	0.936
Gross area sown	0.0175	-2.694^{-4}	0.940
Yield per gross area sown	6.238^{-3}	$+2.361^{-4}$	0.885

All coefficients are statistically significant at the 1% level.

to record a higher trend rate in both area and yield. For all crops, except wheat, the area sown has shown a distinct tendency to slow down since 1967–8. Nor is there any strong evidence of acceleration in yield improvement except for wheat.[3]

There are few systematic analyses of trends in area, yield, and output of crops (either individually or taken together) across regions. What we do have are studies of the changes in these indicators between different points of time during the last three to four decades. The latest and most up-to-date among them (Bhalla and Tyagi, 1989) shows that the rate of change in area and yield of all crops, as well as their relative importance in accounting for the growth of total output between the early sixties and the early eighties, varies widely across states. Yield improvement has been the more important source of output growth in most states. States experiencing more rapid growth of total output also tend to have higher rates of increase in crop output per hectare. There is not much of an association between crop area growth and output growth.[4]

The decomposition of changes in crop output into the contributions

[3]This discussion of cropwise trends is based on Srinivasan, 1979. This is one of the few systematic attempts to test whether or not there is a change in trend of output, area, and yield under major crops before and after the mid sixties. The analysis, however, covers only up to 1977–8. The results may well be different if it were extended to include subsequent years.

[4]The state-wise estimates of the average annual growth rate of area, production, and growth based on the triennial averages for the early 1960s and the early 1980s are as under:

Growth Rates (% per annum)

	Area	Output	Yield
Haryana	1.06	4.92	3.84
Himachal Pradesh	0.59	2.15	1.55
Jammu & Kashmir	0.57	4.37	3.77
Punjab	2.13	6.61	4.39
Uttar Pradesh	0.49	3.27	2.76
Assam	1.32	2.33	1.00
Bihar	0.26	0.55	0.81
Orissa	1.57	1.26	−0.31
W. Bengal	0.54	1.47	0.93
Gujarat	0.05	2.82	2.76
Madhya Pradesh	0.55	1.47	0.91
Maharashtra	0.36	2.15	1.76
Rajasthan	0.87	2.71	1.82
Andhra Pradesh	−0.02	2.40	2.42
Karnataka	−0.05	2.29	2.34
Kerala	0.86	1.64	0.78
Tamil Nadu	0.85	0.91	1.57

of area change and yield changes, while useful, is too simplistic when we are dealing with many crops and many regions whose per hectare yields and the rate of change therein differ. In such a situation the national/regional average output per unit area can be affected merely by a change in the allocation of total area among crops as well as between different geographical units comprising the nation/region without any change in the yield per hectare of individual crops in any component unit. More elaborate decomposition schemes have been devised to isolate the effect of shifts in inter-crop and inter-regional allocation of area from that of changes in the per hectare yield of individual crops *per se*.

One study published in the early 1960s estimated the relative contributions of (a) expansion in total cropped area (keeping crop pattern and yield constant), (b) changes in output due to shifts in crop patterns (keeping area and individual crop yields constant), and (c) changes in output due to changes in yield per hectare of individual crops (keeping crop area and crop patterns invariant), to the observed increase in crop output for the country as whole and in each of the major states between 1951–4 and 1958–61 (Minhas and Vaidyanathan, 1965). This study showed that for the country as a whole, approximately 45 per cent of the addition to output was accounted for by increase in total cropped area, roughly an equal proportion to pure yield increase, and a mere 8 per cent on account of crop pattern shifts. A more recent study (Ray, 1983) of the sources of change in the average annual growth rate of crop output at the national level suggests that changes in crop area became a progressively less important source of change in aggregate output, and that of crop-pattern shifts progressively more important. The contribution of yield increase rose sharply between the fifties and sixties, but did not change much in the subsequent decade. There is great variation in the relative importance of these elements across the states: during the fifties, for instance, area expansion was the major source of output growth in some states; yield improvements *per se* were the main source in some others, with crop-pattern shifts being important in a few.

Dharm Narain (1977) extended the decomposition analysis by introducing the locational shifts in the area under individual crops as an additional component. He argued, and rightly, that a 'relative shift of area under any given crop from states where its per hectare yields are low to those where they are high, would impart a rising trend to its all-India average yield even when its per hectare yield in individual states remained unchanged over time'. His analysis showed that the effect of locational shifts of crop area on national average yields was indeed significant but changing from time to time. It turns out that though the national average output per unit cropped area rose roughly at the same rate between 1952–4 and 1959–61, and between 1959–61 and 1970–2, the major part of the rise in the former period was attributable to locational shifts, while the bulk of the rise in the latter period reflects the effect of yield increase, with only a small fraction being accounted for by locational shifts. The rate of 'pure yield' increase in the sixties—the period of the Green Revolution—is then seen to be dramatically higher than in the fifties (Dharm Narain, 1977).

Unfortunately such decomposition analyses of agricultural output changes for the country as a whole or for all states are not available for more recent periods. Studies for particular states are also relatively few. We do have two major studies at the district level—one by Minhas and Vaidyanathan (1965), dealing with changes between 1951–4 and 1958–61 in 293 districts, and the other by Bhalla and Alagh (1979) covering the experience of 289 districts over the period 1962–5 to 1970–3.[5] Apart from bringing out the enormous differences across districts in the relative contributions of area expansion, crop pattern shifts, and yield improvement to observed changes in output, they also show certain patterns which are suggestive.

The Bhalla–Alagh study shows that among the high-growth districts (concentrated in Punjab, Haryana, and West UP) 'the yield effect constitutes the major and predominant component of growth' and that, 'in general, the contribution of crop pattern changes to growth is much smaller than that of yield and area'. Among the medium-growth districts, the yield effects are not as predominant: area changes exert a much stronger influence and crop-pattern changes are seen to be a relatively more important factor. Among the districts reporting a decline in output—a large number of which are in the Deccan—they noted that in most cases both area and yield fell though there were also

[5]Though the regional/district-level estimates of overall output growth have been extended by Mahendra Dev (1985) and Bhalla and Tyagi (1989) to more recent years, neither has attempted a decomposition of output changes into their component elements.

several cases where total output declined despite substantial increases in area and shifts to high-value crop patterns (Bhalla and Alagh, 1979). Overall, however, the incidence of both area and yield decline is more frequent as one moves from the high-growth districts to those with low growth or decline. Significantly, districts experiencing a decline in output are seen to have a higher relative incidence of a fall in area, a fall in average (pure) yield, and a shift to inferior crop patterns, both individually and in combination.

These findings based on changes between two discrete points in time may not necessarily be a reliable indicator of abiding trends. The patterns tend to change quite dramatically depending on which two time points are being compared. But they do point to the potential usefulness of decomposition analysis in finding out whether there are any distinct patterns of association between different components of output growth and the rate of growth. The existence of such patterns could give useful clues for a better understanding of the reasons for disparate growth.

On the nature and sources of instability in crop output there are two distinct views: one is that higher and growing instability is to be expected along with faster growth because (1) cultivation is being extended to poorer-quality lands whose yields are more sensitive to weather variations; and (2) while irrigation and improved varieties increase the yield-potential of crops by enabling plants to absorb more nutrients more efficiently, the realization of this potential depends crucially on the availability of an adequate and assured supply of soil moisture. Fluctuations in rainfall and associated variations in the quality of irrigation can, therefore, accentuate the fluctuations in yield as more fertilizers and better varieties come into vogue.

This reasoning (advocated by Sen, 1967, and Mehra, 1981) has however been contested. For though output growth of most crops shows greater instability since the mid sixties than before, growth of wheat output—which is among the fastest—has become more stable. Also there is no evidence of any systematic relation across the states, between the growth rate of crop output and the degree of instability in it (Rao et al., 1988). There is reason to believe that the observed increase in instability of crop output at the national level is due largely to a tendency towards more synchronous movements in (a) yield of different crops within each state and across states; and (b) the area and yield of particular crops. 'Increased instability has probably less to do with the improved seed/fertilizer technology than with changes in weather patterns and the more widespread use of irrigation and fertilizers at a time when the supplies of these inputs are not reliable' (Hazell, 1982).[6]

DETERMINANTS OF GROWTH

The decomposition of output growth into its principal components is a useful starting point for exploring the factors responsible for the wide divergences in growth experience between regions and between different periods.

The principal elements of the decomposition scheme are so chosen that their contributions to output growth are determined by more or less independent sets of factors. Increases in gross sown area, for instance, can be derived partly from extension of cultivation to new areas through reclamation of virgin lands or reduction of fallows and partly from increases in double cropped areas made possible by the spread of irrigation, adoption of better crop rotations and moisture conservation practices ... what happens to yields on the other hand depends entirely on the technological relation between inputs and outputs and the quantum of inputs (including fertiliser, water, seeds and labour) used. Aside from availability of irrigation, shifts in crop patterns are a function of relative prices and profitability of crops (Minhas and Vaidyanathan, 1965).

Area expansion

Taking the country as a whole, the net area sown (which is one measure of the extent of land under cultivation) in the early 1980s was some 18 per cent more than in the early 1950s. Most of this expansion took place in the fifties and sixties, there being hardly any growth since. We know in a general way that, triggered by the rapid increase in demographic pressure, cultivation was extended by reducing fallows, reclamation of cultivable wastes, encroachment of forests, pastures and village commons; that this occurred in an unregulated manner thereby aggravating problems of soil erosion, deforestation, and ecological damage which have serious long-term consequences for agricultural development. The privatization of village commons has

---

[6]Ray (1983) also comes to substantially the same conclusion.

important social consequences especially for the vulnerable segments who derive a significant part of their fuel, fodder, and even food needs from common lands.[7] The pace of expansion in cultivated land, the sources of this expansion, the processes by which it occurred, and its consequences also vary across regions. There are, however, hardly any systematic studies of these aspects.

Land use intensity

The intensity of land use has two aspects: one is the proportion of arable land which is actually cultivated during a year; and the other is the cropping intensity. The former is affected by several factors, including the extent of population pressure on land, the availability of moisture, and the state of agricultural technology. It has been shown that inter-district variations in the ratio of cultivated to arable land in east and west UP bear a significant positive correlation to demographic pressure (Ray, 1980). In Karnataka also a similar positive relation between the incidence of fallows and average size of holding (a rough index of demographic pressure) is reported (Nadkarni and Deshpande, 1979). Neither of these studies found a significant or consistent relation between the extent of rainfall and irrigation on the one hand and the intensity of land use on the other. They argue that institutional factors—including size of holdings, alternative income opportunities, relative returns to using available resources on lands of differing fertility, and incidence of absentee ownership—may be more important determinants than agro-climatic factors.

The number of times a piece of land is cropped in any given year as well as the nature and duration of crops grown is also highly variable. The ratio of gross cropped area to net cultivated area—a rough measure of the intensity with which cultivated land is utilized—varies from 1.1 in Kerala to 1.8 in Punjab. A better measure would be the number of months in a year during which crops are grown on a piece of land, but this is not used in computing land use and cropping statistics in India. How often, for how long, and which crops can be grown in a year depends partly on climate and partly on conditions of water supply: the Indian climate permits, in most parts, crop growth practically throughout the year provided moisture is available. Where

[7]See Jodha (1986 and 1990) for evidence on this aspect.

rainfall is highly seasonal and dry-period precipitation is low, only seasonal cropping is feasible in the absence of irrigation. Even with irrigation, the quantity, duration, and assurance of water supplies has a significant bearing on cropping intensity. The proponents of mechanization claim that tractorization facilitates more intensive cropping because it makes for speedier and more timely conduct of cultivation operations in the short period available between successive crops. Demographic pressure may also have a bearing on the outcome. And within these constraints, the allocation of area to different crops is affected by relative costs and returns.

Ray (1985) has explored variations in the intensity of crops using the more refined notion of 'duration of cropping per unit of cultivated area' to measure intensity. He found that districts with a higher duration of cropping per cultivated hectare generally tend to grow more crops in a year and also longer-duration crops. But the latter element is much more prominent in regions with relatively high intensity of cultivation compared to districts with low overall intensity. The study also explores the role of various plausible factors in explaining these variations. Contrary to expectation, neither the proportion of land irrigated nor the quality of irrigation, seems to be the primary (nor always even a significant) determinant of cropping intensity. Other factors (like rainfall, tractorization, labour supply) also show statistically significant association with cropping intensity, but the causal connections are far from clear. The study also highlights the fact that despite a sizeable increase in the percentage of cultivated land irrigated and/or the proportion of tubewell irrigated area (the latter being an index of the quality of irrigation), cropping intensity (and its two component elements, namely, multiple cropping and average duration of crops) shows no rise in two regions (eastern UP and Bundelkhand) and only a marginal increase in the other two (including west UP which has the highest irrigation ratio and where tubewells are most extensive).

A more recent study (Mahendra Dev, 1989) using state and district-level data for different points of time found, however, rainfall and irrigation to be the dominant factors accounting for spatial variations in the ratio of gross cropped area to net sown area. Regions with a higher rainfall, a higher irrigation ratio, and a higher ratio of gross to net irrigated area also tend to have significantly higher cropping intensity. Over time also, changes in cropping intensity are found to be correlated with the spread of irrigation but the latter's impact differs significantly between districts.

As for the effect of mechanization, the balance of evidence does not lend support to the view that tractorization has a large impact on cropping intensity (see Binswanger, 1978). Most of the studies that claim this fail to properly control inter-farm variations in respect of other factors (such as level and quality of irrigation) which have a bearing on the land-use intensity. The one careful investigation into this issue (Bina Agarwal, 1982) in Punjab—the area where mechanization had advanced the furthest—shows that it is the access to energized tube wells which makes for higher cropping intensity. After proper controlling for other differences between farms, tractorization was found not to make any significant difference.

Crop patterns
Climate, rainfall, and their seasonal patterns, soil type, quality, irrigation, and drainage all have a bearing on the type of crops which can be grown in a region. And in any given region, changes over time are also a function of changes in the extent and quality of irrigation, and the relative costs of and returns to competing crops and crop combinations. In addition, the introduction of new seed varieties often alters the optimum time for sowing and harvesting as well as the duration of individual crops. These in turn can make a significant difference to the feasible crop-sequence and combinations. Not so well recognized, but potentially important, is the effect of the expansion and improvement of the transport and credit networks in widening and integrating the market for agricultural produce, and thereby stimulating greater regional specialization in cropping.

That irrigation makes a big difference to cropping patterns can be readily seen from published statistics. But the role of irrigation quality and differences in irrigation impact under varying agro-climatic environments have not been explored. Similarly, the numerous studies on price response of agriculture tend to focus on the effect of relative price changes on the area allocated to particular crops. There is hardly any study which takes a comprehensive look at crop-pattern changes and assesses the relative contributions of the various environmental, technical, and economic factors in explaining the variations in crop patterns across space and time.[8]

Crop Yields

Yield of specific crops per unit area may be viewed as a function of irrigation, fertilizer use, and seed varieties, with prices—or more precisely the relative prices of the crop and its inputs—influencing the level of input use. The three basic technological determinants of yield are, however, closely interlinked often in a synergetic relation. This is brought out in a stylized fashion in Fig. 1.

LU represents the yield response to increased applications of fertilizer (or strictly plant nutrients) on rainfed land using traditional local varieties and conventional practices. HU denotes the response curve on

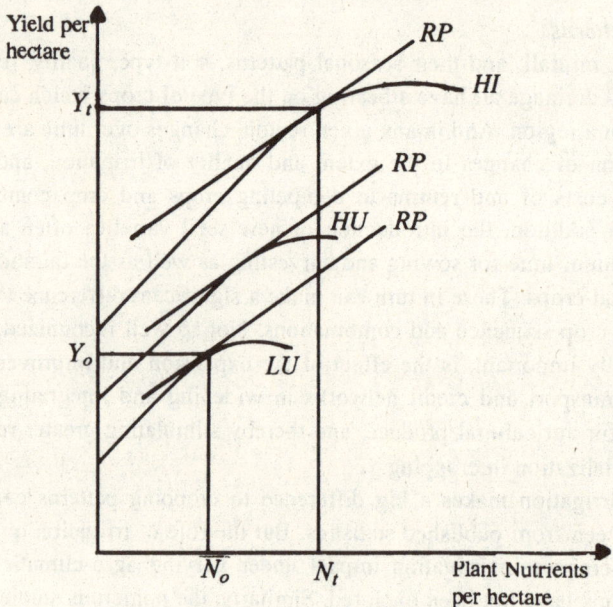

RP: Prices of output relative to unit cost of nutrients

FIG. 1

[8]For the beginnings of an attempt in this direction, see Venkataraman and Prahladechar (1980).

rainfed land using improved varieties and HI the response under an ideal irrigation regime (a regime in which the soil moisture in the root zone of the crop is maintained through all stages of crop growth at levels which protect the plants from any moisture stress) and the best improved variety available. The introduction of improved varieties by itself gives a higher yield than local varieties under a given moisture regime; and often the former can absorb a larger quantum of nutrients, and hence result in a higher maximum yield. Irrigation by itself, in general, has a similar effect. If an ideal irrigation regime is combined with the best available varieties, we get as it were an approximation to the technological frontier at any point of time which is marked by a higher yield for comparable levels of nutrient application, an even greater scope for fertilizer application, and a higher maximum yield physically feasible than would be the case if irrigation or HYV is used. Between LU and HI one can visualize a whole series of fertilizer response curves corresponding to different combinations of irrigation regimes and seed varieties.

At any given point of time, space, and irrigation regime, farmers may be expected to operate on the highest available response curve. The actual amount of nutrients applied will be determined by the costs of fertilizer and associated inputs (including water) relative to the output price. While improvements in fertilizer-cost crop-output ratio can lead to more fertilizer use and higher yields, there are limits to this process set by the available response curves. Over the long run, the pace at which the response curves get shifted upwards and outwards is a far more important determinant of the pace at which productivity will increase.

The magnitude and speed of these shifts depends mainly, though not exclusively, on irrigation and improvement in its quality, the progress of plant breeding and agronomic research, and the efficacy of services in reaching the knowledge of new varieties and improved techniques to the farmers.[9] This is partly a matter of public policy on the volume of resources which are invested in these activities, but only partly. One cannot guarantee profitable new varieties or economically viable improved techniques merely by setting up research facilities. And, as we

---

[9]The techniques of soil-moisture conservation in rainfed lands and the progress of plant-breeding research to evolve more fertilizer-responsive/drought-tolerant/disease-resistant varieties are the other important variables.

shall see later, improvement of the irrigation regime calls for effort in organization and management as well as investment.

Movements in the cost of fertilizers relative to the price of crops are subject to numerous influences which can be broadly grouped as: (a) technological developments which reduce the unit cost of production of plant nutrients; (b) more extensive, faster, and cheaper transport and credit facilities which reduce the effective cost of nutrients to the farmer and/or raise the effective price received by the farmer for his output; (c) state policy operating via taxes, subsidies, and administered prices; (d) the balance between supply and demand for inputs and output in the market; and (e) changes in land tenure affecting the returns to use of water and fertilizers to the actual cultivator. It is obvious that market forces, state policy and structural/institutional changes are all involved in shaping the eventual outcome, via the extent and pace of shift in technical possibilities (represented by the response curves) and the cost–return relationships.

If we visualize the upward and outward shifting of the yield response to plant nutrients as occurring progressively in time, the economic level of yield (assuming profit-maximizing farmers and reasonably efficient markets) at given relative prices increases from Y_0 to Y_f—the magnitude and time profile of this increase being largely a function of the pace of technical progress on the farms. Around this trajectory, fluctuations are possible on account of other factors—the most important of which is the weather. Departures of rainfall from the normal (in terms of both level and seasonal distribution) affect the moisture regime and in effect shift the effective set of response curves around those operative under normal conditions. So long as these departures do not show any trend (or other systematic pattern) over time, weather-induced fluctuations can be taken as being randomly distributed over time. But such àn assumption is not always valid. At any rate given the synergy between water and fertilizers, fluctuations in rainfall—which, in the context of imperfectly-controlled irrigation, obviously affect the soil moisture regimes to some degree—may lead to accentuation of yield fluctuations in times of rapid spread of irrigated, fertilizer-intensive farming.

Conceptually, the above framework has several advantages over the conventional approach of viewing output as a function of the quantum of primary factors (land, labour, and capital) and technical change. The latter is not easy to implement because the relevant time series of capital stock and labour input are simply not available.[10] Attempts to overcome this problem by incorporating irrigation, fertilizers, animal and tractor power and other inputs run into severe difficulties on account of complex complementarities and substitution relations between inputs. It is not surprising, therefore, that econometric estimations of the functional relation between growth of output and various material inputs (the list usually includes irrigated area, HYV area, fertilizers and manures, the use of bullocks and tractors, and, of course, manpower) give results which are difficult to interpret.[11] There seems to be considerable merit in focusing explicitly on the primary role of agro-climatic environment, bio-chemical inputs, and the efficiency of their use on crop yields. The economic and institutional factors as well as state policy are then viewed as determining the shift in response curves and the particular point on the response curves at which inputs are used.

Of the various environmental and bio-chemical determinants of agricultural productivity, irrigation is often cited as the critical factor in as much as it raises cropping intensity, permits changes in crop patterns in favour of more productive crops, and also increases crop yields. That irrigation is indeed an important factor affecting productivity of land is beyond doubt. Inter-regional variations in output per unit of cropped area bear a significant positive correlation to the irrigation ratio. However, irrigation *per se* is not the only factor and at any rate accounts for only a part of the productivity variation. Ranade (1980) found that besides irrigation, differences in crop pattern, and in the level of fertilizer use per unit area are also important. Though irrigation itself influences crop patterns and fertilizer use—in as much as irrigated areas tend to have high-value crop patterns and use more

[10]Reasonably comprehensive estimates of capital stock are available at the national level but not at the state level. Recently some components of agricultural capital stock have been estimated up to the state level by Das Gupta (1984) but these leave out some crucial items, e.g. irrigation. Data on labour time spent on agriculture are available only for a few recent years from NSS.

[11]See for example the studies by Raj Krishna (1964), Ashok Parikh (1970), Mukhopadhyay (1976), Patel and Jha (1978), and Sidhu (1979).

Also see Parikh and Trivedi (1982) for an attempt at estimating production functions with area, irrigation, fertilizers, and rainfall as inputs. The exercise, which is based on data for Andhra Pradesh, seeks to relate aggregate output of selected crops to the selected inputs by pooling cross-section and time-series data.

fertilizers—the variations in the latter are not solely a function of irrigation. Altogether, according to Ranade, about 90 per cent of the inter-regional difference in crop productivity is accounted for by the above three factors. Another view is that the condition of water supply being determined by both irrigation and rainfall, and the crop patterns being a function of water supply, it is more meaningful to view productivity variations in relation to rainfall, irrigation, and fertilizer. Linear multiple regressions—implying a strictly linear and additive relation between the selected inputs and their contribution to productivity—suggest that all three have a significant positive impact on productivity and together they account for about 60–70 per cent of the yield variations.[12]

The relation between irrigation and the growth of productivity is quite complex. Ishikawa (1967) referred to irrigation as the 'leading input' for agricultural growth in Asian countries. In the Indian context S.K. Rao (1971) found some empirical support for the hypothesis that the most important proximate cause of disparities in the growth of crop output during 1952–3 to 1964–5 is the difference in the growth of irrigation. However, the association between the change in irrigation ratio and the productivity changes though statistically significant can 'explain' only a small part of the differences in the growth of productivity. This is not so surprising once we recognize that the impact of irrigation on cropping intensity and pattern, as well as yields, differs significantly across regions.

According to one recent estimate the difference between productivity of irrigated and rainfed lands (expressed as a percentage of the latter) varies from 50 per cent in Bihar to 280 per cent in Maharashtra. The differences are much wider when comparisons are made at the district level (Vaidyanathan, 1988). The data suggest that the productivity differential between irrigated and rainfed land is inversely related to the level of rainfall, that is, irrigation makes a much greater difference to land productivity under conditions of low rainfall than in high rainfall regions. The quality of irrigation is also important though its effect is difficult to measure empirically.

[12]See Mahendra Dev et al. (1989) who finds that 78 per cent of variance in per hectare yields across 56 regions at points of time is explained by these three factors. Mahendra Dev uses normal rainfall in his regressions. The results are substantially the same even if we use actual rainfall.

The impact of irrigation on growth of productivity is even more difficult to disentangle in as much as the pace of advance in bio-chemical technology (especially the development of improved varieties, potential for fertilizer use and its efficiency) is neither uniform across crops and regions nor always strictly complementary to irrigation. Further, the benefits of improved bio-chemical technology can be had not only on new areas brought under irrigation but also on pre-existing irrigated lands. And improvements in cultivation techniques are not confined to irrigated lands. While there is indeed some evidence of a significant positive association between growth of productivity, on the one hand, and a high irrigation-ratio and rapid growth in irrigation, on the other, the relation is neither strong nor consistent.[13]

Attempts to explain changes in productivity between different points in time and across regions in terms of changes in the rainfall–irrigation ratio, and fertilizer uses, show that they have a significant positive impact. Within particular rainfall zones, the impact of changes in fertilizer use and irrigation have a significant positive association with yield changes. The overall explanatory power of this hypothesis is better with relatively well-developed irrigation in all rainfall zones. The underlying notion of linear and additive input–output relations is admittedly simplistic. A more satisfactory formulation must address the non-linearities and the inter-relations between different inputs. Nevertheless, this line of approach seems promising and is capable of further refinement.[14]

Another approach is to estimate the potential production of food-grains on the basis of the observed increases in various inputs (area, improved seed, irrigation, fertilizers, organic manures, soil conservation) and estimated yardsticks of yield response to each input. Such an exercise was conducted in the sixties by a Committee of the Planning Commission for the country as a whole and found the estimated

[13]For a discussion of this point see Vaidyanathan (1988). A multiple regression of growth rate of productivity per gross area on the base-year irrigation ratio and the changes in the irrigation ratio across states gave a positive coefficient for both variables, but only the coefficient for the change was statistically significant. This relation is not corroborated at the district level. There is, however, some indication that regions with low base-year irrigation and those with slow increase in irrigation tend to have a relatively higher frequency of low productivity growth and productivity decline, while the frequency of higher productivity growth is greater among regions with a high irrigation ratio and rapid growth in irrigation.

[14]A study along these lines is currently in progress by the author and Ms Krishna Kumar in MIDS.

potential and the actual trend during the fifties to correspond fairly closely. A later exercise (Vaidyanathan, 1977) compared the increase in actual output with potential increases which might be expected from the expansion in total and irrigated area, changes in allocation of area between different foodgrains, and rise in fertilizer use as between three points of time, namely the early fifties, the early sixties, and the early seventies. The estimates, based on the yardsticks of response in the pre-HYV period, showed that the actual increase was somewhat more than the increase in estimated potential in the first part of the period (i.e. 1950–3 to 1960–4) but considerably less in the sixties, when the highly fertilizer-responsive HYVs spread rapidly. On this basis, it was suggested that during the sixties the productivity of inputs instead of rising, as one would expect from the spread of technology, may in fact have declined. Other studies covering more recent periods also point in the same direction (Sarma and Roy, 1979; Mellor, 1988). Such inferences may however be questioned partly because the estimates of potential output rest on averaging, or because they may be based on rather patchy data on yield responses to inputs (which vary a great deal across crops and regions), and on essentially arbitrary assumptions about the proportion of fertilizers allocated to foodgrains.[15]

It is also necessary to recognize that actual output is a function not only of inputs but also of seasonal conditions. The usual assumption that seasonal conditions vary in a random fashion from year to year may be true when we consider very long periods but not infrequently one sees non-random patterns of variation in rainfall and other seasonal conditions during particular periods for which output behaviour is under study. Moreover, the effect of inputs on productivity and output may not be independent of seasonal conditions. This perception has led to attempts to sort out the effects of seasonal conditions from those of inputs and their productivity in explaining the variations observed in actual output.

---

[15]We have state-level data on the proportion of fertilizer used for different crops in the mid seventies. Most of the papers cited assume that this proportion has remained constant over time. Desai (1982) however cites evidence to suggest that the percentage of fertilizers applied to foodgrains may have increased, and increased substantially.

The fact that these exercises altogether ignore farm-yard manure (which is a significant source of plant nutrients but whose importance varies across space and time), and that they assume a linear and additive production function are also important limitations.

A number of studies seeking to disentangle the effect of weather from those of inputs and technology on output change are now available (Cummings and Ray, 1969; Ray, 1987; Vaidyanathan and Mukherjee, 1980, 1987; Rao et al., 1988). They all show that rainfall has a significant effect on area and yield changes and that in a large majority of states weather-corrected trends are significantly different and generally higher than the uncorrected trends.

Vaidyanathan and Mukherjee (1980, 1987) extended this approach to analysing changes in foodgrain yields at the regional level and by seeking to break up the trend element into the contribution of changes in inputs and changes in the productivity of inputs. The analysis confirms that seasonal conditions have a significant influence on yields, its extent being greater in areas of low rainfall and low irrigation. In such regions the contribution of sustained changes in inputs and technology also seems relatively small. By contrast, in regions with more extensive irrigation, inputs and technology 'explain' a much higher proportion of variance and the overall proportion of variation in yields 'explained' by inputs, technology, and weather together is also much higher. The relative importance of inputs and of technical improvement (reflected in better productivity of inputs) could not, however, be sorted out satisfactorily partly for lack of reliable estimates, both of irrigated area and of fertilizer use by crops over time.

Perhaps some of these limitations can be overcome as more detailed data on fertilizer response to individual crops under different agroclimatic and irrigation types, along with more disaggregated information on patterns of fertilizer use, are available. The cost of Cultivation Surveys, initiated in the early seventies to help the Agricultural Price Commission, also provide a great deal of detailed data on land use, irrigation, crop patterns, input use, and yields for a sample of farms for practically all the states. The potential of this body of data, which now spans nearly two decades and is likely to be a continuing feature, for understanding the dynamics of agricultural production has hardly begun to be exploited. At the same time, more work on the specification of the input–output relations to allow for non-linearities and interactions between rainfall, irrigation, and fertilizers is also essential.

Clearly, we are not in a position as yet to pin down with any reasonable degree of precision the relative importance of irrigation development, bio-chemical inputs, and improvements in technology in accounting for the observed overall growth of crop yields and output, or for the disparate trends across regions. This being the case, it is even more difficult to explicate the concrete role which institutional factors and state policy play in shaping agricultural growth in specific regions.

The thesis that basic changes in agrarian structure (through abolition of the vestiges of feudalism, redistribution of land to the actual tillers, and effective protection of tenants' rights) are essential preconditions to rapid agricultural growth is much too general to be of much use. This thesis has been invoked to explain the relative stagnation of agriculture in east India but without any convincing empirical analysis.[16] In point of fact, even within east India there are considerable variations in growth and according to at least one observer (e.g. Boyce, 1987) parts of Bengal may be growing much faster than generally supposed. Also one has to account for the fact that some of the rapidly-growing areas (e.g. Punjab–Haryana) had a high incidence of tenancy while others (like parts of Gujarat) had a strong feudal tradition. Nor is it always the case that *ryotwari* regions and regions with low incidence of tenancy achieve high growth rates.

At any rate, major changes in agrarian structure do not take place autonomously but as a result of purposive and vigorous intervention by the state. And the ambit of state intervention on agricultural performance extends far beyond agrarian reform, comprehending as it does direct investments in land and water development; strengthening of infrastructure (including electrification, transport, research/extension) essential to support agricultural growth; extending and deepening the access to institutional credit, and maintaining an environment of stable and remunerative prices to stimulate technical progress. The pace of agricultural growth reflects in important measure the cumulative impact of these interventions, even as the regional differences in growth are conditioned by differences in the scale, nature, and effectiveness of such interventions. In what follows we focus on four major areas of state intervention whose crucial importance to agricultural development is beyond dispute: (i) irrigation; (ii) soil and moisture conservation of rainfed agriculture; (iii) the development and spread of

---

[16]Amit Bhaduri (1973) provided a theoretical analysis on semi-feudalism and its effects on agricultural growth, and stimulated an extensive debate on this issue.

bio-chemical inputs and, in particular, fertilizers; and (iv) state policy affecting agrarian institutions and prices.

IRRIGATION[17]

Spread of irrigation

The expansion and improvement of irrigation facilities obviously occupies a central place in Indian agricultural development strategy. Between 1950 and 1989, the State has directly invested some 360 billion rupees in irrigation and flood-control works. This represents somewhat under one-tenth of total public investment during this period, and as much as 40 per cent of public investment in programmes for agricultural and rural development. In addition, the State has, as a matter of policy, made available sizeable amounts of loan finance through institutions like the Land Development Banks to support private investment in agriculture, of which irrigation is an important component.

As a result, according to official estimates, the irrigation potential—i.e. the area which is considered to be irrigable by the projects which have been completed—has nearly trebled from an estimated 22.6 million hectares in the beginning of the First Plan to nearly 80 million hectares at the end of the Seventh Plan. The rate of additions to the potential has also increased from an average of less than 0.7 million hectares per annum in the fifties to nearly 2 million hectares per annum in the Fifth and Sixth Plan periods. Other notable features of the programme include: (1) a progressive shift of emphasis from major and medium irrigation projects to minor works, and especially groundwater; (2) increased emphasis on measures to expedite effective utilization of the potential created; and (3) greater attention to modernization and the improvement of existing systems.

During the first two plans, the potential created under major and medium projects rose by 4.6 million hectares, compared to less than 2 million hectares under minor works. The area under wells and tube wells, which are part of the latter, is estimated to have risen by 1.3 million hectares. The pattern changed drastically from the Third Plan onwards when the advent of the new varieties gave a further fillip to

---

[17]For a general overview of irrigation-related issues, see Indian Society of Agricultural Economics (1976), GOI (1972b), Dhawan (1983, 1985), Vaidyanathan (1986, 1987). A fairly detailed bibliography is available in Vaidyanathan (1986).

groundwater development and government policy supported it by encouraging conjunctive use of ground and surface water in canal commands, investing in rural electrification, and providing farmers loan
assistance for setting up and energizing wells and tube wells on a large
scale and on liberal terms. Consequently, the net area irrigated by
wells rose by an estimated 4.5 million hectares between 1960 and
1970 (nearly 4 times the rate of addition during the fifties) and 6
million hectares in the seventies. The total reached close to 20 million
hectares by 1983–4. If one considers the spread of conjunctive use and
looks at gross area irrigated, the growth of well irrigation may be
greater than the above data would suggest.

Persistent large gaps between potential created and actual utilization
in major and medium projects led to the inclusion of Command Area
Development programmes as a distinct component of the irrigation
programme. This programme was based on the diagnosis that the lags
in the utilization of potential arise from delays in completing tertiary
distribution channels (field channels), the lack of proper drainage
facilities, inadequate care in planning crop patterns suited to local soil
and drainage conditions, and the difficulties of preparing the fragmented landholdings for the efficient use of water. Since farmers who
were expected to take care of many of these aspects did not do so, it
was deemed appropriate for the government to take on greater direct
responsibility for field channel construction and improved drainage, as
well as land consolidation and other on-farm development works. The
outlay on Command Area Development programmes has been rising
progressively both in absolute terms and in relation to the total outlays
on irrigation programmes.

Most of the older systems, dating back from pre-independence
times, need major investments partly to remedy the effects of the long
neglect of maintenance and repairs, and partly to modernize the distribution networks and regulatory structures for more effective water
management. In the earlier phase of planning, most of the attention
and resources were pre-empted by new projects, but gradually the
need for the modernization of existing systems came to be better
appreciated especially in regions like Tamil Nadu, where the scope for
setting up new systems had reached its limit. The Irrigation Commission of 1972 recommended that modernization should be given special
attention.

Impact of irrigation

The impact of these programmes on the extent and quality of irrigation is open to some question: the area reported to be actually irrigated by the land-use statistics is lower than the Plan estimates of the utilization of potential. Both sources of data, however, suffer from numerous deficiencies which makes it difficult to get at the 'true' situation. In the case of land-use statistics, the imprecise definition of irrigated area, the weakness in the machinery for collecting and checking of the data raises doubts about its veracity. The Plan statistics on the other hand are based on concepts of potential and utilization which are loosely defined and ambiguous, and reflect estimates by executive agencies rather than ground-level measurements (see Vaidyanathan, 1987; Government of Andhra Pradesh, 1982).

The growing share of groundwater-based irrigation, the spread of conjunctive use of canal and tank water with groundwater, as well as the improvement of the distribution network and on-farm development works undertaken as part of the command area programmes must have contributed to improving field-level access to water and facilitated better control over the timing and quantum of water application. However, these purely physical and technical improvements can only go a limited way in ensuring that the water supplies are adjusted in accordance with the crop needs. There is not much basis to suppose that the management of surface systems has improved significantly in this respect.

The way irrigation systems are organized, manned, and operated has hardly changed: except for wells and the traditional local systems, most irrigation projects continue to be wholly under the control of the PWD officials; the operating rules for reservoirs and canals based on the original design have rarely been systematically reviewed and modified even though actual experience departs widely from the design assumptions regarding the quantum of water available, the crop patterns, and the technical efficiency of water use. In many cases, the design did not even envisage the possibility of the conjunctive use of groundwater which has since become important. The users are not only not involved in deciding policy but are often unaware of the rationale for the operational rules.

The enforcement of regulations—be it on localization of crops or delivery schedules—is seen to be extraordinarily ineffective partly because some farmers are able, through their political influence or other means, to get the operation or rules modified to their advantage. And large-scale violations of rules have all too often been condoned by the government under political pressure from the concerned farmers. That there has been, generally, no effective counter-pressure from those adversely affected by the violations, however, is rather puzzling.

Large-scale systems, to be managed efficiently, must necessarily rely on a professional bureaucracy guided by clear rules. The view has gradually gained ground that the system managers cannot effectively control both crop patterns and the pattern of water delivery to fit the water needs of individual crops. Also, that it is better to concentrate on guaranteeing delivery of water at the outlets in designated quantities and for a specified duration according to a fixed schedule leaving farmers free to decide what to do with the water.[18] This is certainly an improvement. However, the determination of the schedule as well as regulations concerning the exploitation of groundwater has a direct bearing on how extensive an area will benefit and how the benefits will be shared among the farmers. There is a strong case for involving the *ayacutdars* in making these decisions so that the basis for the decisions and their implications are understood by those affected and that there is an institutionalized basis for them to review/modify the rules in the light of experience. This together with a strong and autonomous management to enforce the rules is essential for improving systems management.

That irrigation makes a significant difference to land productivity is not in doubt; it also generally makes for greater stability in output. However, as pointed out earlier, the magnitude of impact on productivity varies over quite a wide range. That apart, given the qualitative improvement in irrigation, taken together with the introduction of more fertilizer-responsive crop varieties with a higher potential yield, one would have expected productivity of irrigated land to have risen rapidly both in absolute terms and relative to unirrigated lands. The available evidence, however, does not seem to bear out this expectation, at least in Tamil Nadu. In a majority of the districts in this state, it is reported that there is no statistically significant trend rise or fall in

---

[18]This concept underlies some of the improvements being attempted as part of the National Water Management Project funded by the World Bank.

yields of irrigated or unirrigated areas, nor in the ratio of irrigated to unirrigated yields (Vaidyanathan, 1987). But given the weaknesses of the basic data—crop-cutting surveys are not designed to give periodic estimates of irrigated and unirrigated yields at the district level—this cannot be considered definite, at any rate, not universal.

Regional distribution of benefits

The regional distribution of benefits from the spread of irrigation, both in terms of the growth of irrigated area and its impact on production, has been quite uneven: while it is indeed true that the potentialities for irrigation are far from evenly distributed across space, the distribution of ultimate potential is considerably more even than that of area currently under irrigation. However, the inter-regional disparities (measured by the coefficient of variation in the irrigation ratio) have increased somewhat in the post-independence period. And this despite planning and despite 'reduction of regional disparities' being a declared aim of planning. This aggravation of regional disparities, however, is almost exclusively on account of the development of groundwater falling in the sphere of the private sector. The disparities in surface irrigation—which is exclusively the states' responsibility—decreased.[19]

In considering the reasons for disparate growth of irrigation across states we need to distinguish between surface and groundwater. The development of surface irrigation works is for the most part the direct responsibility of the state governments. The extent of unutilized potential varies from state to state as does the availability of concrete projects; the amount of money which a state allocates for surface irrigation is constrained by the overall size of the state plan (in turn a function of its own ability to raise resources, the amount of central assistance available and the claims of other sectoral programmes); and there are varying degrees of 'efficiency' in terms of the number of projects sanctioned relative to the budget available, the care with which projects are designed, and the competence of the construction organization. The unutilized potential is concentrated in relatively few states and under the existing federal system of deciding allocations, it

[19]The coefficient of variation in the ratio of net irrigated area to net sown area rose marginally from 59% in 1961 to 61% in 1978–90. However, the coefficient of variation of net area under canals relative to net sown area has fallen sharply (from 88% to 72%) even as that under wells has risen (88.6% to 91.4%) (Vaidyanathan, 1987).

would be extremely difficult to adjust inter-state allocation for irrigation in such a way as to ensure speedy harnessing of unexploited potential.

Differences in the pace of groundwater development, whose exploitation is mostly with the private sector, cannot be fully explained by differences in exploitable goundwater resources. The most striking example is that of the eastern Gangetic plains which are abundantly endowed with groundwater but whose development has been quite slow especially compared to the explosive growth in the western part of the plains and in Punjab. Even in the Deccan, there is reason to believe that the actual exploitation is well below the potential. The slow pace of development in the Deccan, despite liberal subsidies and loans, is attributed not so much to the low rate of return but to the uncertainty about the rate of return due to wide variations in water yields from wells across space and seasons, as well as the high propensity of the region to drought (Dhawan, 1988). Reducing the uncertainty of water yields (by more liberal remission to farmers striking dry holes while digging wells) and better technical advice from groundwater survey organizations (as to the appropriate location for wells) and measures to augment the yield of wells (by constructing percolation tanks) are suggested as means to stimulate more rapid development.

In the eastern Gangetic plains the problem is very different. The problem of uncertainty in water supply is altogether absent. The well-to-well variations in the rates of return are not due to risk but to variations in the amount of land commanded per well, in turn reflecting differences in landholding size and the extent of fragmentation. The problem of fragmentation is particularly acute in this region and except in east UP—and that too recently—there has been little effort to consolidate landholdings. The process had been completed much earlier in the western plains (and Punjab). Moreover, the landholding size is small so that even after land consolidation, very large segments of the farmer population and a substantial portion of the land resource cannot benefit from their own source of well irrigation (Dhawan, 1983).

The returns to irrigation in this region are also affected because it has a much higher rainfall than the western plains, and hence relatively less need for irrrigation in the kharif season (when in any case controlled irrigation is impeded by floods). The high incidence of tenancy and the insecurity of tenants has also been cited as additional dampening influences (Dhawan, 1983; RBI, 1984; GOI, PC, 1985). However, there are indications (GOI, PC, 1985: 36) that the rate of groundwater exploitation especially in east UP and Bihar has increased at a faster rate than in the rest of India. What accounts for this change, and why it is still localized, remains insufficiently explored.

Distribution of benefits between farmers
Surveys in the early fifties show that in general the small landholdings had a higher irrigation ratio than the large holdings, there being a more or less inverse relation between the size of holdings and the ratio of irrigated to operated area.[20] While this relation still holds, it seems to have become considerably weaker: the irrigation ratio has risen in all classes, but risen rather more in the higher size-class of holdings.

There is no reason to expect as systematic and general the large-farmer bias in the distribution of benefits from big surface works—where geography mainly determines which areas and who gets water. Also, being public systems, there are pressures, however weak, for ensuring equitable distribution. But in the case of wells, which are largely in the private sector, the initial cost of setting up and energization are easier for the large farmers to mobilize than small farmers. Cooperative ownership and operation of wells is exceptional. The development of water markets—i.e. the practice of purchase and sale of well water—in several areas does mean that access to well water is more widely diffused than ownership of wells. However, there are apprehensions that the development of water markets may turn out to be another source of exploitation of small peasants, by overcharging them and even forcing them out of their lands. There is, however, insufficient evidence to judge how well founded this fear is. It seems likely that in areas with relative abundance of groundwater, the development of water markets has enabled small farmers to get access to water at 'competitive' rates.[21]

A third aspect of distribution of benefits from irrigation has to do

---

[20]According to data from the NSS landholding survey, the irrigated area as per cent of the operated area nearly doubled between 1953 and 1971, but it rose considerably more slowly in the smaller holdings than in the large holdings (see Vaidyanathan, 1987).

[21]On water markets and their functioning, see Shah (1988).

with the question of whether available water in a system should be used 'extensively' (i.e. to cover as large an area as possible) or 'intensively' (i.e. to get the maximum output per unit of water). In the former case, a larger number of farmers are benefited compared to the latter. In terms of the overall benefit to society, the extensive pattern is obviously preferable, if it also gives at least as large an increment in output per unit of water used. But there is some question whether this is generally the case.[22] For any given crop, since there is a strong synergetic relation between the availability of water and the ability to exploit the potential of biochemical technology, there would seem to be a strong case for a policy of limiting irrigated area to the extent to which it can be assured timely and adequate water with the given supply in the system.

However, the extent of area irrigable is also a function of what crops are grown, in as much as the water requirements of crops vary: paddy takes several times more than jowar; and sugarcane even more than paddy. It is not obvious that the promotion of water-intensive crop patterns is in all cases desirable in terms of maximizing output per unit of water. This depends very much on the agro-climatic and market conditions which vary from system to system. Even if intensive irrigation makes for large output, a case could be made for adopting less water-intensive systems in the interests of a wider diffusion of benefits. The balance is necessarily a matter of social choice. The choice should be an informed one and made explicitly. Unfortunately, this is not the case in most of our systems.

Some major policy issues

The relative importance to be attached to major and medium works as against minor works has been a recurrent theme in discussions of irrigation investment priorities. Greater emphasis on minor irrigation works in preference to large works is advocated on grounds that they are cheaper, more amenable to decentralized construction and management and—an argument heard more and more in recent times— ecologically safe. The choice is however not as simple as these arguments would suggest.

---

[22]Some studies in Maharashtra claim that the use of water for growing irrigated dry crops benefits a larger area *and* produces more calories per unit water than a water-intensive (sugarcane-based) crop pattern (see Rath and Mitra, 1982).

The mere fact that minor works cost less per hectare of irrigation is not sufficient to establish their superiority. One has to take into account significant differences between different categories of works in terms of the quantum of additional water made available by them during the year, its seasonal distribution and reliability. In general, large storage works tap surface-water flows from a wider catchment and are therefore able to get longer, often more assured, supplies for a longer period in a year than small storages depending on limited local catchments. The productivity impact of the two types of systems is quite different.

In the case of wells, a proper accounting of investment costs per unit area should count the resources spent on infructuous digging in search of groundwater and the costs of extending the transmission and distribution network to supply electricity to the pumps.[23] The scope for different categories of works is also constrained by topography, geology, and other technical factors; and these works are not always independent of each other. Nor is it self-evident that the loss of valuable agricultural or forest land due to submergence by reservoirs relative to the area benefited is invariably less in the case of minor works. The question of the appropriate balance between different categories of works has to take into account all these considerations in a comprehensive manner while evaluating alternative integrated strategies for developing a given river basin.

The present system of planning and management of irrigation works does not address these issues systematically and explicitly. Though the need for it is recognized and legislation exists, there is a remarkable reluctance to set up the necessary organizations. Irrigation planning continues to be done on a project-by-project basis; decisions on projects are made in response to local pressures or, more often, because politicians in power are anxious to cultivate support among their constituents. This has led to a weakening in the technical quality of projects, in terms of the quality of design, the veracity of cost-and-benefit estimates, and the objectivity of technical and economic evaluation. It has also been responsible for taking on far more projects than can be completed in reasonable time with the available resources. Together with the opportunities for corruption which such projects

---

[23]For one of the few systematic and careful analyses of costs and benefits of well irrigation, see Deepak Lal (1972).

offer, these have contributed to extraordinary delays in project comple-
tion, high costs, and the inability to ensure adequate water supply to
the designed *ayacut*.[24]

These deficiencies compound the difficulties of the government in
imposing water rates on users to cover even operational expenses, not
to speak of capital costs. Numerous committees have specified that
irrigation charges must cover operational costs and leave a sufficient
margin to earn a reasonable return on investment. Betterment levies to
recover a part of the invesment from beneficiaries have also been
legislated. But these charges have proved consistently inadequate to
cover even current costs, partly because the rates are set too low, partly
because no adjustments are made to offset the inflation on costs, and
also because of the laxity in collecting whatever is due and to enforce
prescribed penalties for violation of the rules regarding water use.

Political pressures by farmers as a class seeking various forms of
concessions from the state is, of course, an additional factor. But it can
be argued that if project managements, in fact, did deliver water in
designated amounts and according to a schedule, if the user charges of
each system were seen to be applied for the maintenance and management of that system rather than merged into some common pool, if
users were more directly involved in operating the systems, and if the
charges did bear a reasonable relation to the increases in productivity,
the farmers would be willing to pay much higher rates than at present.
A reasonable level of water rates is *essential* both to recover the cost
of providing irrigation services and to create incentives for more
careful and economical use of water.

RAINFED AGRICULTURE

While more extensive and better irrigation facilities have an unquestionably important role in raising productivity, the fact remains that
nearly 70 per cent of the country's cultivated area is rainfed and
contributes around 40 per cent of the total output. Even after the
potential for irrigation has been fully exploited, about half the land
will—on a conservative estimate—remain solely dependent on rainfall.
The rate of growth of productivity on rainfed lands will therefore have

---

[24]For more detailed references on some of these issues, see Vaidyanathan (1986).

a significant bearing on the overall rate of agricultural growth, and on the prospects of achieving greater regional balance in this growth.

Successive five year plans do recognize the importance of developing rainfed agriculture and incorporate a variety of programmes for the purpose.[25] Though there is gradually greater appreciation of the problems of rainfed farming in high rainfall tracts, the actual programmes tend to focus more on arid and semi-arid tracts marked by a low and highly-variable rainfall, and by a high propensity to drought. Building on a much longer tradition of research in dry farming, especially in the old Bombay Presidency, the Plan strategy aims at soil-moisture conservation and land improvement in these tracts along with research to evolve superior crop varieties and agronomic practices. Contour bunding, land consolidation, construction of percolation ponds, and other devices to augment and conserve soil moisture figure prominently in these programmes. Over the years greater awareness that effective soil-moisture conservation requires planning on an area basis has led to the formulation of Drought-Prone Programmes, the Desert Development Programmes, and Hill Area Programmes. The concept of integrated planning of land and soil-moisture conservation on a watershed basis represents a further stage in the evolution of thinking on this matter. At the same time, research in dryland agriculture has been intensified and organized on a more systematic basis through the All India Coordinated Research Project for Dryland Agriculture. However, by all accounts these programmes have not had the impact that the HYVs and irrigation have had. There are several reasons for this.

In the first place the scale of outlays has been quite meagre: in the Seventh Plan, for instance, the allocation for soil and water conservation was about Rs 740 crores which is barely 7 per cent of the total projected public-sector outlay on agricultural development programmes other than irrigation and flood control. The proportion was about the same even in the Third Plan. By contrast, the amounts allocated for irrigation and flood-control projects in the Seventh Plan was nearly 22 times the amount envisaged for soil and water conservation; in the Third Plan, the outlay on the former was only 9 times the amount spent on the latter. Thus the relative importance attached to irrigation

[25]For a recent detailed review, see Jodha (ed.) (1989).

over the improvement of rainfed lands has, if anything, increased over time.

Second, the programmes for rainfed agriculture have largely been focused on the relatively dry (or arid and semi-arid) tracts. However, the extent of unirrigated land under cultivation in the medium and high-rainfall zones (750 to 1150 mm and over 1150 mm) is nearly twice as large as in the dry regions (with annual rainfall below 750 mm). These areas need measures to check and control flooding during the rainy season and an efficient drainage network to prevent excessive water accumulation in fertile but low-lying areas, particularly for the plains in high-rainfall tracts. Both the nature of the problem and the remedies are different compared to dryland farming. In point of fact, a great deal of research on land use, moisture control, and cropping practices in each of these diverse agro-climatic environments is required in order to come up with appropriate techniques and programmes for raising the productivity of unirrigated land.

Unfortunately, research seems to have been largely concentrated on the dry zone. The All India Coordinated Programme for Dryland Agriculture, the ICRISAT (International Crop Research Institute for Semi-Arid Tropics), and the Arid Zone Research Station are all focused on the problems of the dry zone. There is no effort of comparable scope or scale for research into the problems of rainfed agriculture in the medium and high-rainfall zones. Similarly, while there is an extensive literature on the problems of the arid and semi-arid zones, it is hard to come by systematic and serious analyses of the regions with relatively high rainfall. The Plan programmes, like research, seem overly preoccupied with the dry regions.

The main thrust of research has been on (a) improving the environment of crop growth through better conservation of soil moisture combined with techniques to make more effective use of available soil moisture; and (b) improving the yield potential of individual crops under unirrigated conditions. Contour bunding, gully plugging, land consolidation and reshaping along contours, percolation ponds, and preparation of land well ahead of the monsoon belong to the first category. The breeding of seed varieties with higher yield potential, greater drought resistance, and improved adaptation to local rainfall patterns belong to the latter category. The general assessment is that the improvements resulting from this research have been substantial in some respects, though not as dramatic as in the case of HYVs. The improvements in crop-specific technologies are judged to be more significant than those concerning soil-moisture conservation.

Advances in crop-specific techniques demonstrate that sizeable increases in yields are feasible, but the *magnitude* of the increases in yield potential is smaller than that under good irrigation and also subject to larger variability. The greater variability of the environment of rainfed compared to irrigated agriculture makes adaptive research to develop varieties and practices suited to specific local conditions much more important in the case of the former. It is also suggested that such research should pay greater attention to (a) ways of increasing the efficiency of fertilizer use, meeting the taste, cooking, and other qualities of grain, and strengthening pest and disease resistance of the staple crops; (b) improving cropping systems rather than individual crops. This points to the necessity for a major reorientation of crop-related research along with an increase in the scale of the effort to evolve systems suitable for the varied agro-climatic conditions under which rainfed agriculture is practised.[26]

The performance of better varieties, crop systems, and agronomic practices, however, depend crucially on improvement in the soil-moisture environment of rainfed agriculture. The relatively slow progress in this respect arises in part from the fact that the need to evolve techniques suitable for the wide variety of agro-climatic conditions of unirrigated agriculture has not received sufficient recognition in the planning of research. The other important consideration is whether the improved systems of soil-moisture management are financially feasible and economically viable. This aspect has received surprisingly little attention in the planning of dryland agriculture programmes. There is hardly any systematic assessment, *exante* or *expost*, of the costs and benefits of soil-moisture conservation programmes.

In addition, significant improvements in the soil-moisture environment of rainfed areas, even when they can be shown to be economically attractive in terms of the additions to productivity of land and overall output relative to the costs involved, cannot be implemented by individual farmers. They often require major changes in field boundaries, plot locations, and land-use patterns affecting wide areas and a

[26]For a critical assessment of the research on dry farming technology, see Jodha (1986).

large number of farmers and farming communities. The potential of improved techniques can be realized only if the affected farmers can be collectively persuaded to accept all these changes and the associated costs. The mere fact that the state is willing to subsidize a part or all of the costs is not sufficient to secure acceptance of, or at any rate continuing compliance with, the changes. For even if a technically well-conceived programme for land and water management in an area can be shown to yield a large increase in the output and incomes of that area taken as a whole, the fact that all affected farmers may not gain equally, and that the extent of gain for individuals is inherently uncertain and also contingent on how others behave, makes it extraordinarily difficult to implement a ccommon programme whether by consensus or by fiat. This aspect has been pretty much neglected in the Plan programmes, including the much heralded integrated watershed development projects; nor is there much by way of systematic effort to see what can be learnt from the experience of numerous community initiatives promoted by voluntary organizations to tackle this problem.[27]

Altogether the scope and scale of the state's effort at raising the productivity of rainfed agriculture through direct investment and research-support appears too limited to have had much of an impact. And, yet, rainfed agriculture in India is not stagnant altogether. (Nor, it needs emphasizing, have irrigated tracts always sustained high rates of growth.) The experience in terms of the growth of overall output and of productivity per unit of land, across districts where rainfed agriculture is predominant, is extremely varied. Of special interest is the fact that several of the districts (notably in Gujarat and Karnataka) with a very low level of irrigation development have experienced growth rates of crop output equal to and higher than the national average.[28]

This suggests that there are forces generating growth independently of government plans. It is possible that farmers on their own are responding to growing market opportunities by investing in land improvement; perhaps greater specialization and even technical innova-

[27]Some idea of the experience of such efforts can be had from Chopra et al. (1988) and Society for Promotion of Wasteland Development (1990). For an overview of the institutional aspects of watershed development, see Vaidyanathan (1990).

[28]The Bhalla–Alagh study shows that between 1960–3 and 1975–7, 27 out of the 72 districts with less than 750 mm rainfall recorded growth rates of more than 4.5% p.a. Among 38 districts with irrigation ratios less than 20%, 7 posted growth rates exceeding 4.5% p.a.

tion is taking place independent of state-sponsored research. To some degree these processes may be facilitated by government programmes for expanding and improving infrastructure and for expanding the institutional credit into rural areas. What explains the relatively high growth in some districts with predominantly rainfed cultivation, and slow growth or decline in others would seem obviously important questions to explore. But studies of regional variations in Indian agriculture have barely got out of the descriptive stage. Analytical work to pin down the causes of variations are as yet rare and what exists is quite unsatisfactory.

BIOCHEMICAL INPUTS

Given the soil-moisture environment, biochemical technology (of which the genetic potential of the seed varieties and the intensity of fertilizer use are perhaps the most important) is crucial in determining the yields per unit area. The strengthening of the research network to breed better strains of all important crops adapted to varying agro-climatic conditions and to evolve agronomic practices for their optimum performance; extension services to propagate these varieties, together with associated inputs and cultivation practices, among farmers; and enlarging the supply of fertilizers and other inputs as well as the network for distributing them—all these have been a prominent feature of the agricultural programmes since independence.

The results of plant-breeding research have however been quite uneven. While there are instances of dramatic breakthroughs (especially in wheat, rice, and to some extent, cotton), achievements in other crops (notably pulses and oilseeds) have not been impressive. The reason for this uneven progress is beyond the scope of the present essay. But it may be noted in passing that the technical problems of breed improvement differ as between crops and environments. Also, the results depend on the direction and priorities of research as well as the way they are managed. It has been suggested that inadequate resources for research on rainfed agriculture, inadequate attention to local adaptive research, and neglect of farming systems in favour of crop-specific research are weaknesses of the present research. Apart from this, deficiencies in the arrangements for production and distribution of seeds of certified quality are believed to impede the realization of the benefits from the work of research institutes in improving plant varieties.

It is fairly well established that for any given seed variety, the potential for fertilizer (or more generally plant nutrient) absorption as well as the productivity per unit of applied nutrient is higher on irrigated land than under rainfed cultivation. Improved seed varieties—especially the more recent high-yielding varieties—are capable of absorbing more nutrients and using them more efficiently. The extent of this improvement, however, depends a great deal on the quality of water control. The larger and more assured the supply of soil moisture relative to the crops' needs in different stages of crop growth, the greater the potential for raising productivity through fertilizer use. Where the quantum of soil-moisture availability is inadequate relative to the needs of a crop and/or its timeliness and quantum of supply cannot be ensured, the yield impact of both improved seed varieties and fertilizers is reduced and also becomes more uncertain.

There is ample evidence that the diffusion as well as intensity of fertilizer use is markedly higher on irrigated than on rainfed lands. Experimental data also show that HYVs can absorb a much larger quantum of nutrients and give a higher yield per unit of nutrient than traditional varieties. Given this, one would expect the extent and quality of irrigation together with the spread of HYV to have a significant bearing on fertilizer use. There is indeed a strong positive correlation between the intensity of fertilizer use/hectare and the spread of irrigation across regions. However, a closer look shows high variation in both the diffusion and the intensity of fertilizer use across regions and crops on irrigated as well as unirrigated lands. And the bulk of the fertilizer use is accounted for by a few crops.[29] The quantum of fertilizer consumption has risen rapidly from a mere 0.5 million tonnes of plant nutrients in 1950–1 to over 9 million tonnes in 1987–8. This has unquestionably been a major factor contributing to the growth of yield and total agricultural output. The extension of irrigation, its qualitative improvement, and the spread of new varieties have been the important factors contributing to the spread of fertilizer use. We have inadequate data to assess trends in diffusion and intensity

[29]According to NSS data for 1971–2 nearly three-fourths of the fertilizers used (by value) in India was concentrated on irrigated land and two crops (rice and wheat) accounted for close to two-thirds of the consumption (*Sarvekshana*, Oct. 1978; also Desai and Singh, 1973; Desai, 1986; Nagaraj, 1980; NCAER, 1978).

across crops and regions. The quality of irrigation, the prices of fertilizer relative to that of crops, the coverage and quality of extension, the farmers' accessibility to distribution outlets and credit, and agrarian relations are obviously relevant but there are hardly any studies which explore the relative contribution of these factors in explaining the inter-crop and inter-regional differences in fertilizer consumption or in their behaviour over time.

A number of studies of trends in aggregative fertilizer consumption confirm the role of irrigation and HYVs but suggest that the shifts in relative prices have not had a marked influence on changes in fertilizer use. In fact there are phases when fertilizer consumption has continued to grow despite a sharp rise in the price of fertilizer relative to crop prices. This has led some observers to emphasize the role of non-price factors—especially extension, the distribution network, and research to improve the productivity of fertilizers—in promoting fertilizer use.[30]

Without underrating the relevance of these factors, it is nevertheless important to recognize that they ultimately act on the returns to fertilizer use via the cost of fertilizer or its yield response: the extension of a modern transport network and wider access to institutional credit reduces the costs of procuring fertilizers; extension services, by increasing the farmer's awareness of the effect of fertilizers and helping him to adapt fertilizer use to his specific soil–crop environment, could reduce the perceived risks associated with fertilizer use; propagation of better methods of application of nutrients has a direct bearing on the productivity of, and returns to, fertilizer use. These aspects have again not been examined systematically.

There is persuasive evidence that fertilizers are not being used efficiently. Apart from the fact that the growth in output has not been commensurate with the increased fertilizer use, an independent analysis—based on a detailed estimate of fertilizer response functions by crops and region, and calculations of the optimum allocation of fertilizers to achieve a specified output level with given cultivated land and irrigated area—corroborates that the level of fertilizer use per unit of incremental output is much higher than necessary (Parikh and Srinivasan, 1974).

This apparent, and growing, inefficiency in fertilizer use has been variously attributed to the government's policy of concentrating on

[30]This is specially emphasized by Desai (1982).

HYVs and the intensive use of fertilizer in favoured areas; the possibility that the response curves obtained from fertilizer trials may not be representative of the average farm conditions; and the substitution of fertilizers for traditional organic manures.[31] While no definitive conclusion can be drawn on the precise reasons, there seems to be general agreement that the efficiency of fertilizer use is much less than it ought to be. From every point of view—reducing the scale of investments for expanding fertilizer production, reducing the cost of fertilizer per unit of crop output, and minimizing the adverse ecological impact of excessive fertilizer use—the priority should be on more efficient use of fertilizers. In view of the historical experience that the growth of fertilizer use is not particularly sensitive to changes in the relative prices of fertilizer to crops, the manipulation of fertilizer subsidies is unlikely to make a significant difference in the potential impact of measures to promote a wider diffusion of fertilizer use across crops and regions. The impact of systematic efforts to promote more efficient use of fertilizers by farmers is likely to be much greater and preferred on every ground.

INSTITUTIONAL FACTORS

We have so far concentrated on the impact of the proximate technical factors affecting agricultural productivity and growth, namely the physical environment, biochemical technology, and the changes therein. The nature and pace of the changes in the latter are however not autonomous but conditioned by the agrarian structure, the mode of production, and state policy. These factors together influence the scale, the composition, and the quality of investments in land and water improvement, research and extension, and a variety of facilities supporting agricultural production. They also affect the private profitability of changing crop patterns and cultivation techniques and the use of yield-raising inputs. It must be borne in mind that, from the social viewpoint, not only the pace of growth but also its impact on the distribution of wealth and incomes between different groups involved in agricultural production is important.

[31]For a discussion of these aspects see Parikh and Srinivasan et al. (1964), Parikh (1978), and Vaidyanathan (1978).

Agrarian relations

The British rule had brought about far-reaching changes in India's land system primarily with a view to safeguarding the government's command over land revenue. In the process, private property in land had come to be formally recognized by law. Ownership of land, at the time of independence, was highly unequal; while the vast majority of cultivators were peasant proprietors engaged in personal cultivation of their land, a large proportion of cultivable land was in the hands of relatively large landowners—including especially the zamindars of UP, Bihar, and Bengal who held vast estates which were cultivated either with the help of tenants or wage labourers. This agrarian structure has long been recognized to be both iniquitous and inimical to progress. Some limited efforts at land reform even during the British period (especially tenancy reform) were made. A section of the Congress party advocated the necessity for radical land reform to ensure 'land to the tillers' and there was indeed a spurt of land reform legislation in the wake of independence. These reforms had three main components: (1) abolition of the zamindari estates; (2) tenancy reform; (3) imposition of ceilings on land ownership.[32]

Zamindari abolition and tenancy reform were expected to correct the gross inequalities in land ownership, and simultaneously—by giving the actual cultivators ownership or at least more favourable and secure long-term rights in land cultivated by them—create conditions for increasing land productivity. The intention behind land ceilings was primarily to take over land from those who had more than a specified size, and distribute the surplus among those who did not have any land, or had very little, thereby achieving a more egalitarian land distribution.

There is a general consensus that land-reform legislation was riddled with loopholes favouring large landowners who were also in a position—by virtue of their political power, influence over local officials, and ability to sustain litigation—to thwart the implementation of even the limited changes envisaged by the land reform. Zamindari abolition was perhaps the most successful: it led to the breaking up of large feudal estates and conferring ownership rights on the cultivators. Tenancy reform did not make much headway except in a few states like Kerala and West Bengal. It is well known that the ceiling legisla-

[32]For a good overall review of the progress of land reforms, see GOI, Planning Commission (1963), Joshi (1975), and Bandhopadhyay (1988).

tions did not yield much surplus land for redistribution to the landless or to those with holdings of a non-viable size.

Data from the National Sample Survey do not show any significant change in either the degree of landlessness or the extent of inequality in land ownership anywhere since 1960.[33] What it suggests is a progressive decline in the average size of holding and near stable distribution around the mean. This suggests that increase in demographic pressure has been the dominant influence. While there is no marked change in the degree of inequality in land ownership, there is ample evidence of significant shifts in the distribution of land between castes, at least in some regions. In Tamil Nadu, for instance, the locus of land control has shifted dramatically from upper castes to lower castes, including Harijans, partly due to tenancy laws and partly because the upper castes have tended to move out of such areas into urban occupations.[34]

The NSS also shows a more or less universal trend for the reported area under tenancy to decline. How far this reflects a genuine reduction and now far it is due to increasing concealment is difficult to establish. There is no doubt that the decline in some regions is real. In Punjab–Haryana, the advent of the HYV–private tube wells combination has made personal cultivation so much more profitable that those who had leased-out land have resumed self-cultivation; and increasingly those with small bits of land are seen to be leasing it out to larger farmers to take advantage of the benefits of new technology. In Kerala and West Bengal, tenancy reform is known to have been quite effective but it should not be assumed that the resulting redistribution of ownership rights necessarily benefited the small tenants. In Kerala, the bulk of tenancy was with farmers with medium-size holdings.[35]

The imposition of ceilings and redistribution of surplus land among the landless and small holders was also expected by some to help raise

[33]Data from the NSS landholding surveys suggest that the Gini coefficient (GCC) of total assets (in nominal terms) across classes changed little between 1961–2 and 1971–2, but declined in 1981–2. In 7 out of 14 states GCC of nominal value of assets declined progressively over this period. But these findings have to be interpreted with caution for several reasons. For a detailed discussion, see Vaidyanathan (1990).

[34]For a documentation of the phenomenon in Tamil Nadu, see Sundari (1991), Guhan and Mencher (1982), Guhan (1983), Athreya (1984), Guhan and Bharathan (1984).

[35]For an account of changes in the nature and extent of tenancy in Punjab and Haryana, see Bhalla and Talib (1981) and S. Bhalla (1977). For an account of the process of tenancy reform in Bengal, see Bandhopadhyay (1988), and for the impact of the Kerala reform, see Raj and Tharakan (1983).

productivity: this expectation was based on the apparent tendency, revealed by several surveys of the fifties, for land productivity to be substantially higher on the relatively small holdings compared to the large ones. Smaller holdings, it was argued, had an incentive to use underemployed family labour more intensively on their land. This interpretation of the inverse relation between farm size and productivity has however come to be questioned. It is suggested instead that much of the difference in productivity and labour input could be due to the fact that smaller farmers tend to have relatively more of irrigated land and also better quality land.[36]

The disadvantages of small and marginal farmers in terms of access to technology and resources needed to exploit the potential for raising yields as well as the implications for the distribution of gains from technological improvement (especially of high yield varieties) has been the subject of much debate. (For a sampling see Frankel, 1971; Rao et al., 1975; B. Das Gupta, 1977). It was widely feared that the HYVs were inherently biased in favour of large farmers and that, together with the trend toward mechanization in the agriculturally dynamic regions it would lead to a worsening of real income distribution in rural areas. In the event, it turns out that though large farmers may have an initial advantage, the use of HYVs and fertilizers has, over a period of time, spread to all classes of farmers; and that where HYVs have produced rapid growth, employment and rural wage rates have risen. However, large and medium farms are better placed to exploit groundwater; HYV technology is available for only a few crops and that too under irrigated conditions and in the high growth tracts of north-west India, there has been a significant displacement of tenants and a corresponding increase of wage labour. All of these have a bearing on the trend in overall income distribution between classes and regions. We know that disparities in production per capita have widened in the last twenty years. But evidence on interclass distribution of assets and consumption (mostly from the NSS) do not show any aggravation of inequality, while the evidence of wage rate and employment in rural areas is rather ambiguous. These are extremely important questions but lack of space precludes an adequate treatment

[36]Various aspects of size productivity relations have been debated extensively during the fifties and sixties, mostly in the columns of the *EPW*. See Rudra and Sen (1980) for a statement pulling together the various strands of the debate.

here. This paper is largely confined to a discussion of the characteristics and determinants of growth in agricultural production.

Management of common production resources

Be that as it may, there is hardly any question that a large number of relatively small and fragmented holdings made the task of propagating improved techniques and getting them to be properly used more difficult. Small farmers are traditionally at a disadvantage in getting access to credit at a reasonable rate of interest and in marketing the produce at reasonable prices. That they have, typically, to pay a higher interest for their capital needs, and accept a lower realization for their products, makes innovations economically less attractive for them. Moreover, certain kinds of investments essential to get the full benefits of new technology—and especially groundwater—are not economically viable on an individual basis for most small and marginal farmers.

Measures, which of necessity have to be primarily institutional, to remedy these disadvantages are therefore as important a component of reform in agrarian structure as land reform in the narrower sense. A number of steps have been taken to mitigate these disadvantages including land consolidation, cooperatives, and small and marginal farmers' development programmes. Land consolidation, essentially a means to overcome the disavantages of fragmentation, has not made significant progress except in Punjab, Haryana, and UP. In these states consolidation is known to have given a big fillip to groundwater irrigation. But elsewhere, even where consolidation is recognized to be essential for making fuller and more effective use of irrigation resources, the state governments have been remarkably reluctant to pursue the programme vigorously.

Cooperatives for credit and marketing are, in principle, a way of increasing the potential returns to land improvement and improved techniques for its members. They have been actively fostered and promoted by the state since the beginning of the century and cooperative credit has expanded greatly since independence. But they have belied their expectations. Cooperative marketing does not play a significant role in agriculture. Cooperative credit has grown massively but the societies are dominated by the large landowners and, instead of serving as a means to pool local surpluses for mutual benefit, have become more or less exclusively a channel for finance from outside with liberal subsidies from the state. That there have been no democratic elections to the management committees of cooperatives in several states for a long time has weakened them further. The bulk of the benefits of concessional lending and the rather permissive attitudes in the matter of recovery of dues must have benefited the bigger farmers far more than small farmers. Whether the cheapening of the cost of borrowed capital has stimulated productive investment and technical progress among them is in some doubt.

The failure of the co-ops to meet the needs of small farmers led to a special state-sponsored programme to channel funds, along with technical assistance and inputs, to the 'small' and 'marginal' farmers both to augment their productive asset base through physical investments and to make effective use of these assets by providing the necessary working capital. Whether all the resources channelled through these programmes in fact reach the 'target' groups, and whether they have led to a significant and continuing improvement in the productivity and incomes of these groups remains very much an open question.

On the whole, the weight of accumulated evidence suggests that the large holdings have not only been able to thwart any major change in the pattern of rural land distribution, but the various interventions (including credit expansion) have reinforced the economic advantage of large-sized holdings in exploiting such new techniques as HYV and groundwater irrigation. There is evidence that the inverse relation between farm size and productivity per unit land has considerably weakened in some agriculturally dynamic areas.

If institutional changes in the field of credit and marketing have not been as effective as expected, necessary changes in other important spheres have suffered serious neglect. As mentioned earlier, the effective use of irrigation resources, flood control, soil and moisture conservation on rainfed lands, all require organizations capable of regulating the use of land and water effectively in the collective interest of the beneficiary farmers.

In the case of large irrigation systems serving extensive areas and a large number of farmers, the proper preparation of land for effective irrigation, regulation of the kinds of crops grown and their extent, as well as the coordination of water deliveries with the requirements of the crops are all essential. In the case of groundwater, though the construction and operation of wells may be with individual farmers, regulation of the distribution of limited groundwater both to prevent over-exploitation and to ensure equitable access, again requires appropriate organization, rules, and procedures. Likewise, significant improvement in the productivity of rainfed lands—involving changes in the existing pattern of land use, the maintenance of *bunds*, the checking of dams and tree-cover on a continuing basis, the realignment of field boundaries, and possibly changes in the location and use of plots owned by individuals—cannot be brought about without the consent and cooperation of concerned farmers and villages.

How to achieve this consent to the once-for-all changes involved and ensure continuing compliance with the rules is an extremely important aspect of reform in agrarian institutions. There are inherent uncertainties about the magnitudes of the benefits accruing from these regulations, the manner in which the benefits will be distributed, and the extent of benefit which particular individuals will get. It is not only a matter of formulating regulations concerning allocation based on clear, consistent, and technically sound principles. These principles have also to be seen and accepted as fair by those affected, even as the management charged with implementing the regulations must show that it will enforce the regulations effectively and impartially. To achieve voluntary consensus on these issues in the face of inadequate information and uncertain outcomes is impossible. At the same time, a set of rules and regulations imposed by an outside authority (like the PWD) without any consultation with those affected is unlikely to be effective. In point of fact, the state either avoids the problem altogether or makes a set of regulations which are not always clear, consistent, and technically sound, and which are not enforced or enforced in a lackadaisical manner. The latter is typical of irrigation management while the former is characteristic of land consolidation and soil conservation.

Role of state policy

State intervention in agriculture, of course, extends far beyond attempts to change agrarian relations. Public investments, the policy regarding taxes and subsidies, and pricing and distribution of farm inputs are other interventions which have a profound bearing on agricultural growth. We have already referred to the massive investments by the government in irrigation, land improvement, research and extension, and other infrastructural support for agriculture. At current prices, according to CSD estimates, direct public investment in agriculture has arisen from Rs 329 crores in 1970–1 to over Rs 2,500 crores in 1984–5. In real terms, however, the growth is considerably smaller—the level in 1984–5 being barely 60 per cent higher than in 1970–1. In fact, the quantum of public investment in agriculture had peaked in 1980–1 at a level slightly more than double the 1970–1 level and has since fallen off. The cumulative direct public investment in agriculture during this period represents about a third of the total investment in agriculture in current prices, and about 40 per cent in real terms.

Apart from direct investment, loans by term-lending financial institutions (like NABARD) finance a significant and growing proportion of private investment in agriculture: in 1973–4, the long-term loan by these institutions for agriculture amounted to Rs 438 crores which was about 32 per cent of the estimated total gross fixed investment by the private sector in agriculture. By 1984–5, the volume had risen to Rs 2,435 crores which is nearly 54 per cent of the total private capital formation in agriculture in that year. Short and medium-term loans to finance working capital needs through cooperatives and public sector banks has also grown apace from Rs 950 crores in 1973–4 to Rs 9,500 crores in 1984–5. They constitute between 12 and 16 per cent of the estimated total value of current material inputs used in the agricultural sector (Rath, 1987). The interest rate charged on loans to agriculturists is substantially less than the rates for non-agricultural borrowers, with even lower rates for small and marginal farmers.

The agricultural sector, like the rest of the economy, is liable to both direct and indirect taxation. Land revenue is the most important direct tax in agriculture. Income from agriculture is exempt from the federal income tax, but is liable to taxation by the state governments. Land revenue, once an important source of government revenue, has progressively diminished in importance partly because the rates have not been revised for a long time and partly because of exemptions of certain categories of land from this tax and, in some cases, abolition of land revenue itself. The coverage of agricultural income tax is limited and amounts realized quite small. Altogether, total collection of direct taxes from agriculture has increased from around Rs 107 crores in 1960–1 to around Rs 220 crores in 1984–5. As a proportion of net income from agriculture, these taxes amounted to about 1.6 per cent in 1960–1 and a mere 0.4 per cent in 1980–1. By contrast, the incidence of direct taxes (income and corporate tax) relative to non-agricultural incomes is much higher and has remained more or less constant between 4.5 and 5 per cent. Indirect taxes are much more important and have over the years become the dominant source of tax revenue. Since the rural areas spend relatively less of their income on urban manufactures subject to excise, customs, and sales tax, the overall incidence of indirect taxes on the agricultural population is lower than in urban areas, though it is increasing over time. The overall incidence of taxation relative to incomes in agriculture is thus lower. But since, on the average, incomes per head in the agricultural sector are also relatively low, this cannot be taken as evidence of agriculture as a whole being undertaxed.[37] More plausible is the proposition that the better-off persons/families in agriculture are taxed much less than their non-agricultural or urban counterparts.

The rural areas, in general, and agriculture, in particular, benefit from a variety of direct and indirect subsidies.[38] Apart from the free education, health, and other general infrastructural and social services provided by the state, the agricultural sector specifically benefits from subsidies. These may be in the form of outright grants to help particular classes of farmers in times of distress or to help them build a better productive asset base (e.g. through the IRDP). But for the most part subsidies are indirect, being given by supplying inputs needed for agricultural products at rates which do not fully cover their cost. The fertilizer subsidy (which was of the order of over Rs 6,000 crores in 1990–1) is the most visible. There are, as already noted, significant elements of concealed subsidy in the pricing of irrigation, electricity, and agricultural credit.

The collection of water rates from surface irrigation is not adequate to cover even operating costs, leave alone depreciation or even a modest interest on capital. According to a recent estimate (Mundle and Rao, 1990), the loss is currently of the order of Rs 4,500 crores per annum and rising at an alarming rate. It is also well known that the marginal cost of supplying electricity to rural areas is much higher than in urban areas (because of the extra investment in transmission and distribution network, line losses), and yet agricultural users are

[37]For a discussion of various aspects of direct taxation of agriculture, see GOI (1972a); on relative incidence of indirect taxes on rural and urban areas, see Chelliah and Lal (1978).
[38]For a recent comprehensive assessment of implicit subsidies, see Mundle and Rao(1991). On the larger question of intersector resource transfers, see Mody, Mundle, and Raj (1985).

charged much lower rates than industry. In fact, several states have exempted certain classes of agriculturists from paying any charge while several others have switched to fixed rates based on horsepower of pumps irrespective of the volume of power consumption. Substantial subsidies also accrue to farmers getting access to cooperative and commercial bank credit at rates much below those charged to other sections and, of course, the market rate. The laxity in collection of interest and principal repayments in time, and the periodic decisions to 'write off' arrears also, in effect, subsidize farmers.[39]

The subsidies on all these accounts are rising: according to one estimate (Subba Rao, 1985) the total subsidies for agriculture and rural development rose from Rs 764 crores in 1974–5 (about 2.7 per cent of GDP from agriculture) to Rs 2,560 crores in 1980–1 (about 6 per cent of agricultural GDP). Subsidies on water, fertilizer, and electricity alone have risen from Rs 720 crores to Rs 1,584 crores in this period. Estimates for more recent years are not available but there is doubt that the quantum has risen substantially since.

The state has also exerted a significant influence in the prices of agricultural products. Since the early sixties, the government has been committed to a policy of guaranteed support prices to production, and it now covers practically all important crops. The Agricultural Prices Commission, set up in 1965, advises the government on the level of support and procurement prices to be given to various crops. In making its recommendation, the Commission has to balance a number of considerations including costs of production, market conditions, the need to maintain overall price stability, and the optimum use of resources. The relative importance to be attached to these considerations has been a matter of continuing debate both at the analytical and political level. Among the major issues under contention is the relation

[39]For comprehensive estimates of various subsidies to agriculture and alternative ways of estimating them, see Subba Rao (1985) and Gulati (1989). Subba Rao shows that a disproportionately large share of the benefits of these subsidies accrues to richer regions and better-off farmers. However, it would be incorrect to assume that the entire benefit of these subsidies accrues to farmers. A part, perhaps a substantial part, is due to inefficiency (over-capitalization, over-manning, poor use of capacity) in the production and distribution of inputs. Moreover, the impact of these elements on agriculture (overall, by regions and classes) cannot be considered in isolation from terms of trade, taxation, policies regarding prices and public distribution; and the nature, magnitude, and effectiveness of public investment in agriculture. This calls for a general equilibrium type analysis. For a recent attempt at exploring comprehensively various policy options in respect of agriculture in such a framework, see Narayana et al. (1991).

between support prices and costs of production; and the question of parity between agricultural and other prices.

There is a consensus on the general principle that support prices should cover the costs of production, and the Agricultural Prices Commission, in fact, uses the data from the detailed cost-of-cultivation surveys conducted in all major states as a major input in formulating its recommendations. The purchase prices fixed by the Commission for rice and wheat at any rate are found to be 'in general close to (or above) the weighted average costs of production' (Subba Rao, 1985a: 27). Actual prices announced by the state governments have, in general, been higher than the APC recommendations. Moreover, support prices being uniform across the country, regions with relatively low costs and/or declining unit costs tend to get a disproportionately large benefit under the present regime. It has been argued that this reflects the ability of the farmers in the more advanced, surplus-producing states to influence price policy in their favour; while the general tendency to fix prices higher than the APC recommendations and the acceptance of the principle of parity prices—i.e maintaining a reasonable balance between agricultural and non-agricultural prices— reflects the power of the farm lobby generally.[40]

While the political influence of the farm lobby is not to be mini-mized, it needs to be noted that, at least in some states for some time in the past, a system of compulsory procurement at prices below the market price was in vogue; while in others the restrictions on the movement of foodgrains across state borders tended to depress open-market prices in states with a surplus, thereby facilitating procurement by public agencies at the prescribed procurement prices. But over the years, movement restrictions have been progressively relaxed and are now minimal, thereby removing the potential source of discrepancy between the free-market and procurement prices. Moreover, the rate of productivity gain in the major surplus-producing regions (namely Pun-jab, Haryana, and West UP) has fallen off sharply of late, and this implies that unit costs in these tracts may well be rising. The market price has been the leader price and the procurement price the reluctant

---

[40]For a detailed exposition of the political economy of agricultural price formation in terms of the power of the large farmers, and their alliance with the bourgeoisie, see Mitra (1977).

For a recent discussion of the issues, see Rath (1987), Kahlon and Tyagi (1983), Tyagi (1987), and Nalini Vittal (1988).

follower. Regardless of the principle of price fixation, the prices actually fixed by the state seem to be based on the simple rule of thumb that if the market price rises for one or two years the procurement price should be raised by about half to two-thirds of the increase in wholesale price.

One of the arguments advanced by the 'farm lobby' in support of higher prices is that the prices of inputs used in cultivation has risen much faster than that of output, and that the overall terms of trade have shifted against agriculture. The prices of key inputs—especially fertilizers and diesel oil—have indeed risen faster than output prices as a result of the oil shocks. As for the overall terms of trade, several questions are still under debate—these concern commodities whose prices should enter the calculation: what are the appropriate prices (farm harvest, wholesale, retail) to be used, what are the relative weights to be given to various commodities and services. Despite differences in concept and methods of estimation, all the available studies point to broadly similar patterns of change over the last three decades: the agricultural sector's terms of trade improved steadily from the late fifties to the early seventies, and have been falling since 1974–5 (see Sundrum, 1987: 120–3; Ahluwalia, 1985: 43–6).

These trends have two aspects: one relates to their implications for income distribution between farmers and the rest of the economy, and the other to their impact on productivity growth. A fall in agriculture's terms of trade means that the farmers are getting less of manufactures and other non-agricultural products per unit of their output. In the context of growing output and marketed surplus, this need not necessarily imply a reduction in the absolute real income, but it certainly means that farmers are not as well off as they would have been with stable terms of trade. Even a relative worsening of the terms of trade for agriculture will, it is argued, dampen the incentives for growth as it reduces the returns to investment in current input and capital improvement. This is too simplistic an argument in as much as it ignores technical progress and the fact that there is much scope for improving the efficiency of input use even with known technology. Agricultural growth does not depend only or even mainly on getting the price right. An oversimplistic and, therefore, excessive preoccupation with price can do harm by distracting attention from the harder but more important tasks of technological innovation and of removing institutional and other non-price constraints which stand in the way of such innovations becoming a reality on the farmers' fields.

TABLE 1

PUBLIC SECTOR PLAN OUTLAYS IN AGRICULTURAL DEVELOPMENT

(Rs crores)

	First Plan 1951–6	Second Plan 1956–61	Third Plan 1961–6	1966–9	Fourth Plan 1969–74	Fifth Plan 1974–9	Sixth Plan 1980–5	Seventh Plan 1985–90
1. Agriculture and cooperation	211	216	528	547	1649	3217	7323	12687
2. Rural development	79	219	288	97	115	604	6297	14195
3. Special area programmes	—	—	—	—	—	168	1580	3436
4. Irrigation and flood control	434	515	937	794	1191	4752	10930	16718
5. Total (1 to 4)	724	950	1753	1438	2955	8741	26130	47036
6. Total public sector plan outlay	1960	4600	8576	6625	15779	39426	109292	222170
7. (5) as % of (6)	36.9	20.7	20.4	21.7	18.7	22.2	23.9	21.2

Source: GOI, Ministry of Agriculture, Directorate of Economics and Statistics, Agricultural Statistics at a Glance (1990).

TABLE 2

SELECTED INDICATORS OF AGRICULTURAL GROWTH IN INDIA
1950–1 TO 1986–7

Units	1950–1	1960–1	1970–1	1980–1	1986–7
Net area source (million ha)	118.7	133.2	140.3	140.0	140.1
Gross cropped area (milion ha)	131.9	152.8	165.8	172.6	176.9
Cropping intensity (per cent)	111.1	114.7	118.2	124.7	126.2
Gross irrigated area (million ha)	22.6	28.0	38.2	49.8	55.6
Fertilizer consumption (million tons) (N+P+K)	65.6	292.1	2177.0	5515.6	8644.9
Institutional credit[1]					
Short term (millions of rupees)	229	1828	5193	20433	45183
Medium and long-term (millions of rupees)	13[2]	315[2]	1595[2]	13464	31930
Index nos. for all crops[3] (1967–8 to 1969–70 = 100)					
Area	78.7	95.3	101.9	106.1	103.4
Production	60.1	84.5	108.8	131.7	154.1
Yield	78.5	91.1	105.6	118.7	137.6

Sources: GOI, Ministry of Agriculture, Directorate of Economics and Statistics, Agricultural Statistics at a Glance, New Delhi, 1990.

Notes: [1] Cooperatives, commercial banks, and regional rural banks.
           [2] Excluding term loans of commercial and regional rural banks.
           [3] Triennial average centred around each year.

TABLE 3
DEVELOPMENT OF IRRIGATION, 1950–1 TO 1989–90

(million hectares)

	Cumulative irrigation potential				Gross irrigated area	
	Major and medium	Major surface works	Ground-water	Total	As per plan	As per land-use statistics
1950–1	8.62	7.48	6.5	22.6	22.6	22.6
1960–1	13.25	7.51	8.3	29.1	27.8	27.98
1968–9	17.01	7.60	12.5	37.1	35.3	35.43
1979–80	25.56	9.08	22.0	56.64	52.68	49.21
1989–90	31.83	12.25	34.78	79.74	69.23	55.64[1]

Source: Planning Commission.
Note: [1] relates to 1986–7 (provisional).

REFERENCES

AGARWAL, BINA (1982), *Mechanisation in Indian Agriculture—An Analytical Study based on the Punjab*, Allied Publishers, New Delhi.

AHLUWALIA, ISHER J. (1985), *Industrial Growth in India*, OUP, Delhi.

ATHREYA, V.B. (1984), Vadamalaipuram: a resurvey, W.P. No. 50, Madras Institute of Development Studies (MIDS), Madras.

BAGCHI, A.K. ed. (1988), *Economy, Society and Polity—Essays in the Political Economy of Indian Planning*, Oxford University Press, New Delhi.

BANDHOPADHYAY, N. (1988), The story of land reforms in India, in Bagchi, ed., *Economy, Society and Polity*.

BHADURI, A. (1973), Agricultural backwardness under semi-feudalism, *Economic Journal*, March; reprinted in *Unconventional Economic Essays: Selected Papers of Amit Bhaduri*, OUP, Delhi, 1993.

BHALLA, G.S. and Y.K. ALAGH (1979), *Performance of Indian Agriculture: A District-wise Study*, Sterling, New Delhi.

BHALLA, G.S. and B.D. TALIB (1981), Agrarian structure and peasant movements in the Pubjab, Jawaharlal Nehru University, New Delhi, mimeo.

BHALLA, G.S. and D.S. TYAGI (1989), Patterns in Indian agricultural development: a district level study; Institute for Studies in Industrial Development, New Delhi.

BHALLA, SHEILA (1976), New relations of production in Haryana agriculture, *EPW, Review of Agriculture*, March.

_____ (1977), Changes in average and tenure structure of land holdings in Haryana 1962–1972, *EPW*, March.

70 A. VAIDYANATHAN

BINSWANGER, H.W. (1978), The economics of tractors in S. Asia: an analytical review, ICRISAT, Hyderabad.

BLYN, GEORGE (1966), *Agricultural Trends in India 1891–1947: Output Availability and Productivity*, University of Pennsylvania, Philadelphia.

BOYCE, JAMES K. (1987), *Agrarian Impasse in Bengal: Institutional Constraints to Technical Changes*, OUP, Bombay.

CHELLIAH, R.J. and R.N. LAL (1978), Incidence of indirect taxation in India, 1973/4, NIFPR, New Delhi.

CHOPRA, K., G.K. KADEKODI, and V.M. MURTHY (1988), Sukhomajri and Dharwala watersheds in Haryana: a participatory approach to management, Institute of Economic Growth, Delhi, mimeo.

CUMMINGS, RALPH W. and S.K. RAY (1969), 1968–69 Foodgrains production: relative contributions of weather and new technology, *EPW Review of Agriculture*, September.

DAS GUPTA, A.K. (1984), *Growth and Composition of Agricultural Capital Stock in Indian States 1961–1977*, Hindustan Publishing Corporation, Delhi.

DAS GUPTA, B. (1977), *Village Society and Labour Use*, OUP, Delhi.

DESAI, GUNWANT (1982), Sustaining rapid growth in India's fertiliser consumption, *IFPRI*, Washington, DC.

_____ (1986), Policies for growth in fertiliser consumption—the next stage, *EPW*.

DESAI, GUNWANT and SURENDER SINGH (1973), Growth of fertiliser use in the districts of India: performance and policy implications, IIM, Ahmedabad, mimeo.

DHAWAN, B.D. (1983), Leading issues in irrigation policy: a review article, Institute of Economic Growth, New Delhi, mimeo.

_____ (1985), Output impact according to main irrigation sources: empirical evidence from some selected states, Institute of Economic Growth, Delhi, mimeo.

_____ (1988), *Irrigation in India's Agricultural Development: Productivity, Stability and Equity*, Commonwealth Publishers, New Delhi.

_____ (1989), *Studies in Irrigation Management*, Commonwealth Publishers, New Delhi.

_____ (1990), *Studies in Minor Irrigation with Special Reference to Groundwater*, Commonwealth Publishers, New Delhi.

FRANKEL, FRANCINE (1971), *India's Green Revolution: Economic Gains and Political Costs*, Princeton University Press, Princeton.

Government of Andhra Pradesh (1982), *Report of the Commission for Irrigation Utilization*.

GOI, Ministry of Finance (1972a), *Report of the Committee on Taxation of Agricultural Wealth and Income*, New Delhi.

GOI (1972b), *Report of Irrigation Commission*, New Delhi.

GOI, Planning Commission (1963), *Progress of Land Reform*, New Delhi.

GOI, Planning Commission (1973), *Report of the Task Force on Agrarian Relations*, New Delhi, mimeo.

GOI, Planning Commission (1985), *Report of Study Group on Agricultural Strategies for Eastern Region of India*, New Delhi.

GUHAN, S. (1983), Palakuruchi: a resurvey, Working Paper No. 42, MIDS, Madras.

GUHAN, S. and J. MENCHER (1982), Iruvelpattu revisited, Working Paper No. 28, MIDS, Madras.

GUHAN, S. and K. BHARATAN (1984), Dusi: a resurvey, Working Paper No. 52, MIDS, Madras.

GULATI, ASHOK (1989), Input subsidies in Indian agriculture: a statewise analysis, *EPW*, June 24.

HAZELL, PETER (1982), Instability in Indian foodgrain production, IFPRI, Research Report 30, Washington, DC.

HESTON, ALAN (1977), National income, in Dharma Kumar, ed., *The Cambridge Economic History of India 1957–1970*, vol. 2, Orient Longman, New Delhi.

Indian Society of Agricultural Economics (1972), Seminar on the Role of Irrigation in the Development of Indian Agriculture.

ISHIKAWA, SHIGERU (1967), *Development in Asian Perspective*, Kinokuniya, Tokyo.

JODHA, N.S. (1986), Research and technology for dryland farming in India: some issues for future strategy, *IJAE*, July–September.

_____ (1990), Rural common property resources: contributions and crisis, Society for Promotion of Wastelands Development, New Delhi.

JODHA, N.S., ed. (1989), Technology options and economic policy for dryland agriculture: potential and challenge, Indian Society of Agricultural Economics, Bombay.

JOSHI, P.C. (1975), *Land Reforms in India*, Allied Publishers, Bombay.

KAHLON, A.S. and D.S. TYAGI (1983), *Agricultural Price Policy in India*, Allied Publishers, New Delhi.

KRISHNA, RAJ (1964), Some production functions for the Punjab, *IJAE*, July–December.

KRISHNA, RAJ and RAY CHOUDHRY (1980), Some aspects of wheat and rice price policy in India, World Bank Staff Working Paper 381.

LAL, DEEPAK (1972), *Wells and Welfare: An Exploratory Cost–Benefit Study of the Economics of Small-Scale Irrigation in Maharashtra*, OECD Press, Paris.

MAHENDRA DEV, S. (1985), Direction of change in performance of all crops in Indian agriculture in the late 1970s, *EPW*, December 21–8.

MAHENDRA DEV, S., S.M. DESHPANDE, and E. KAMIAH (1989), Estimation of yield functions with binary choice models: an analysis of agro-climatic regions in India, mimeo.

MEHRA, SHAKUNTALA (1981), Instability in Indian agriculture in the context of the new technology, IIFRI, Research Report 25, Washington, DC.

MELLOR, JOHN W. (1988), Food production, consumption and development strategy, in Robert E.B. Lucas and Gustav F. Papanek, eds., *The Indian Economy: Recent Development and Future Prospects*, Westview Press, Colorado/OUP, Delhi.

MITRA, ASHOK (1977), *Terms of Trade and Class Relations*, Frank Cass, London.

MINHAS, B.S. and A. VAIDYANATHAN (1965), Growth of crop output in India: 1951–54 to 1958–61, *Journal of the Indian Society of Agricultural Statistics*, 17, 2.

MODY A., S. MUNDLE, and K.N. RAJ (1985), Resource flows from agriculture: Japan and India, in Kazushi Okhawa and G. Ranis, eds., *Japan and the Developing Countries: A Comparative Analysis*, Basil Blackwell, Oxford.

MUKHOPADHYAY, S.K. (1976), *Sources of Variations in Agricultural Productivity: A Cross-Section Time-Series Study of India*, Macmillan, Delhi.

MUNDLE, S. and GOVINDA RAO (1991), Volume and composition of Government subsidies in India, 1987–8, *EPW*, June 24.

NADKARNI, M.V. and R.S. DESHPANDE (1979), Underutilisation of land—climate or institutional factors, *IJAE*, April–June.

NAGARAJ, R. (1980), Determinants of fertilizer use and its growth, unpublished M.Phil. dissertation, Centre for Development Studies, Trivandrum.

NARAIN DHARM (1977), Growth of productivity in Indian agriculture, *IJAE*, January–March.

NARAYANA, N.S.S., K.S. PARIKH, and T.N. SRINIVASAN (1991), *Agricultural Growth and Redistribution of Income: Policy Analysis with a General Equilibrium Model of India*, North-Holland, Amsterdam/Allied Publishers, Bombay.

National Council of Applied Economic Research (NCAER) (1978), Fertilizer demand study: survey data on pattern of fertilizer use on selected crops, 1975–76 and 1976–77, New Delhi, mimeo.

PARIKH, ASHOK (1970), Cropwise, districtwise production functions, *IJAE*, January–March.

PARIKH, A. and P. TRIVEDI (1982), Impact of irrigation and fertilizers on the growth of output in Andhra Pradesh, *IJAE*, April–June.

PARIKH, K.S. (1978), HYV fertilisers: synergy or substitution: implications for policy and prospects for agricultural development, *EPW, Review of Agr.*, March.

PARIKH, K.S., T.N. SRINIVASAN et al. (1974), Optimum requirement of fertilizers for the Fifth Plan period, ISI, New Delhi, mimeo.

PATEL, R.G. and D. JHA (1978), Output growth and change in Maharashtra agriculture: a district-wise study, *IJAE*, June–September.

RAJ, K.N. and M. THARAKAN (1983), Agrarian reform in Kerala and its impact on the rural economy: a preliminary assessment, in A.K. Ghose, ed., *Agrarian*

Reform in Contemporary Developing Countries, Crown, Helm and St Martin's Press.

RANADE, C.G. (1980), Impact of crop pattern on agricultural productivity, *IJAE*, April–June.

RAO, C.H. HANUMANTHA (1975), *Technological Change and the Distribution of Gains in Indian Agriculture*, Macmillan, New Delhi.

RAO, C.H. HANUMANTHA, S.K. RAY, and K. SUBBA RAO (1988), *Unstable Agriculture and Droughts: Implications for Policy*, Vikas, New Delhi.

RAO, K. SUBBA (1985a), Farm prices—a survey of the debate, in M.L. Dantwala et al., eds., *Indian Agricultural Development since Independence*, Oxford IBH, New Delhi.

_____ (1985b), Incentive policies and India's agricultural development: some aspects of regional and social equity, *IJAE*, October–December.

RAO, S.K. (1971), Interregional variations in agricultural growth, 1952–53 to 1964–65—a tentative analysis in relation to irrigation, *EPW*, July.

RATH, N. (1987), Agricultural Growth, Investment and Credit in India, Sir A. Ramaswamy Mudaliar Memorial Lecture, University of Kerala, Trivandrum (mimeo).

RATH, N. and A. MITRA (1982), Economics of Irrigation in Water Scarce Regions: A Study of Maharashtra, Gokhale Institute of Politics and Economics, Pune.

RAY, S.K. (1977), Variation in crop output, Institute of Economic Growth, Delhi, mimeo.

_____ (1980), Change in agriculture in eastern and western regions of UP, Institute of Economic Growth, Delhi, mimeo.

_____ (1983), Growth and instability in Indian agriculture, Institute of Economic Growth, Delhi, mimeo.

_____ (1985), *Intensification of Agriculture: A Study of the Plans of Uttar Pradesh*, Hindustan Publishing Corp., New Delhi.

_____ (1987), Instability in Indian agriculture revisited, Lecture delivered at National Symposium on Growth and Instability in Indian Agriculture, Indian Agricultural Statistics Research Institute, New Delhi.

Reserve Bank of India (1984), *Report of Committee on Agricultural Productivity in East India*, Bombay.

ROY, PRANNOY (1981), Transition in agriculture: empirical indication and results (evidence from the Punjab), *Journal of Peasant Studies*, January.

RUDRA, A. and A. SEN (1980), Farm size and labour use: analysis and policy, *EPW*.

SARMA, J.S. and SHYAMAL ROY (1979), Foodgrains production and consumption behaviour in India, 1960–77, IFPRI, Research Paper No. 52, Washington, DC.

SEN, S.R. (1967), Growth and instability in Indian agriculture, *Journal of the Indian Society of Agricultural Statistics*.

SHAH, TUSHAR (1988), Groundwater markets and small farmer development, *EPW*, March 26.

SIDDHU, D.S. (1979), *Price Policy for Wheat in India*, S. Chand, New Delhi.

SRINIVASAN, T.N. (1979), Trends in agriculture in India, 1949–50 to 1977–8, *EPW*, Special Number, August.

SUNDARI, T.K. (1991), Caste and agrarian structure: a study of Chingleput District, Oxford IBH and Centre for Development Studies, Trivandrum.

SUNDRUM R.M. (1987), *Growth and Income Distribution in India: Policy and Performance since Independence*, Sage, New Delhi.

Society for Promotion of Wasteland Development (1990), Profile of Activities, New Delhi.

TYAGI, D.S. (1987), Domestic terms of trade and their effect on supply and demand in agriculture, *EPW*, March.

VAIDYANATHAN, A. (1977), Performance and prospects of crop production in India, *EPW*, Special No.

___ (1978), HYV and fertiliser: synergy or substitution: a 'comment', *EPW*, June.

___ (1986), Water control institutions and agriculture: a comparative perspective, *Indian Economic Review*.

___ (1987), Irrigation and agricultural growth, *IJAE*, October–December.

___ (1988), India's agricultural development in a regional perspective, R.C. Dutt lecture, Centre for Studies in Social Sciences, Calcutta.

___ (1990), Integrated watershed development: some major issues, *Wasteland News*, Supplement to volume VI, no.4.

VAIDYANATHAN, A. and C. MUKHERJI (1980), Growth and fluctuation of food grains yields: a statewise analysis, *IJAE*, April–June.

___ (1987), Statewise analysis of agricultural growth, in Prem Narain et al. (eds.), *Recent Advances in Agricultural Statistics*, Wiley Eastern, New Delhi.

VENKATARAMAN, L.S. and A. PRAHLADECHAR (1980), Growth rates and cropping pattern changes in agriculture in six states: 1950–1975, *IJAE*, April–June.

VIDYASAGAR, R. (1980), Decomposition of growth trends and certain related issues, *IJAE*, April–June.

VITTAL, NALINI (1988), Intersectoral terms of trade in India: reality and hope, *EPW, Review of Agriculture*, September.

Unfree Labour and Indian Agriculture

ASHOK RUDRA

1. THE CONCEPT

The concept of free and unfree labour is one that occupies a place of fundamental importance in Marxian political economy and historiography. Free wage labour is supposed to be one of the distinguishing characteristics of the capitalist relations of production, if not the only one, that is, its *differentia specifica*. We shall see that this question is a highly problematic one and one of the main purposes of the present paper is to discuss some of these problems. However, the importance of the concept reaches beyond capitalism. That is because, in Marxian historiography, the concept of different degrees of unfree labour plays a crucial part in defining different stages of development through which human society passes. This historiography has for its central theme the idea of 'progress'. Progress is conceived of as increasing the freedom of man from all its bondages. More particularly, there is, in what we shall call vulgar Marxism, the grand vision of history as a sequence of systems of production[1]—in the case of Europe: slavery, feudalism, capitalism, and socialism. These systems are supposed to correspond to higher and higher degrees of freedom enjoyed by the producer. Thus, feudal serfs are more free than slaves, capitalist workers more free than serfs, and so on. The uni-linear scheme of slavery,

[1]In Marxian historiography, one talks of a sequence of 'modes of production'. We are deliberately avoiding the term 'mode' in view of the great deal of confusion that is associated with it. We have argued elsewhere (see Rudra, 1988b) that while present-day Marxists treat the term 'mode of production' as a technical term occupying a central position in Marx's conceptualization of society and history, Marx himself never invested the term with any precise meaning and used it interchangeably with such other terms as 'systems of production', 'kinds of production', etc. We have argued that the term 'mode of production' does not add anything more to the concept of relations of production. For instance, we think that Marx's view of history can be understood as one involving a succession of dominant relations of production. In view of our strongly held position, we are insisting on using the phrase 'system of production'.

feudalism, capitalism is no more accepted to have universal validity.[2] However, whatever be the sequences of social systems in different parts of the world, all pre-capitalist societies have been marked by labourers being unfree, a higher development of society being associated with a higher degree of freedom of labourers. Therein lies the importance of the concept of free labour; therein also lie all its difficulties.

Marx's definition

The following passage is one of the most frequently quoted from Marx, supposedly containing the full essence of the concept of free labour:

... free labourers, in the double sense that neither they themselves form part and parcel of the means of production, as in the case of slaves, bondsmen, and co., nor do the means of production belong to them, as in the case of peasant-proprietors; they are, therefore, free from, unencumbered by, any means of production of their own.[3]

Marx elaborates on this idea in the following passage:

The immediate producer, the labourer, could only dispose of his own person after he had ceased to be attached to the soil and ceased to be the slave, serf or bondsman of another. To become a free seller of labour-power, who carries his commodity wherever he finds a market, he must further have escaped from the regime of the guilds, their rules for apprentices and journeymen, and the impediments of their labour regulations. Hence, the historical movement which changes the producers into wage workers, appears, on the one hand, as their emancipation from serfdom and from the fetters of guilds ...

But, on the other hand, these *newfreedmen* became sellers of themselves only after they had been robbed of all their own means of production, and of all the guarantees of existence afforded by the old feudal arrangements.[4]

Marx harps on this theme of freedom in the double sense in various other places.[5] It is quite clear from the context that Marx is talking not

---

[2]For detailed discussions see Sawer (1977), Melotti (1977), and Rudra (1988a).
[3]Marx (1954), p.174.
[4]Marx (1954), p. 715.
[5]For instance this worker must be free in the double sense that as a free individual he can dispose of his labour-power as his own commodity, and that, on the other hand, he has no other commodity for sale, i.e. he is rid of them, he is free of all the objects needed for the realisation of his labour-power' (Marx, 1954, pp. 272–3).

Another example: 'free from the old relations of clientship, bondage and servitude, and secondly free of all belongings and possessions, and of every objective, material form of being, free of all property, dependent on the sale of its labour capacity or on begging, vagabondage and robbery as its only source of income' (Marx, 1954, p. 507).

of free or unfree labour in general but only of the contrast between the conditions of labour under feudalism and capitalism. Labour in socialism is also supposed to be free but Marx is clearly not talking of labourers under socialism. Nor is he talking of slaves. Slavery is a form of unfreedom where the direct producer does not own the means of production, hence if and when he becomes 'free' he cannot do so in the double sense of the feudal serf to become wage labourer.

The interpretation of the concept of free labour which has been most generally accepted is that of 'commodified' labour, that is labour that has become a commodity. It goes along with a definition of capitalism as an economic system in which commodity production has become generalized in the sense of having supplanted all other forms of production (e.g. production for self-consumption, production by self-employed workers, production for barter, production for distribution as in the traditional Indian village community, etc.) and in which labour has also become a commodity. By 'free' is meant 'free wage labour' and by that is meant such labour which exchanges in a 'labour market' against its value, like any other commodity.

We may note that on this matter, Marx has an unexpected and strange bedfellow in Max Weber. As is well known, Weber was also a serious student of capitalism, though he held different views from Marx on several important matters. But he also thought that a characteristic feature of capitalism is that 'services of labour are the subject of a contractual relationship which is free on both sides'.[6] It may however be an exaggeration to say that 'Weber considered capitalism and free labour to be ... synonymous',[7] a position that has been ascribed commonly to Marx.

Daniel Thorner's explanation

While Marx is indeed the fountain-head of this particular seminal idea, he is not to be relied upon for a clear explanation. Lucidity was not his special virtue; his love for a literary style that is much too compressed and pregnant with various layers of meanings—many of them half-articulated—has been the delight of Marxologues who received from him generous rations of ambiguous matters to be explained, clarified, rationalized, and controverted. But it has also been the despair of those

[6]Weber (1978), pp. 127, 128.
[7]Miles (1987), p. 2.

who might want to draw lessons for action. From this point of view, we find the clearest, if not the most profound, explanation of the concept of free and unfree labour in the following words of Daniel Thorner:[8]

A free labourer is one who is able to accept or reject the conditions and wages offered by the employer. If he wishes, he may refrain altogether from working. Once having taken a job he can decide to give notice and quit. Economic stringency may indeed compel a free labourer to agree temporarily to terms he does not consider favourable. But his basic right to refuse work or to seek alternative employment remains uncompromised.

An unfree, or bond labourer, by contrast, is one whose bargaining power is virtually non-existent, or has been surrendered. Such a labourer does not possess the right or has yielded the right to refuse to work under the terms set by his master. Through custom, compulsion, or specific obligation, the bond labourer is tied to his master's needs. He can neither quit nor take up work for another master without first receiving permission.

The fact that a labourer is under contract—whether formal or informal, oral or written—does not tell us whether he is free or unfree. There are contracts which signify bondage and contracts which state the terms of free agreements arrived at freely ... A free labourer who enters into a contract to work for a stipulated period of time for a certain employer does not thereby surrender his freedom; he is merely exercising it in a particular fashion. The crucial question is whether he can leave unconditionally at the end of the specified period. If so, will he be in a position to negotiate again with the same employer or to open negotiations with other employers on a basis of unimpaired bargaining power? ... Similarly, if the emoluments provided in the contract are markedly less than the going local rates, there is again a strong suspicion that the relationship is not a free one.

Extra-economic coercion

One important point that has always been emphasized is that while talking about free and unfree labour one is concerned with the absence of freedom which arises from constraints due to factors outside the domain of economics. The most characteristic term used in this connection is 'extra-economic coercion'. One elaborates the qualification 'extra-economic' by resorting to such phrases as politico-juridical, customary, etc.[9] The idea is that there is no society where the act of

[8]Thorner (1962).
[9]Thus, Takahashi (1978) writes, 'The feudal landlords, in virtue of that ownership, use "extra-economic coercion" directly, without the intervention of the laws of commodity exchange, to take the surplus labour from the peasant producers ... It is an obligation laid on

producing goods and services can ever be totally free. There are lots of constraints within which labourers have to work. But in a capitalist economy these constraints are all economic in nature, whereas in pre-capitalist economies labourers are subjected to various restrictions imposed by political powers as well as social institutions.

2. DIFFERENT KINDS OF UNFREE LABOUR

In this section we shall quickly review some of the different kinds of unfree labour that have been seen in history. The most important and the easiest to identify is, of course, the outright slave. A slave may be defined as

> one who owns or controls neither his own labour power nor the means of production with which he produces, and whose entire product is forcibly appropriated by another... The slave is normally outside the dominant community in which he performs his labour, either because he has in some manner (debt, for example) lost his membership in it, or because he originally belonged to another community from which he was alienated by purchase or warfare or the like. Because of his external relationship to the dominant community, the slave can be bought or sold or otherwise alienated and exchanged, and is, as a labourer, subject to an amount of direct force normally greater than that found in other labour relationships.[10]

It may be noted that in this definition the slave is engaged in the act of production—sometimes even the production of commodities. Such a slave has to be distinguished from slaves who provide their masters with various personal services. Such domestic slaves or palace slaves have been much more common in the history of mankind than slaves engaged in production, which alone lies at the base of the conception of the slave mode of production. The most familiar example of such a mode is provided by ancient Greece and Rome. There, too, instances of

---

the producer by force and independently of his own volition to fulfil certain economic demands of an overlord whether these demands take the form of services to be performed or of dues to be paid in money or in kind ... This coercive force may be that of military strength, possessed by the feudal superior, or of custom backed by some kind of judicial procedure, or the force of law.' Similarly Laclau (1971) talks of 'a general ensemble of extra-economic coercions weighing on the peasantry'. Again, Dobb (1978) talks of 'political constraint and the pressure of manorial customs'.

[10]Padgug (1976), p. 4.

most labourers being slaves or most of production being carried out by slaves constitute small parts, temporally and spatially, of Greco-Roman history. Such instances are even less important in other histories. Thus, for instance, in India, there were domestic and palace slaves not only in the Hindu period, not only under the Sultanate and the Mughal Empire, but even during the colonial period. However, slave labour constituting the basic means of production has never been widespread in India.

The next most familiar form of unfree labour, thanks to the Euro-centrism of world history, is the feudal serf. The serf is more difficult to define than the slave, not only because of geographical and temporal variations of lord–peasant relations in European history, but more so because of the lamentable habit, not only of the layman but also of the scholar, to use terms connected with European feudalism in a loose way. Present-day Marxists use the following definition: 'serf labour . . . is required by custom or law to provide either a certain quantity of labour power or a proportion of the product of labour power for the use of the non-labouring class.'[11] This usage diverges widely from the category that has been described as serf labour in historical accounts of feudalism which, incidentally, is not a Marxian concept at all but happens to be a classificatory term used by medieval historians of Europe. That category of labourers cannot be defined by themselves but require to be defined in terms of their duties, obligations, and subservient relationship vis-à-vis other classes such as lords and vassals and as a part and parcel of such institutions as the fief and the manor. In that historical context the serf (or the villein) is clearly distinct from various other categories of labourers in feudal society, all of whom were subject to extra-economic coercion. The use of the specific term 'serf' for the general purpose of describing all producers subjected to extra-economic coercion is due, largely, to Maurice Dobb, and the attempt by some Marxists during the last few decades to treat feudalism not as a social organization of a certain period in European history but as a mode of production applicable to all human history.[12]

Miles (1987) in a recent study of unfree labour mentions quite a few other similar kinds of labour that came into existence during and as a

[11]Miles (1987), p. 32.
[12]For an account of this attempt at universalization of feudalism and a critique of the same, see Rudra (1988b).

result of the spread of the political and economic power of Western Europe over the rest of the world. Thus, he talks of Convict Labour

which was the predominant form of labour exploitation in the Australian colonies in the late eighteenth and early nineteenth centuries (and was also utilised in Canada in the nineteenth century) and which exhibited features similar to those of slave labour . . . Although the convict was not a commodity available for sale or purchase, the powers that accrued to the non-producer as a result of the purchase of human beings as commodities were, in the case of convict labour, gained by the state. These powers invested in state officials were transferred when convicts were assigned to private individuals for whom they would provide labour and who thereby became responsible for the convict's material reproduction.

Then, Miles cites the case of Labour Tenancy

which was widespread in the South African colonies and later in South Africa. This relation of production was closer to serfdom than to slave labour . . . The labourer retained a significant degree of economic independence by remaining responsible for the production of the means of reproduction, and by owning the tools necessary for production . . . The relations of production were shaped by the establishment of private property rights in land and by a legal prohibition on land ownership by the labourers who therefore could gain access to the land as a means of production only by providing labour power directly to the landowner.

Miles further talks of Contractual Servitude

which was evident in the South African and the Australian colonies during the nineteenth century . . . Contractual servitude approximated to both nineteenth century indentured labour and contract migrant labour . . . The central feature of this form of unfree labour (as with indentured and contract migrant labour) lay with the contract itself which bound by legal means the labourer to the non-labourer for varying periods of time (up to five years).

Finally, Miles mentions Indentured Labour in which

form of unfree labour, the non-producer had a monopoly of the means of production and recruited and retained labour power by means of a formal, legal contract. Under the terms of this contract, the producer alienated the use and product of his/her labour power to the non-producer for a specified period of time and the non-producer assumed responsibility for the provision of the means of subsistence and reproduction, supplemented in certain circumstances by the payment of a small cash wage.

All these examples, with the exception of Indentured Labour, are from outside India. Indentured Labour prevailed in the Indian plantations; under this system a large number of labourers from south India migrated to Africa. From within India, the most commonly referred-to type of unfree labour used in production is what is generally termed 'bonded labour'. One definition of such a labourer is provided by the Commissioner for Scheduled Castes and Scheduled Tribes:

The prominent feature of the system is that a man pledges his person or sometimes a member of his family against a loan. The pleader or his nominee is released only on its discharge. Until then the man himself or the member of the family is required to work for the creditor against his daily meals. Since he gets no money, he has to depend upon someone in the family to procure the sum required for his release and this, of course, is rarely available. The relationship lasts for months and sometimes years, occasionally for an entire lifetime and not infrequently follows the male heir.[13]

The Labour Department of Bihar uses a very similar definition for a bonded labourer:

... a rural worker who is indebted to a propertied household and has to remain at the beck and call of his creditor throughout till he pays off the loan. Meanwhile, he does not receive any money payment but only meals. Thus, by paying no wages and by charging compound interest the creditor-employer keeps the labourer in bondage and manages to secure service not only from him but also his family.[14]

Bonded labourers, properly speaking (as distinguished from merely indebted peasantry), are a fast disappearing species in India. While surely it is possible to discover some examples of such labourers scattered in remote corners of India's vast countryside, it is debatable if they constitute a significant feature of the agrarian scene in the country. A great deal of details about such labourers, which go in different parts of the country by such names as, e.g., Padiyal, Hali, Sevakia, Gothi, Sonkiya, Jane, Jutha, Vet, Sagri, Khundit-Mundit, Vaula, Nadappu, Vallurkavu, Paunam, Harvahi, etc. are to be found in an early special issue of the *Indian Journal of Agricultural Economics* (1948) and a recent book edited by Utsa Patnaik and Manjari Dingwaney (1985).

[13]*Report of the Commissioner for Scheduled Castes and Scheduled Tribes, 1962–63.*
[14]Quoted in Sinha (1975).

3. PROBLEMS

In this part we shall discuss some of the difficult problems that are given rise to by the concept of free and unfree labour. The problems we shall discuss can be put in the form of the following questions.

(a) Is the existence of free labour a *sufficient* condition for defining a system of production as capitalist?

(b) Is the existence of free labour a *necessary* condition to define a system of production as capitalist?

(c) What kind of constraints are to be recognized as rendering labour unfree?

We shall see in the following that the answer to the first two questions above are in the negative. In other words, we shall show that free labour is neither a sufficient nor even a necessary condition for systems of production that have been regarded as capitalist. As to the third question, we shall see that there is considerable difference of opinion among scholars as to the particular constraints that render labour unfree.

Not a sufficient condition

Some present-day Marxists insist that free wage labour is not only an important characteristic feature of the capitalist mode of production but is also sufficient to define it: that is, free wage labour is both a necessary and a sufficient condition for capitalism to exist. The matter is something on which some discussion is called for. In the debate on the mode of production in Indian agriculture that took place in the seventies in the pages of the *Economic and Political Weekly*, some of the participants, the present writer included, took the stand that while wage labour is indeed a necessary condition for capitalism, it is not a sufficient one. Thus, I for instance advanced the following four criteria for a system of production to be capitalist:[15]

(1) Surplus is extracted from free sellers of labour power in a market for commodities.

(2) Surplus is realized through exchange in a market for commodities.

(3) Surplus is reinvested, giving rise to a continuous process of accumulation of capital.

---

[15]My detailed discussions are to be found in Rudra (1978) and Rudra (1982).

(4) Pursuit of profit leads to a continuous process of technological progress.

The opposite point of view was strongly defended by Paresh Chattopadhyay who wrote:

Labour takes the form of 'wage labour' only when labour power is a commodity used for the production of exchange value, and 'wage labour' connotes nothing but the 'single relation' between wage labour and capital, the other name for the capitalist relation. Hence, wage labour implies capital just as capital implies wage labour.[16]

This indeed is a very clear statement and it is surprising that there should have been any serious differences on this point. All of us, Paresh Chattopadhyay included, agree that employing labourers for wages is not sufficient to characterize capitalism, but that it is essential that the labourers produce surplus value which is reinvested to give rise to accumulation of capital. What Paresh Chattopadhyay is insisting upon is that Marx, in his original German, economized on words by using a single phrase to denote the employment of labourers by paying them wages and the reinvestment of surplus generated by them. The difference, if any, is therefore only semantic.

Not a necessary condition
Free labour cannot be regarded as a necessary condition for capitalism for the reason that if it were so we would have to treat the following two systems as falling outside capitalism:

(a) The system of production involving the use of slaves in America during the centuries between the colonization of the New World and the abolition of slavery.

(b) Present-day agriculture in the advanced capitalist countries of Western Europe.

American slavery and capitalism A tricky problem with equating capitalism to free labour is proposed by the phenomenon of the large-scale use of slave labour in the American plantations. The rise of this particular enterprise coincides in history with the rise of capitalism in Western Europe. There is no link whatsoever between this slave economy and those of ancient Greece and Rome. The problem is how

---

[16]Chattopadhyay (1980).

to characterize this system of production in terms of the concept of mode. If the form of labour exploitation is the only criterion by which to identify a mode of production then these American plantations have to be understood as embodying the slave mode of production. Yet this has not been an accepted characterization among Marxists. One reason is that it would make nonsense of the idea of slavery preceding feudalism and therefore being much behind capitalism with little development of the forces of production to the capitalist mode of production. American slavery however coexisted and interacted with the most advanced capitalism of its day.

The problem can be dealt quite satisfactorily in the framework of analysis of the Dependency School, for whom the unit of modal characterization is the world as a whole. Thus, Gunder Frank would treat American slavery as a particular form of exploitation of the Periphery by the Centre. Similarly, Wallerstein would treat this type of slavery as one among several forms of labour control utilized by the world capitalist system. But for the majority of Marxists who do not go along with the Dependency School there is no easy solution. They cannot characterize American slavery as capitalist, as the free labour criterion is grossly violated. On the other hand, to characterize it as the slave mode of production raises certain questions: are the internal contradictions of American slavery the same as or even similar to those of Greek and Roman slavery? Do these slave modes of production exhibit the same laws of motion? If so, what are these laws? And how can we explain that the American slave economy was an extension of the emergent capitalist economy of Europe? To the best of our knowledge these questions have not been answered by anybody. Wallerstein has been pilloried for his heretical views but no one has succeeded in giving a satisfactory modal explanation of American slavery.

Agriculture in present-day Western Europe We now come to a problem which seems not to have caught the attention of the Marxist scholars who go along with the wage labour definition of capitalism. The paradoxical fact is that in the advanced capitalist countries of Western Europe wage labour has practically disappeared from the agricultural sector. That there has been a very sharp decline in the fraction of the working force engaged in agriculture is well known. What seems to have escaped the attention of the Marxist scholars is that the population that has been left engaged in agriculture are almost all self-cultivators. Mechanization has proceeded so far as to almost totally supplant wage labourers. The typical farm in countries of Western Europe now consists of

(a) labour supplied by the family members of the owner of the farm;

(b) a huge collection of modern machinery;

(c) services of much larger machinery supplied by big firms specializing in hiring out machinery and machine operators to different farms in turn.

In view of the fact that the farms absorb predominantly family labour and only marginally the hired labourers of the servicing firms, should we describe these farms as peasant farms and therefore non-capitalist or even pre-capitalist? It seems to us that most Marxists would reject as absurd the characterization of these highly capital-intensive activities as pre-capitalist. These farms being organically linked with the servicing firms which are huge capitalist enterprises, would it make any sense to treat them as not constituting integral parts of the highly advanced capitalism of Western Europe?

If therefore we agree to continue to treat Western Europe as being capitalist, we have to accept that a capitalist system can include parts where production takes place with no wage labour at all.

What kind of constraints?

We have seen in Part 1 of the paper that the constraints that are supposed to make labour unfree in pre-capitalist socities have to be extra-economic in nature. The distinction between economic and extra-economic constraints is, indeed, extremely penetrating and illuminating. No doubt this distinction is one of the most incisive contributions of Marxian Political Economy to social science. Yet, it would be a mistake to think that the distinction is easy to apply. As is so common in the social sciences, the concept may be used without much difficulty in the context in which it was first constructed. Thus, the slave-owners' right over the life and death of the slave was ensured by law and enforced by the state. In the same way the feudal serf's attachment to the soil was ensured by feudal law and was enforceable by the court, whether of the Lord or of the Crown. Similarly, the various dues like tolls, banalities etc. had the same status for serf as well as non-serf peasants in the eyes of the law and of the civil administration. The customary rights of villagers over the commons, forest land etc. was also an extra-economic coercion applying upon labourers.

Bonded labourers The distinction, however, becomes clouded when we change the context and come, say, to the case of the debt-bonded labourers in Indian agriculture. There is no law that ties the labourer to his employer and the police will not come to force the labourer to work for that particular employer. The labourer took the loan voluntarily, and knows full well the terms of the contract. He is bonded in the sense that he cannot leave the employer before repaying his debt in full. But debt is an economic institution; how can we say then that the lack of freedom of the indebted or bonded agricultural labourer is extra-economic in character?

After all, an employee of the government or a modern private firm, who might have taken a loan from his employer also cannot leave without clearing his debts. We do not consider such an employee as akin to a feudal serf. We have no difficulty in accommodating him in the capitalist system. Where then can we draw the line of distinction between indebted peasants and government servants/private sector employees who might have taken a loan from their employers?

I think that the answer lies in the following:

There is such a phenomenon as some labourers being attached to certain employer families over years, sometimes over generations, in an unequal relation of mutual dependence, the basis of the relation being some loan taken a long time back. In such cases, quite often, both the parties have lost track of the loan accounts in terms of principal and interest, which accounts are in any case outrageous and totally arbitrary. It is the non-significant part played by the loan accounts and the essential part played by the relation of personal dependence and personal domination which qualifies the coercive relationship as being extra-economic.[17]

It follows that all those labourers who habitually take small amounts of advances from their employers do lose their freedom temporarily but they do not, by that token, become subject to extra-economic coercion. The same applies to farm servants who may work for several years at a stretch for the same employers. We are making this point, as

[17]Rudra (1982), p. 422.

it has been a common practice in this country among vulgar Marxists to characterize the Indian rural society as semi-feudal merely because of the existence of the phenomena of casual labourers taking loans from their employers and farm servants working for the same employer over many years.

Free peasants in medieval India?   Yet another problem is given rise to by Marxist scholars being selective about the kinds of extra-economic constraints that are recognized as rendering labour unfree. Thanks once again to the Euro-centrism of Marxism, Indian scholars debating about the supposed modes of production prevalent in pre-colonial India have tended to consider only such restrictions on labourers as occurred in European feudalism. Thus, it would appear that both R.S. Sharma, who is the principal advocate of Indian feudalism and Harbans Mukhia, who opposes the thesis,[18] are only concerned about such un-freedom as restricts the mobility of labourers. Sharma's main plank of argument is that there is plenty of evidence about gifts of lands and villages being made by kings to Brahmans. His interpretation is that all the residents of the donated villages become subject to the arbitrary powers of the persons receiving such gifts. Mukhia's principal contention seems to be that in pre-colonial India, State power did not make itself felt inside the village economy, its coercive powers being applied only to communities as a whole, of which the ultimate unit was the village. He takes considerable pains to emphasize that for the medieval Indian peasantry, the 'process of production was free of extraneous control and whose class struggle therefore was of a different order from that of feudal lords and peasants in Europe'.[19] Mukhia, thus, explicitly takes the position that a peasantry may be regarded as free as long as it is not affected directly by State power. State power, indeed, is one important source of extra-economic coercion.[20] But, by what logic does one ignore the pressures exerted on the individual peasant by the village society? It is strange that neither Sharma nor Mukhia makes any serious references to the caste

[18]The latest versions of their views are to be found in Mukhia (1985) and Sharma (1985) in a special number of the *Journal of Peasant Studies.*
[19]Mukhia (1985), p. 233.
[20]There are indeed instances of State-enforced restrictions like 'legal prohibition on land ownership by the labourers', cited by Miles, but surely rendering labour unfree to such extent is not the only form of extra-economic coercion.

system and the system called *jajmani* which regulated the activities of and exchanges between different family groups in a village.

Mukhia permits himself to assume that the nature of social conflict remained extraneous to the production system because he assumes that 'exploitation of the peasantry had come to be pivoted on revenue collection'.[21] Revenue collection, indeed, constituted a contradiction between peasants and the State. However, what reason is there to assume that there were no other contradictions? Mukhia seems to assume that all tillers of the soil were revenue-paying peasants and vice versa. It appears to be a very far-fetched assumption especially in the light of what we know of servile labourers. If tilling the soil was not carried out by people of the upper castes, if it was carried out by different categories of the untouchables forced to work for their *jajmans*—a very plausible presumption based on whatever we know of our rural society in the past—there would indeed be exploitation and coercion inside the village society and outside the revenue collecting system.[22]

It is true that this coercion was not enforced by any politico-juridical means. However, the sanctions of the caste system and the traditions of the village society are surely as much extra-economic as any laws enforced with the help of the police.

We have argued elsewhere[23] that the peasantry, even in contemporary India, is far from being free. We have shown that people refrain from participation in different agricultural operations on grounds of religion, caste, and sex. Thus, for instance, upper-caste Hindu men will not touch the plough; lower-caste Hindu families will sometimes work in the family field but not go out to work as labourers for any employer; Muslim women will not go out to work at all. These restrictions are extra-economic in nature and they prevent the labour of the concerned person from being commodities. A commodity, we may remind ourselves, is something that circulates impersonally and freely in a market. It cannot be said that labour, even in our present-day

---

[21]Mukhia (1985), p. 246.

[22]We are glad to find that our views agree with those of Irfan Habib. He writes about Mukhia, 'He finds a "free peasantry" already existing in pre-colonial India, so, of course, there could be no feudalism ... These conclusions presume a rather idyllic picture of pre-colonial India (without acute tensions) for which there is little justification.' See Habib (1985).

[23]Our arguments and supporting empirical data are presented in Rudra (1984).

agriculture, hindered by various taboos, has reached that degree of free circulation that characterizes a commodity.[24]

Apart from such taboos, there are other constraints on peasants in present-day India that indicate the continuing vitality of the Indian village as an organic social unit. Thus, we have shown that the production relations between agricultural labourers and their employers, landlords and their tenants, moneylenders and their clients, etc. quite often do not transgress the boundaries of the village. Different villages, even in the same neighbourhood, are like islands, cut off from each other. As a result wage rates, rental shares, interest rates, etc. vary enormously from one village to another, even in a small neighbourhood. We have argued that even in present-day India the village society imposes a patron–client kind of relationship on different parties entering into production relations. Patron–client exchanges are, by their very nature, contrary to the exchange of commodities. If in present-day India actual tillers of the soil are far from being free on account of the factors mentioned above, is it not taxing one's credibility too much to assert that the peasantry in medieval India was free?

REFERENCES

CHATTOPADHYAY, PARESH (1980), Mode of production in Indian agriculture—an afterword, *Economic and Political Weekly*, Review of Agriculture, June.

DOBB, MAURICE (1978), A reply, in Hilton, *Feudalism to Capitalism*.

HABIB, IRFAN (1985), Classifying pre-colonial India, *Journal of Peasant Studies*, Special Issue on Feudalism and Non-European Societies, 12, April.

HILTON, RODNEY, ed. (1978), *Transition from Feudalism to Capitalism*, Verso.

LACLAU, ERNESTO (1971), Feudalism and underdevelopment in Latin America, *New Left Review*, 67, May–June.

MARX, KARL (1954), *Capital—A Critical Analysis of Capitalist Production*, 1, Foreign Languages Publishing House, Moscow.

MELOTTI, UMBERTO (1977), *Marx and the Third World*, Macmillan.

[24]The question as to the kind of constraints to consider for judging whether labour is free or unfree ought not to give rise to any complications if one strictly adheres to the commodity definition of free labour as in the following: 'the distinction between free and unfree labour is one which turns on the presence or absence of a commodification of labour power; unfree labour is non-commodified or only formally commodified, while free labour exists where the individual retains access to his/her labour power as private property and can freely dispose of it within a labour market.'

MILES, ROBERT (1987), *Capitalism and Unfree Labour: Anomaly or Necessity?*, Tavistock Publications.

MUKHIA, HARBANS (1985), Peasant production and medieval Indian society, *Journal of Peasant Studies*, Special Issue on Feudalism and Non-European Societies, 12, April.

PADGUG, ROBERT A. (1976), Problems in the theory of slavery and slave society, *Science and Society*, XL, 1.

PATNAIK, UTSA and MANJARI DINGWANEY, eds. (1985), *Chains of Servitude: Bondage and Slavery in India*, Sangam Books.

RUDRA, ASHOK (1978), Class relations in Indian agriculture, *Economic and Political Weekly*, June 3, 10, and 17.

____ (1982), *Indian Agricultural Economics: Myths and Realities*, Allied Publishers.

____ (1984), Local power and farm-level decision-making, in *Agrarian Power and Agricultural Productivity in South Asia*, Meghnad Desai, Susanne Hoeber Rudolph, and Ashok Rudra, eds., Oxford University Press, Delhi.

____ (1988a), *Some Problems of Marx's Theory of History*, R.C. Dutta Lectures on Political Economy, 1985, Centre for Studies in Social Sciences, Orient Longman, Calcutta.

____ (1988b), Pre-capitalist modes of production in non-European societies, *Journal of Peasant Studies*, 15, April.

SAWER, MARIAN (1977), *Marxism and the Question of the Asiatic Mode of Production*, Martinus Nijhoff, The Hague.

SHARMA, R.S. (1985), How feudal was Indian feudalism?, *Journal of Peasant Studies*, Special Issue on Feudalism and Non-European Societies, 12, April.

SINHA, ARUN (1975), More laws against bonded labour in Bihar, *Economic and Political Weekly*, 10, October.

THORNER, DANIEL (1962), Employer–labour relationships in agriculture, in *Land and Labour in India*, Daniel & Alice Thorner, Asia Publishing House.

TAKAHASHI, KOHACHIRO (1978), A contribution to the discussion, in Hilton, *Feudalism to Capitalism*.

WEBER, MAX (1978), *Economy and Society: An Outline of Interpretive Sociology*, University of California Press, Berkeley.

Some Aspects of Technological Change and Innovation in Agriculture

NIRVIKAR SINGH*

1. INTRODUCTION

This essay aims to selectively survey some explanations of why technological change and innovation in agriculture may be less than optimal. Many of the theories described are based on some kind of lack of information. However, non-information based explanations are also common and plausible: externalities and public goods are venerable economic concepts. The nature of technological change, or the 'production of knowledge' easily admits such analyses, and they have recently proliferated. So I attempt some evaluation as well as listing of explanations. While the rest of this essay is mainly theoretical, I begin with a discussion of India's recent experience with technological change in agriculture.

The most straightforward summary statistic for agricultural performance is the growth in real agricultural output. According to the Asian Development Bank's figures, real agricultural output in India grew from 1971 to 1989 at an average annual rate of 2.1 per cent.[1] This translates into an aggregate increase of about 40 per cent. This period postdates the beginning of the 'green revolution': by the mid-seventies, output growth in India was slowing down. Much of the growth was confined to certain crops, especially wheat and rice. In many other

*I am grateful to Kaushik Basu for his guidance and Deepali Singhal for proofreading help. Joni Tannheimer and Cheryl Van De Veer did an excellent job of preparing the manuscript and figures. Partial financial support came from the UCSC Academic Senate and the Division of Social Sciences.
[1]These figures are from *The Economist* magazine's recent survey of India (*The Economist*, 1991).

crops, output grew slower, or stagnated. Also, the benefits of the green revolution were concentrated in a few regions, so that income disparities between the states widened. Finally, farm labour productivity increased by considerably less than 1 per cent a year in this period, as the agricultural labour force continued to grow along with the overall population.

To what extent do the aggregate statistics reflect the effects of technological change? There are statistics at the state level on changes in tractor ownership, irrigated area, fertilizer consumption, and area under high yielding varieties (HYV).[2] For example from 1966 to 1972, tractor ownership in Punjab increased by 298 per cent. From 1972 to 1977, the increase was 57.3 per cent. Corresponding figures for Tamil Nadu, at the other end of the spectrum, were 64.7 per cent and 20.4 per cent. Punjab registered similar large increases in other categories, while several other states lagged. Most significantly by 1980–1, 96.3 per cent of the net area sown in Punjab was under HYV. In several other states it was only around 20 per cent. Combined with data on yields, there emerges a clear and obvious connection between investment and technological change on the one hand, and agricultural output on the other.

Somewhat better than such casual empiricism are attempts to quantify the contribution of technological change to growth. A recent example is the work of Das and Pant (1991), that starts from a micro-theoretic model of farmer behaviour. They estimated equations for wheat for Punjab, and rice for Tamil Nadu and Andhra Pradesh. They decomposed growth in output into five components: growth due to (1) neutral technical progress,[3] (2) changes in output prices, (3) changes in the share of labour, (4) expansion of inputs, and (5) a component measuring the bias of new technology. For Punjab, for 1971–88, this last component, rather than neutral technical progress, was the most important. For Andhra Pradesh, from 1972–84, there was no evidence of a positive contribution of either neutral or biased technological change. Finally, for Tamil Nadu from 1971–82, biased technological change was the most important single component. Das and Pant interpret their results in a plausible manner, that the mere use of new technology in the form of new seeds would be useless or

[2]These data are from Zarkovic (1987).
[3]This term will be defined more precisely in section 2.

harmful unless accompanied by an increase in the use of complementary inputs such as machinery and fertilizers.

A different sort of decomposition, at the aggregate level, was undertaken by Hayami and Ruttan (1985).[4] They sought to explain the differences in agricultural productivity of various countries from that of the US. The factors considered included: (1) different endowments of internal resources, such as land and livestock; (2) different use of technical inputs, such as fertilizer and mechanical power, (3) different investment in human capital through general and technical education; and (4) different size of farms, which might generate economies or diseconomies of scale. The results for India are summarized in Table 1. From there, it may be seen that about half the difference in labour productivity to that of the United States was due to the differential use of technical inputs and differences in general and technical education. Both these factors may be considered embodiments of superior technology in the US versus India.

TABLE 1
ACCOUNTING FOR DIFFERENCES IN AGRICULTURAL LABOUR PRODUC-
TIVITY OF INDIA FROM UNITED STATES

Year	Output per worker	Difference from US as per cent of US	Percentage of difference explained by			
			Internal resources	Technical inputs	Human capital	Scale economies
1960	2.2	97.7	28.0	25.0	29.0	26.4*
1980	3.1	98.9	29.2	24.9	24.7	27.3*

*Sum of components exceeds total due to estimation residual.
Source: Hayami and Ruttan (1985, p. 154), Timmer (1988, p. 311).

So far, we have looked at India's agricultural performance by itself, and in relation to the United States. How has it compared with that of other Asian countries? For the period 1971–9, Sri Lanka, Malaysia, Thailand, Indonesia, the Philippines, Pakistan, and South Korea all outdid India in the growth of real agricultural output. Malaysia's average annual growth rate of 4.7 per cent meant a doubling of output compared to India's 40 per cent increase in the same period. Similarly, farm labour productivity growth was higher in other Asian countries:

[4] A summary and evaluation of their results is in Timmer (1988).

in South Korea, it increased by 5 per cent a year between 1970 and 1985, over five times the growth rate for India.

The picture that emerges from the data and examples is one of moderate growth, fuelled in part by technological change, but clearly also of *relative* stagnation. The goal of economic theory must be to understand this phenomenon of relative stagnation. The next sections will present some possible explanations, after reviewing basic concepts. The focus is on the failure of technological change to occur optimally. Many of the explanations will be abstract or general enough to apply to non-agricultural settings as well. Often the difference of agriculture is one of degree. However, the sum total of these differences, including seasonality, geographical dispersion, uncertainty, and decision-making, makes agriculture essentially different. This will partly emerge from the choice of theoretical models and issues.[5]

2. GENERAL CONCEPTS

Typically, technological change in agriculture involves improvements in the biological processes by which plants and animals grow and yield output, or in the mechanical functions that are necessary for the biological processes to carry on more efficiently than in a natural setting.[6] Biological–chemical innovations, such as hybrid seeds, pesticides, and fertilizers, all tend to be yield-increasing and thus save on land. Mechanical technology can have a yield effect when it permits more timely cultivation, cultivation of heavy soils, or irrigation of dry lands, but it mostly makes agricultural work less physically burdensome and saves on labour: tractors, harvesters, and such machines are the most obvious examples.

As the above examples indicate, technological change is usually embodied in new inputs. However, the standard economic approach is to treat inputs as belonging to aggregate categories—land, labour, and capital—and to analyse technological change as a shift in the production function (the mathematical expression of feasible, efficient output–input combinations). Much of the economic analysis has been

---

[5]For a detailed discussion of agriculture and its special place, see Timmer (1988). For a survey of issues of technological change and innovation in industry contexts, see Kamien and Schwartz (1983).

[6]This discussion is based on Timmer (1988).

conducted in macroeconomic or industry contexts, but is applicable to agriculture as well.

2.1 Microeconomic foundations

Technology can be defined as 'the sum of knowledge of the means and methods of producing goods and services' (Bannock et al., 1978). In the usual context of a firm in a static equilibrium, it is fairly unobjectionable to represent technology by a production function that specifies the maximum levels of output(s) for different combinations of inputs. In practice, however, efficiency may not be achieved because of information and organization costs. Johansen (1972) has emphasized this point. Of course, suitably expanded specification of inputs can get round this issue, but this makes the concept of a production function less operational, especially at the aggregate or macro level. At any aggregate level, the aggregation itself raises conceptual issues. Further difficulties arise when one compares across countries. Much knowledge pertinent to agriculture is not proprietary, yet as was il-

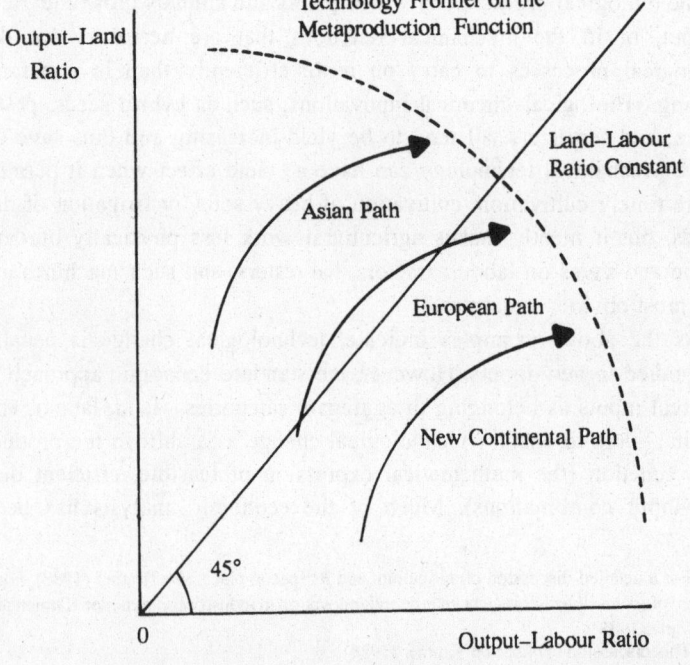

FIG. 1

lustrated by the comparison of productivity in India and the United States described in the introduction, the differences across countries are great, and not completely explained by differences in the use of conventional inputs. Hayami and Ruttan, whose work on this has been extensive, introduce the term 'metaproduction function' (see Fig. 1) arguing that the underlying technologies that describe the cross-country technology frontier are potentially available to all countries at a point in time. Again, one has to appeal to additional costs to explain why some countries are inside the technological frontier.

Having raised these definitional or semantic issues, I will not attempt to resolve them. Instead, I will use the term 'technology' fairly loosely, allowing the context to identify its implications.[7] A further semantic issue is also not tackled head on. Sometimes the distinction is made between 'invention' and 'innovation'. The former refers to the production of new knowledge, and the latter to its application. In

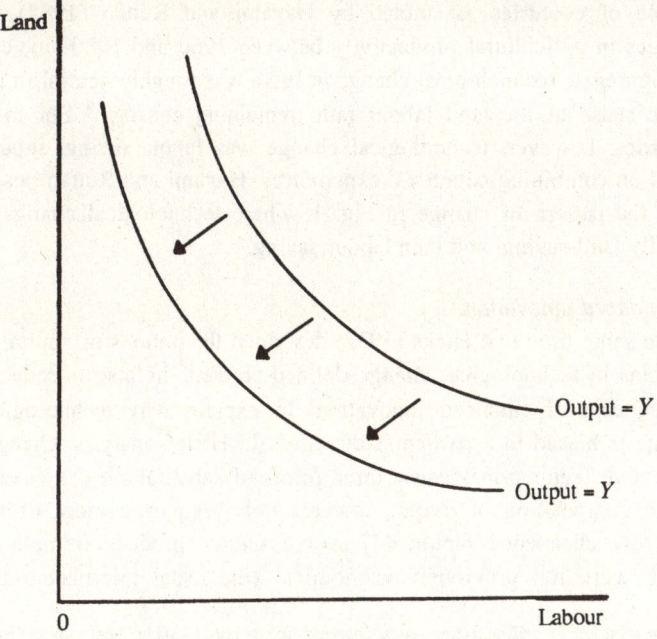

FIG. 2

[7]A further discussion is in Boyce (1987).

practice, it is hard to maintain this distinction, just as it is hard to define 'technology'. Therefore, I shall use the terms technological change and innovation loosely as well, and somewhat interchangeably. Either can refer to a shift in the production function in the usual microeconomic model of production. An illustration with two inputs is in Fig. 2, where technological change moves a representative isoquant inwards.

While I have avoided precision with regard to the exact situation represented by the isoquant in Fig. 2, it will be useful to define some common terms that characterize the nature of technological progress in terms of the way the production function or its isoquants shift.

For given factor prices, technological change is 'Hicks-neutral' if the ratio of inputs, in this case the land–labour ratio, does not change in response.[8] If the technological change increases the land–labour ratio it is 'labour-saving', while if it decreases the ratio it is 'land-saving'. In either case, the change is 'biased'. Empirical evidence for a large sample of countries assembled by Hayami and Ruttan (1985) for changes in agricultural productivity between 1960 and 1980 suggests that aggregate technological change in India was roughly neutral in the above sense of the land–labour ratio remaining constant.[9] For most countries, however, technological change was labour-saving, though based on combining countries' experiences, Hayami and Ruttan postulated the pattern of change in Fig. 1, where technological change is initially land-saving, and then labour-saving.

2.2 Induced innovation

At the same time that Hicks (1932) described the notions of neutrality and bias in technological change defined above,[10] he also introduced the concept of 'induced innovation' to explain why technological change is biased in a particular direction. In Hicks' analysis, changes in relative factor prices cause three forms of substitution: (1) change in the composition of output, towards items requiring more of the relatively cheapened factor; (2) use of known production methods which were not previously economical (the usual microeconomic

[8]The modifier for neutral technological change is necessitated by subsequent growth theory concepts of 'Harrod-neutral' and 'Solow-neutral' change, in which the capital–output and labour–output ratios, respectively, are constant.

[9]See Hayami and Ruttan (1985), p. 121 or Timmer (1988), p. 307.

[10]The concept of neutrality can be traced to Pigou (1920).

notion of factor substitution); and (3) 'the search for new methods of production which will use more of the now cheaper factor and less of the expensive one' (Hicks, 1932, p. 120). The last of these is induced technological change.

Hicks' hypothesis that a significant component of technological change is induced provoked a large literature, including critiques and refinements. A good discussion of the issues, including references, is in Samuelson (1965), who also provided a formal analysis from a macro-economic perspective, with exogenously given or growing factor supplies. Subsequently, Kamien and Schwartz (1968, 1969) analysed the case of induced innovation for a firm maximizing the present value of a stream of profits. Both these analyses concentrated on conditions under which technological change would be neutral or biased in a particular direction. Hayami and Ruttan (1985) extended the concept of induced innovation to public research, and to the rate as well as the direction of technological change, though they didn't provide a formal analysis. They also attempted to make these ideas empirically operational. For example, they related the rise in yields per acre in Japan to historical movements of the fertilizer–rice price ratio. Notions of induced innovation are also implicit in estimations such as those of Das and Pant (1991), summarized in the introduction. A further discussion of conceptual and empirical issues relating to induced innovation in agriculture may be found in Boyce (1987, pp. 21–3) and Hayami and Ruttan (1985, pp. 84–93). Here I will concentrate on clarifying how induced innovation can be modelled in standard economic terms.

Following Kennedy (1964) and Samuelson (1965), let $F(a(t)A, b(t)L)$ be the production function at time t, where A is the quantity of land, L the quantity of labour, and $a(t)$ and $b(t)$ measure land and labour-augmentation. For a particular exogenous rate of spending on technical advance, the maximal rates of factor augmentation that can be achieved are related through

$$b'(t)/b(t) = f(a'(t)/a(t)) \qquad (1)$$

where $f' < 0$ and $f'' < 0$. The function f is analogous to a production possibility frontier, as is apparent from Fig. 3.

In Samuelson's formulation, the point on this 'innovation possibility frontier' that maximizes the instantaneous rate of cost reduction is what obtains in equilibrium. Kamien and Schwartz (1969) go a step

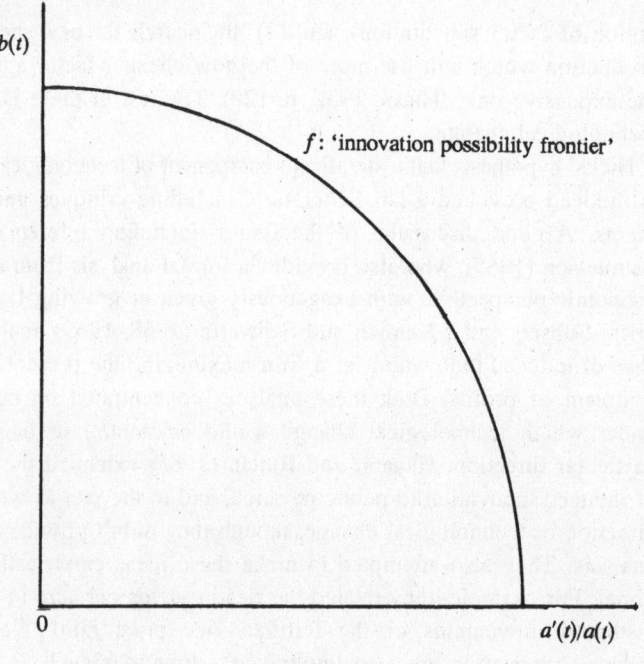

FIG. 3

further, by comparing this myopic rule with the case of maximizing the present value of profits: they examine a firm's decision-making, rather than the macroeconomic context of Samuelson. Kamien and Schwartz (1968) also look at long-run optimization of the direction of innovation, but with a slightly different specification of the innovation possibility frontier.   The production function is $F(A, L; a, b)$ where a and b are parameters of the production function, e.g. for the Cobb–Douglas form, F is $aA^b L^{1-b}$. Now the innovation possibility frontier is given by

$$I(a'(t), b'(t)) = M, \qquad (2)$$

where M is fixed research expenditure. This is not too different in concept and implications from (1).

The most general formulation, of Kamien and Schwartz (1979), allows research expenditure to be a choice variable also. Hence there is a family of innovation possibility curves, described by

$$b'(t)/b(t) = f(a'(t)/a(t)) \cdot g(M(t)) \qquad (3)$$

As $M(t)$, the rate of expenditure on technological change, increases, the innovation possibility curve shifts out, i.e. $g'(M) > 0$. Furthermore, $g'' < 0$ to capture the notion of decreasing marginal returns to a higher rate of investment in technological change.

All these analyses concentrate on deriving conditions under which technological change is neutral or biased in a particular direction. The Hicksian notion of induced innovation is captured by results on how changes in the factor price ratio cause movements along the innovation possibility frontier. In all these cases, however, the direction of innovation is 'optimal' in either the long-run or short-run sense. If one is to use these theories as a basis for explaining why innovation or technological change in Indian agriculture has lagged or been less than optimal—as suggested by cross-country comparisons of performance as described in the introduction—one must focus on the position of the innovation possibility frontier, and why it might be lower for India than another country. What one has done is to focus on the investment aspect of technological change, as captured above in expenditure $M(t)$, rather than the direction of induced innovation, as a key issue. Therefore I do not pursue the application of these models further in this essay.

2.3 Investment and public good aspects

When one examines investment in technological change, with a view to explaining its possible sub-optimality in Indian agriculture, there are two avenues. The one which has been most explored in the specific context of agriculture is the set of explanations based on asymmetric information and credit constraints. These kinds of explanations can apply to any kind of investment, not just investment in knowledge. I consider them in sections 3 and 4.

The second avenue focuses on the special properties of investment in knowledge. Knowledge is a valuable input in production that can be used simultaneously in more than one activity. If one farmer uses a new technique of soil rotation or cultivation, it does not reduce the availability of that technique for other farmers. In the language of public goods, knowledge is a non-rival good. Romer (1990a, b), in particular, has emphasized this aspect of knowledge.[11] He emphasizes that non-rivalry, rather than non-excludability—the other attribute of

[11] See Romer's papers for numerous other references.

public goods—is what matters. Since a production process can be replicated by doubling all rival inputs, without increasing the level of knowledge, increasing the latter as well implies increasing returns to scale. Formally, following Romer (1990a, p. 98), if R is the set of rival inputs, N the set of non-rival inputs, and $F(R, N)$ denotes output, then for integer values of λ,

$$F(\lambda R, \lambda N) > F(\lambda R, N) = \lambda F(R, N). \tag{4}$$

The implication of increasing returns is that there is a fundamental difficulty in decentralizing optimal allocations. In other words, market outcomes may not be efficient.

Romer (1990b) and others have developed the detailed implications for growth of the increasing returns created by the public good properties of knowledge. Unlike the standard neo-classical growth model, growth rates may not converge, and may not be optimal. These models are aggregative in nature, but have as much relevance for agriculture as for any other part of the economy. I describe some of their features, and then discuss the lessons for understanding India's experience with technological change in agriculture.

Romer models production of consumption goods with the following Cobb–Douglas form:

$$Y = H_Y^\alpha L^\beta \int_0^A x(i)^{1-\alpha-\beta}\, di. \tag{5}$$

Here Y is output, L is labour input, and H_Y is human capital. Human capital embodies those aspects of knowledge that are rival, since one person may have a specific skill without another person sharing that skill. For convenience, there is a continuum of capital goods, indexed by i. $x(i)$ is the amount of good i used in production. A is the measure of shareable knowledge. Hence both kinds of knowledge are used in production. It is assumed that the relative prices of the existing capital goods are fixed by the technology, and that units are chosen so that these prices are 1. With this assumption, the aggregate capital stock is well defined, as $K = \int_0^A x(i)\, di$. If all the $x(i)$'s are the same, then (5) reduces to a familiar three-input Cobb–Douglas function. Also, if all inputs are increased in proportion, output increases in the same proportion, so that there are constant returns to scale.

In this model, technological change is an increase in A. This means an increase in the number of capital goods. These capital goods are the embodiment of new designs, blueprints, etc., which are assumed available to everyone. Hence A is the stock of non-rival knowledge. If each researcher, j, possesses human capital H^j, and access to A, her rate of production of new designs is assumed to be $\delta H^j A$. Hence, the rate of production for the economy is

$$dA/dt = \delta H_A A, \qquad (6)$$

where $H_A = \Sigma H^j$ is the amount of human capital used in research. $H_A + H_Y = H$ is then the total amount of human capital available, assumed fixed. The formulation in (6) incorporates increasing returns—it is homogeneous of degree two. The justification and implications of this specification are discussed in detail in Romer (1990b). What I wish to emphasize is that the specification implies that the balanced rate of growth for the economy depends on its parameters and on the *stock of human capital*. Increasing the stock of human capital in this economy leads to a permanent increase in the economy's growth rate. Furthermore, this rate of growth is lower than what would be selected by an omniscient social planner.

In order to explore implications of alternative specifications of technological change, Rivera-Batiz and Romer (1991) examined a somewhat polar case, where knowledge is produced by a technology similar to that of the manufacturing sector:

$$dA/dt = BH_A^\alpha L^\beta \int_0^A x(i)^{1-\alpha-\beta} \, di \qquad (7)$$

Here B is a constant scale factor. Now there are constant returns in the research sector as well, but there is a form of increasing returns in this alternative economy also. To illustrate this, substitute $x(i) = \bar{x} = K/A$ in (7), to obtain

$$dA/dt = BH_A^\alpha L^\beta K^{1-\alpha-\beta} A^{\alpha+\beta}. \qquad (8)$$

Hence, in terms of the basic inputs, H_A, L, K, A, there is a form of increasing returns to scale. In this specification, also, growth is suboptimal and positively related to the stock of human capital. It is also, unlike the first specification, positively related to the economy's endowment of labour.

These models are abstract, and their implications are not specific to agriculture, nor to LDCs. This is not a weakness. It can be argued that India's manufacturing sector growth has also been sub-optimal and that its industrial policies have slighted technological change. However, here I concentrate on implications for agriculture. If growth is driven by the stock of human capital, an obvious policy is to increase this stock. In the above models, human capital is fixed. There are models where human capital is also endogenous, e.g. Becker, Murphy, and Tamura (1990), which may provide better guidance on how precisely equilibrium human capital can be increased. In the Romer formulation, there is a further policy response which will increase growth, namely shifting human capital from production to research. Research does not have to mean sophisticated biotechnology; it could also mean better animal husbandry or crop-rotation techniques. Some of this knowledge, of course, exists in other countries. It may simply need to be adapted to Indian conditions. Another implication of growth models of the above type is also germane here: economic integration, by increasing access to knowledge, increases growth. This can apply to freer interaction with other economies, as well as to greater integration of the *domestic* economy.[12] There are caveats to this result,[13] but they may be quibbles in the Indian case.

While human capital and public knowledge may be relatively new components of formal growth models, the importance of human capital, and of the education of farmers in particular, has long been recognized and documented.[14] Hayami and Ruttan's (1985) cross-country studies found that human capital was consistently important in explaining productivity differences (recall Table 1 in the introduction). Rosenzweig (1982) used micro-data for India to document how more educated farmers are more likely to adopt new productive innovations and accelerate the diffusion of such innovations. Chaudhri (1968) and Sidhu (1976) are among other studies for India with similar con-

---

[12]See Hayami and Ruttan (1985, Ch. 9), for more on the possibilities of international transfer of agricultural technology.

[13]See Rivera-Batiz and Romer (1991), as well as other references therein.

[14]Schultz's work (1963) on human capital is seminal. Griliches (1964) provided empirical evidence for the importance of education of farmers in the United States.

clusions.[15] A related piece of positive evidence, which also incorporates the non-rival aspect of knowledge, is a study for India that notes that adoption rates for HYVs are higher for members of farmers' organizations (Reddy and Kivilin, 1968).[16]

How does India compare with other countries? The easiest comparison is aggregate spending on education: for India, this was 3 per cent of GNP in 1987. This was far below the shares of GNP spent in many other Asian countries, e.g. Thailand at 4.2 per cent of GNP and Malaysia at 8.5 per cent.[17] It has also long been argued that India's allocation of education spending is sub-optimal: too much on higher education and not enough on primary education (Blaug et al., 1969). More specifically for agriculture, the evidence suggests that government spending on agriculture has been misdirected: too much on transfer payments and subsidies, and not enough on investment, some of which might be interpreted as embodying technological change (real investment in irrigation fell by 8 per cent between 1980–1 and 1987–8), and some of which could promote economic integration within India (rural roads in particular). Thus there are no surprises in this aspect of India's agricultural development: its relatively poor performance in terms of growth of yields is correlated with a relative lack of public policy to broadly foster technological change.

3. INFORMATION AND INCENTIVES

Asymmetric information has become a popular explanation for many kinds of economic phenomena, in particular the observed richness of pricing structures and contractual provisions, and the possible sub-optimality of market outcomes. The two best-known examples of this approach in the context of agriculture (particularly in LDCs) are theories of sharecropping and of interlinking[18] of rural markets. While much of this literature has been focused on forms of contracts and their implications in the presence of imperfect information, a seminal piece, that of Bhaduri (1973), attempted to explain the absence of

---

[15]See Zarkovic (1987), pp. 39–40 and Schultz (1988), pp. 597–8 for further references.

[16]Ahmed (1981) contains further discussion and empirical examination of this issue.

[17]These figures and others below are from *The Economist*'s (1991) survey of India.

[18]See the collection of essays in Bardhan (1989), as well as the pieces by Stiglitz (1988) and Bell (1988).

technological change or investment in agriculture, albeit without explicit consideration of informational aspects. Since then, a few papers have addressed technological change in agriculture in these contexts, and I summarize them in this section.

3.1 Moral Hazard

Moral hazard refers to the incentive to shirk or otherwise cheat by someone whose actions cannot be monitored. In the agricultural context, it applies to a worker or tenant whose effort cannot be observed by a landlord. A fixed-rent tenancy avoids moral hazard, since the tenant bears all the marginal costs and benefits of his effort, but it also leaves him with all the risk. Sharecropping—with or without lump-sum payments or other contractual provisions such as cost-sharing and credit terms—may represent an optimal tradeoff between risk-sharing and incentive provision, given the absence of insurance markets[19] and the inability to monitor. In this context, a technological improvement—an upward shift of the production function—may not be adopted because it does not benefit the landlord.

This argument for technological stagnation was developed by Braverman and Stiglitz (1986).[20] They analyse a general model as well as give a simple illustration. I present the latter. Ignoring uncertainty, and assuming initially that the terms of the contract are fixed, consider the technological change represented in Fig. 4. The initial technology is denoted by $f(e)$. The marginal return to effort is very high up to e^*, and that is the level of effort supplied by the tenant. The new technology is represented by $\hat{f}(e)$ which provides more output for each effort level. However, now diminishing returns set in at a much lower level of effort *and* at a lower level of output. The tenant now chooses e^{**}, making the landlord worse off. The tenant must be better off, since he could still choose e^* and have more output. But the landlord will reject this innovation.

Two points must be emphasized. First, such a situation would not arise if the landlord were able to monitor and enforce a particular level of effort. So the moral hazard is essential. Second, the argument holds even though the improvement is costless, e.g. the new technology or

---

[19]These may, in turn, be absent because of other forms of moral hazard or lack of information.

[20]An earlier treatment based on moral hazard was due to Newbery (1975).

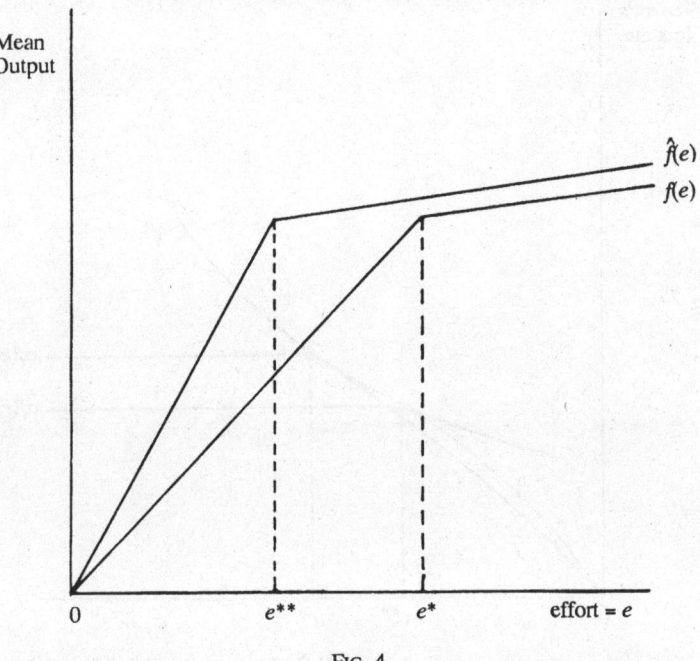

FIG. 4

technique has already been discovered and is freely available. In fact, a fixed cost of adoption of the new technique would strengthen the argument.

More realistically, the landlord might be able to alter the terms of the contract as the new technique is adopted. Suppose the contract is a pure sharecropping contract (without other payments) and let α be the tenant's share. It is typical in such models to assume that the landlord has all the bargaining power, or that tenants compete for landlords, so that the tenant always receives his reservation utility level, say V^*. The same kind of situation can arise, as illustrated in Fig. 5. The landlord can increase his share of a given output, but if this has the usual negative effect on the tenant's effort, it may reduce the landlord's income, or at least not increase it sufficiently to offset the negative impact of the new technology, as illustrated in Fig. 4.

The above illustration assumed away uncertainty, which helps justify sharecropping in the first place. Braverman and Stiglitz derive the general expression for the effect of a change in technology on the

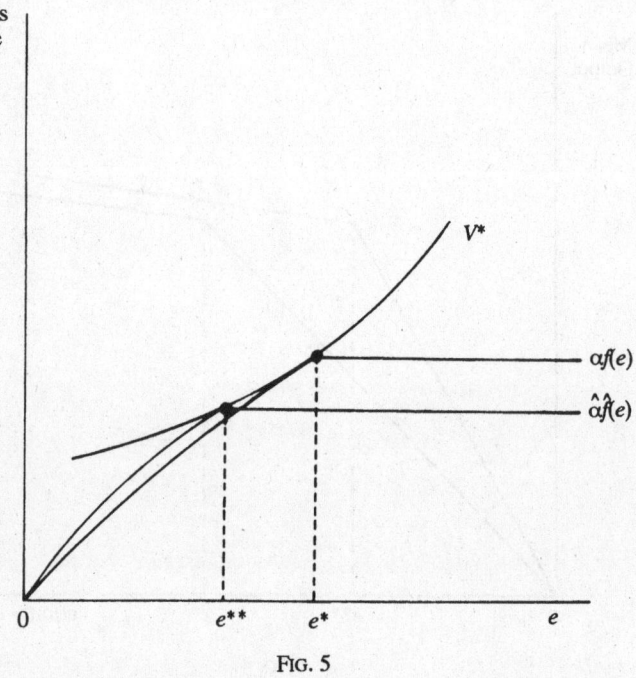

FIG. 5

landlord's income, allowing for uncertainty. The outcome of their algebra[21] is the same as the illustration: if the new technology leads to a reduction in effort, this might outweigh the direct effects of the change in the technology, and the landlord's ability to adjust the contract.

Braverman and Stiglitz further analyse the effects of technological innovation in the case of moral hazard by looking at what may happen to the utility possibility frontier. With costless monitoring, a technological improvement must push the utility possibility frontier outward. With moral hazard on the other hand, it may shift inward, based on the argument above. A more interesting case is illustrated in Fig. 6.

The initial utility possibility frontier goes through $C_0 M_0$, while the new frontier goes through $C_1 M_1$. With the new technology, the monopsony equilibrium, where the landlord keeps the tenant at the latter's minimum acceptable utility (perhaps subsistence), shifts from M_0 to

---

[21] See equations (10)–(12) in Braverman and Stiglitz (1986), p. 322.

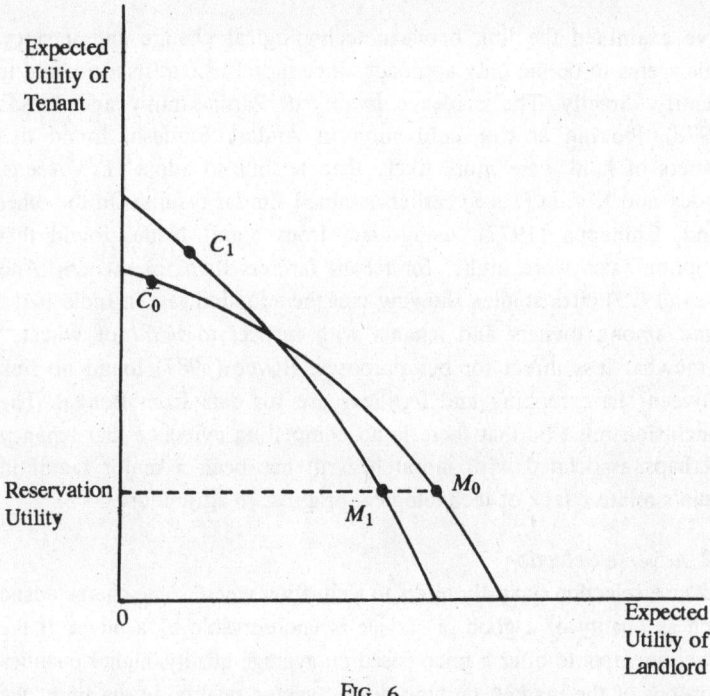

FIG. 6

M_1. Hence the landlord will reject this innovation. However, the competitive equilibrium shifts from C_0 to C_1, and the new technology in this example would be adopted in a competitive environment.

In a subsequent paper, Braverman and Stiglitz (1989) extended the analysis of the link between technological change and the ownership of resources. Their argument was that if technological change is capital-using and access to capital is restricted (due to market imperfections such as those caused by lack of information), technological change might make land more valuable to richer farmers, and lead to greater inequality in land ownership. This, in turn, could lead to a replacement of owner cultivation by tenant farming such as sharecropping, an exacerbation of incentive problems in production, and even lower productivity. Furthermore, returning to their earlier analysis, this reorganization could reduce the likelihood of other forms of innovation being adopted, so that technological change would lack momentum.

How can the experience of technological change in Indian agriculture be related to analyses based on moral hazard? Several studies have examined the link between technological change and tenancy. This seems to be the only approach since moral hazard itself is hard to identify directly. The evidence is mixed. Parthasarathy and Prasad (1978), looking at rice cultivation in Andhra Pradesh, found that owners of land were more likely than tenants to adopt HYV seeds. Reddy and Kivilin (1968) earlier obtained similar results. On the other hand, Chinappa (1977), using data from Tamil Nadu, found that adoption rates were higher for tenant farmers than for owners. And Vyas (1975) cites studies showing that the adoption rate in India is the same among owners and tenants with respect to HYV of wheat.[22] Somewhat less direct for our purposes, Boyce (1987) found no link between sharecropping and fertilizer use for data from Bengal. The conclusion must be that there is no compelling evidence that tenancy (perhaps associated with moral hazard) has been a major factor in India's relative lack of technological progress in agriculture.

3.2 Adverse Selection

Adverse selection typically refers to a situation where some characteristic such as quality of a good or service is unobservable by a buyer. If the buyer attempts to offer a price based on average quality, higher qualities drop out of the market, pushing down average quality. In the limit, the market may collapse. Akerlof's (1970) seminal piece on adverse selection dealt with used cars. Here I present an example developed by Samuelson (1984), where I interpret the good being traded as 'knowledge'. After presenting the basic example, I discuss the special issues raised by the non-rivalrous character of knowledge as a good, and then the relevance of the issue for the case of Indian agriculture.

Initially, suppose that the new technology is embodied in some investment good, such as a new machine. The cultivator or the landlord is the potential buyer of the new machine. The machine is worth v to the seller, and $w(v)$ to the potential buyer. Also, $dw/dv > 0$ and $w - v > 0$. These assumptions mean that v is akin to quality or value—the more valuable it is to the seller, the more valuable it is to the buyer—and that the machine is always worth more to the buyer than to the seller, so that there is room for mutually beneficial trade.

If the buyer knows w, we have a conventional exchange situation,

---

[22]Cited in Zarkovic (1987), p. 43. See also Ahmed (1981), p. 15, for references to inconclusive studies for other countries as well.

and the farmer would adopt the new technology. However, it is plausible that with a new technology, the buyer will *not* know w. Instead, assume that the buyer knows $w(v)$, and has a continuous probability density function $f(v)$ over the interval $[a, c]$. The seller knows $w(v), f(v)$, as well as v: this captures in the simplest manner the idea that the seller is better informed about the new technology than is the buyer.[23]

Suppose that the transaction proceeds by the buyer offering a first-and-final offer which the seller can accept or reject (this is optimal for the buyer—see Samuelson, 1984 for all results and proofs in this kind of model). If $b \in [a, c]$ is the buyer's bid or offer, the seller will accept it, and the technology will be transferred, if and only if $v \le b$. Hence the buyer's expected value is not $E(w)$, but $E(w \mid v \le b)$. The latter is the conditional expected value of the new machine for the buyer, given that the seller accepts the offer. Subtracting b from this gives the buyer's expected gain from the transaction, and the buyer would choose b to maximize this.

The precise expression for the conditional expected gain of the buyer is

$$\int_{a}^{b} [w(v) - b][f(v)/F(b)] \, dv, \tag{9}$$

where $F(v)$ is the cumulative distribution function. So this integral must be non-negative for a mutually beneficial agreement. Now consider an example.[24] Suppose v is uniformly distributed on the interval $[0, 1]$ and that $w = \Delta + kv$ where $\Delta, k \ge 0$. It can be shown that the relevant expression for the buyer is $H(b) = \Delta + (k - 2)b$. For $\Delta > 0$, there must be a small enough $b > 0$ that provides the buyer with a positive expected gain. However, the transfer will not always take place, even though both buyer and seller know that there are gains to trade. A more extreme situation is where $\Delta = 0$ and $1 < k < 2$. Then the new technology is never transferred. For example, if $w = 1.5$ v, and the buyer offers b, he acquires on average something worth $b/2$ to the seller, and $1.5b/2 = 0.75b$ to himself. So no positive bid will give the

[23]In fact, $w(v)$ and $f(v)$ are 'common knowledge'. Here the seller is perfectly informed, but it is also possible to introduce uncertainty for both buyer and seller.

[24]This is Example 1 in Samuelson (1984), but it is very similar to Akerlof's (1970) original example.

buyer a positive expected gain. This was exactly Akerlof's example for used cars. The set-up, though, is quite general, and it seems appropriate for contexts in which the good for sale is some new machine embodying technological change: lack of information on the buyers' part seems plausible, especially in the case of LDC farmers.

Suppose now that the technological change is pure knowledge, e.g. better ways of soil preparation or cultivation. Now a buyer can sell the same good to more than one seller: knowledge is non-rival or shareable. If n is the number of potential (identical) buyers, mutually beneficial agreements can occur if $nw > v$, or $w > v/n$. As long as the knowledge is excludable, that is, it cannot be passed on from one buyer to another, the analysis can proceed as before. Alternatively, one could think of the knowledge being provided simultaneously to the n potential buyers, through a farmers' cooperative. Note that here the usual public good free-rider problem is not an issue, because it is being assumed that the seller knows buyer valuations. Typically, however, there may be excludability problems, and in practice this kind of knowledge is not produced and provided by private sellers, but by state and national governments. The role of government in the US and Japan in pursuing and encouraging agricultural research and extension is well documented in Hayami and Ruttan (1985, Ch. 8). Even with government provision of knowledge, however, if the objectives of the provider and receiver of the knowledge differ, an adverse selection phenomenon can still arise. Even if the knowledge is not sold to farmers, there are effort and opportunity costs of providing and using new knowledge.

A major point to emphasize is that the discussion above provides a role for education complementary to that outlined in section 2.3. Education cannot only increase productivity directly through enhancement of human capital, but it can also facilitate the acquisition of productive new technology or knowledge. In the illustration above, if the buyer knows w, the mutually beneficial agreement always occurs. General education thus can play a role supporting education in specific techniques or procedures.

In practice, it is hard to separate the two types of education and their effects. Hence, the references provided in section 2.3 for the Indian case must also suffice here. However, a further piece of evidence, from Hayami and Ruttan (1985), may be adduced. In their decomposition of differences in agricultural labour productivity between the US and several other countries, they noted that productivity was nearly twice as high in the Philippines as in India, despite very similar resource endowments, and that the difference between these two LDCs was explained almost solely by different levels of general and technical education. Hayami and Ruttan equate this with human capital, but this section has provided a further rationale for how education can enhance technological change and productivity. While quantification of benefits is impossible based on such an abstract example as presented here, the thrust of the analysis is additional support for paying attention to rural education in India.

3.3 Bargaining

The model in the previous section involved one form of non-cooperative bargaining. In this section, I briefly examine the consequences for technological change of an alternative approach to bargaining. This is the cooperative solution, based on a set of axioms proposed by Nash. Original references and a detailed discussion of this approach may be found in Roth (1979). Bell (1988, 1989), in particular, has applied the Nash bargaining approach to analysing agricultural contracts and innovation.

In the context of a landlord–tenant relationship, one can consider the locus of possible outcomes in terms of utilities for the two participants (or expected utilities if there is uncertainty). This is a utility possibility frontier, such as those drawn in section 3.1. An additional element in this approach is the disagreement point, say (d_L, d_T). This represents the expected utilities the two parties would get if they were unable to reach an agreement. In fact, Nash's axioms imply that they will agree on a point (u_L, u_T) on the utility possibility frontier that maximizes $(u_L - d_L)(u_T - d_T)$. The Nash bargaining solution is illustrated in Fig. 7. To contrast this with the 'principal–agent' approach of section 3.1, suppose d_T is the tenant's reservation utility. Then the outcome of the earlier analysis would be A, if the landlord chooses the contract terms to maximize his own utility subject to the tenant receiving his reservation utility. The Nash bargaining approach does not require any incentive problem, or moral hazard, but can be applied to such situations. A detailed analysis of the landlord–tenant contract outcome with and without costless monitoring is in Bell (1989).

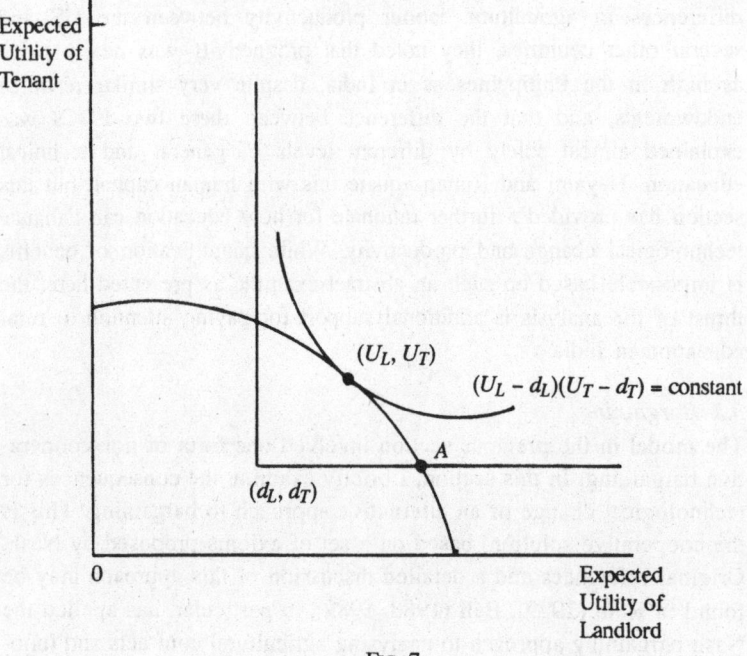

FIG. 7

In the case of moral hazard, Bell (1988, 1989) provides an argument for why the bargaining and principal–agent solutions may lead to different outcomes in terms of adoption of innovation. The reasoning is somewhat similar to Braverman and Stiglitz (1986), as will be clear from comparing Fig. 8 with Fig. 6 in section 3.1. In Bell's argument, if an innovation increases risk, and the tenant's absolute risk-aversion is decreasing with income, the landlord may not be able to manipulate the terms of the contract to his advantage at the tenant's reservation utility level. Near the Nash bargaining solution, however, the tenant is better off, and therefore more willing to bear risk. There may be contracts that make both landlord and tenant better off in that neighbourhood. Fig. 8 illustrates this possibility. The initial utility possibility frontier passes through M_1B_1, the new one through M_2B_2. The landlord who can drive the tenant down to his reservation utility will reject the innovation. In the bargaining case, the innovation will be adopted.

Several remarks are in order at this stage. First, one can generalize the Nash bargaining solution to involve maximizing $(u_L - d_L)^a(u_T - d_T)^{1-a}$, so that $a/(1 - a)$ is the landlord's relative bargaining power. As a increases, the bargaining solution moves towards the point M on the utility possibility frontier. Hence, in the illustrated situation, there is some level of bargaining power of the landlord above which the innovation will not be adopted. One might wish to treat this as exemplary of a connection between 'feudalism' and technological stagnation. However, generalizations are tricky: utility possibility frontiers for the two situations may cross more than once, since they need not be convex. Second, this kind of illustration is superficially reminiscent of Bhaduri's original (1973) analysis of technological 'backwardness'. A discussion of that analysis and links to the above is taken up in section 4.1. Finally, note that, with different assumptions (albeit less plausible), the utility possibility frontiers could cross in the opposite way from Fig. 8, so that increased bargaining power of the

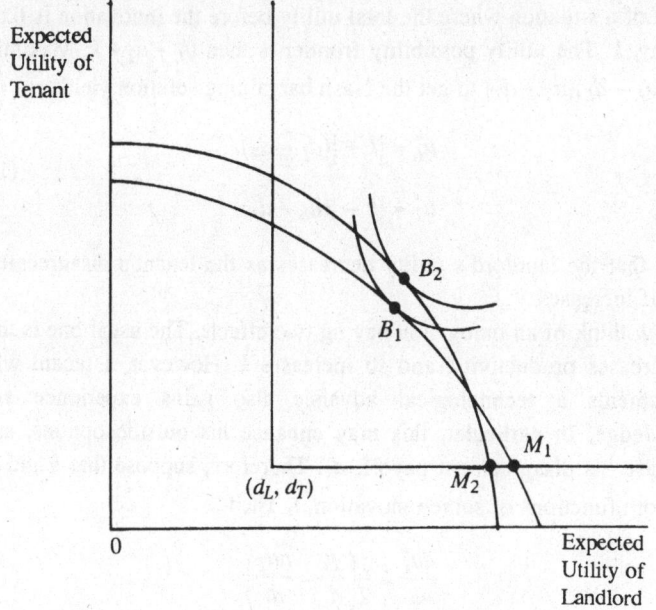

FIG. 8

landlord is associated with greater likelihood of adoption of innovations.

This last possibility emphasizes the need for an empirical examination of the link between bargaining power or degree of competition and the adoption of innovations. The difficulty is in measuring bargaining power. Farm size might be a proxy—inversely related to a tenant's bargaining power—but it probably more directly measures the effects of economies of scale on innovation. Hence this issue remains somewhat open.

To conclude this section, I present another, novel application of the Nash bargaining solution in analysing agricultural innovation. This focuses on the disagreement payoffs and the human capital aspect of technological change. Boyce (1987) has provided the following comments on the general issues raised by Bhaduri's model of lack of innovation: 'the attraction of whatever new income they could obtain is outweighed by the attendant risks to their [landlords'] positions of power' (p. 44).[25] I attempt to model this idea very simply.

Assuming away risk, moral hazard, and other such factors, we may think of a situation where the total utility before the innovation is fixed at, say, k. The utility possibility frontier is then $u_L + u_T = k$. Maximizing $(u_L - d_L)(u_T - d_T)$ to get the Nash bargaining solution yields:

$$u_L^* = \tfrac{1}{2}k + \tfrac{1}{2}(d_L - d_T)$$
$$u_T^* = \tfrac{1}{2}k - \tfrac{1}{2}(d_L - d_T) \tag{10}$$

Note that the landlord's utility decreases as the tenant's disagreement payoff increases.

Now think of an innovation having two effects. The usual one is that it increases productivity, and so increases k. However, a tenant who implements a technological advance also gains experience and knowledge. In particular, this may enhance his outside options, and increase his disagreement payoff, d_T. Therefore, suppose that k and d_T are both functions of some innovation, i. Then

$$\frac{du_L^*}{di} = \frac{1}{2}\left(\frac{dk}{di} - \frac{dd_T}{di}\right) \tag{11}$$

If this is negative, i.e. if the innovation enhances the tenant's disagreement payoff more than it increases the size of the pie to be shared, the landlord will reject it. Additionally, if there are different kinds of innovations, a landlord will only wish to adopt those that do not greatly enhance the tenant's position. This model therefore captures very simply the idea that landlords may wish to protect their relative power, and reject innovation for that reason. How plausible or relevant it is remains something that, like Bell's bargaining model with moral hazard, awaits empirical analysis. Till then it remains, to my mind, an appealing approach, consistent with the emphasis on education and human capital in previous sections.

4. CREDIT, QUITS AND SUBSISTENCE CONSTRAINTS

As the title of this section implies, it contains a miscellany of additional perspectives on sub-optimal technological progress. A weakly unifying theme is the existence of market imperfections. I first argue that interlinking of credit and other markets in itself cannot be the basis for an explanation of lack of innovation. Then I present some recent models that incorporate the possibility that tenants may quit and lose the benefits of investment in land.

4.1 Interlinking
Interlinking or interlocking refers to the interaction of two economic agents in two or more markets simultaneously. The typical example is that of a landlord who is also a moneylender to his tenant. Bhaduri (1973) was a seminal piece in this area. While a considerable literature has evolved on understanding interlinking and its static efficiency and welfare properties (see, e.g. Bell, 1988, for a survey), Bhaduri's main thrust was in fact the supposed dynamic inefficiency of interlinking. Bhaduri argued that a landlord would resist innovation because the innovation would permit the tenant to climb out of a debt trap that otherwise kept him in a form of bondage, thereby reducing the landlord's income. Thus Bhaduri related lack of innovation in agriculture— particularly with the Indian case in mind—to the interlinking of the land/labour market with the credit market. Bhaduri did not provide an explicitly theoretical rationale for the interlinking, but models of imperfect information, with moral hazard and adverse selection, have been used extensively to provide such a rationale.

There have been two sets of criticisms of Bhaduri's analysis. One set has focused on how the tenant's borrowing responds to innovation.

There is in fact no presumption that the tenant will borrow less in response to innovation. The more serious criticism has been the inconsistency in the application of the landlord's power in Bhaduri's model. The landlord is powerful enough to block innovations and keep the tenant in debt, but not powerful enough to extract the surplus generated by innovation. In fact, Bhaduri's model is unrealistic as well as inconsistent. An early criticism was made by Newbery (1975). Subsequent evaluative discussions, which also reference the large literature generated by the model, include those of Basu (1984), Braverman and Stiglitz (1986), Boyce (1987), and Bell (1988).

The outcome of this scrutiny is the conclusion that interlinking *per se* cannot explain technological stagnation in agriculture. What is true instead is that the same kinds of factors that can explain interlinking, such as moral hazard and adverse selection, can also explain lack of technological change in agriculture. Such explanations were used in section 3; the models presented there had no interlinking incorporated. Yet one could provide similar analyses for situations where the landlord was also a moneylender for the tenant. For example, Fig. 8 could depict utility possibility frontiers for such situations, before and after innovation (see Bell, 1988, for such an interpretation).

Basu (1984) makes two further points in his evaluation of Bhaduri's argument. One is that while it is important to pay attention to the credit market, it may be that landlords and tenants are both credit constrained as far as innovation goes, rather than landlords being monopolistic moneylenders who can manipulate the tenants' credit. So landlords may be unable rather than reluctant to innovate. Evidence for this comes from Byres (1972), Griffin (1974), and Newbery (1975). A similar argument is provided in section 4.3, where subsistence constraints and the absence of credit prevent innovation from occurring.

A second point is that even if credit is available, technological change may not occur. In addition to the possibilities discussed in section 3, which are based on contractual relationships, Basu emphasizes the customary system of rewards and obligations (CSRO), a concept due to anthropologists. Basu quotes examples from Epstein (1967) of the CSRO thwarting innovation: labour-saving innovations were not adopted because landlords had an obligation to support a fixed number of labourers, and innovations that required more effort were not adopted because landlords had no obligation to pay more for extra effort. To some extent, such examples might be explained by conventional economic insurance motives. However, Epstein also examined villages where customary relations were weak, and the inhabitants were more receptive to innovations. As Basu suggests, this seems a fruitful approach for further economic modelling. Akerlof (1984), for example, has shown how 'extra-economic' aspects such as the CSRO can be incorporated in rigorous economic models. Phenomena such as interlinking and technological stagnation may both be better understood in this manner, even if one does not cause the other.

4.2 Tenant Quits

Basu (1989) has recently provided a novel explanation for lack of agricultural innovation based on asymmetric information about the probability of tenants quitting. Hence, it is also an adverse selection model. Tenant quits are important in the model because it is assumed that the landlord cannot raise the tenant's rent after the innovation. This may be due to legal constraints or to the CSRO discussed in section 4.1. The landlord can also not evict tenants, so must rely on their quitting to reap any benefits from the innovation. Tenants, on the other hand, may be unwilling to invest in technological change precisely because they may quit and not be around to enjoy the benefits. The argument that landlords will not innovate because they cannot raise rents or evict tenants goes back to Johnson (1950), but is incomplete without the added features of tenant quits and adverse selection provided by Basu.

The kind of innovation that Basu considers is a sunk investment in land. Once it has been adopted, it cannot be separated from the land and sold off without loss of value. Soil improvement, new irrigation facilities, and tube wells are examples of such innovation. Mathematically, the innovation is characterized by an ordered pair (X, C) where C is the cost of adoption and X is the subsequent benefit. The assumption that $X - C > 0$ means that the innovation is socially worthwhile.

After adoption, but before the benefits are realized, the tenant may quit. The probability of quitting is q. In the simplest version of the model, q is exogenous, but Basu (1987) also allows q to be endogenously determined. If the tenant quits, the landlord can extract the additional output X from subsequent tenants. If the tenant does not quit, he retains the additional output X.

Assuming risk neutrality for both parties, the landlord's expected profit if he innovates on his own is $qX - C$. If the tenant innovates on his own, his expected gain is $(1 - q)X - C$. Each of these can be negative, even though $X - C$ is positive, so neither landlord nor tenant will then innovate on his own. However, there exist cost-sharing arrangements that will provide positive expected returns for both. An example is if the landlord pays qC and the tenant pays $(1 - q)C$. Hence, as long as the quit probability is common knowledge, there is no problem, assuming that both parties are able to finance their cost shares of the innovation. The socially-beneficial innovation will always be adopted.

More realistically, though, the landlord may not know how likely it is that the tenant will quit. Basu considers a situation where there are many indistinguishable tenants of the landlord, with different quit probabilities. Alternatively, the landlord could have a single tenant whose quit probability is unknown, but drawn from a known distribution. Let this distribution have the cumulative distribution function $F(q)$ with continuous probability density $f(q)$. One can also work, as Basu does, with a finite rather than a continuous distribution.

Let d stand for the landlord's cost share. The landlord has to choose a value of d that will maximize his expected return. Since he does not know q, he cannot make d depend on q (so $d = q$, which we know would work, is ruled out). The tenant with quit probability q has an expected profit of $(1 - q)X - (1 - d)C$. Hence only tenants with $q \le q^*(d)$ will wish to accept the innovation with the proposed cost-sharing, where $q^*(d) = 1 - (1 - d)C/X$. Hence, the landlord's expected gain from the innovation, with cost share d, is

$$\int_0^{q^*(d)} (qX - dC)f(q)\, dq. \tag{12}$$

Adverse selection is built into this expression, because the tenants with the highest quit probabilities, who are most preferred by the landlord, are absent from its calculation. And if the landlord tries to improve matters for himself by reducing d, his cost share, he risks hurting himself even more by shrinking the pool of potential tenants who would accept the innovation with cost sharing.

For example if the tenant's quit probabilities are distributed uniformly on $[0, 1]$, i.e. $f(q) = 1$ on that interval, it turns out that for any positive d, the landlord will wish to decrease d. Hence he sets $d = 0$. In this case, tenants with low enough quit probabilities, $q \leq 1 - C/X$, will bear the whole cost of the innovation, while other types of tenants will not invest. If, for example, $X = 5$ and $C = 3$, $1 - C/X = 0.4$, so innovation takes place only 40 per cent of the time, even though it is always socially beneficial.

In other situations, cost sharing can occur. Suppose that the distribution of quit probabilities is given by $f(q) = 2q$, $0 \leq q \leq 1$. Compared to the previous example, it is more likely that a given tenant has a high quit probability, which the landlord would prefer, since he benefits from the innovation only if the tenant quits. This leads to cost sharing. The optimal value of d for the landlord is $d^* = (X - C)/C$, with $q^* = 2(X - C)/X$, provided $X \leq 2C$. For the previous values of X and C, $d^* = 2/3$ and $q^* = 4/5$. Innovation would now occur 64 per cent (16/25) of the time, with the landlord paying two-thirds of the cost of the innovation.

Basu (1987) considers in more detail the nature and properties of the equilibrium of his model. In particular, he shows that an increase in mobility of tenants—a shift of the distribution of q to the right—can increase, decrease, or leave unchanged the chance of the innovation being adopted. What matters is the shape of the distribution as well as its position. This should be clarified by noting that for a *given* distribution of quit probabilities, innovation will only be undertaken by tenants with quit probabilities *below* a given value, q^*. In this sense, mobility and innovation are negatively correlated in the model.

The empirical relevance of the model is hard to judge. Migration from rural to urban areas is clearly a fact of life in India as in other LDCs. But the literature on migration has focused on the determinants of migration. The empirical question raised by Basu's model is the effect of migration or mobility on innovation in agriculture, and I am unaware of any study of this link.

A further complication for future empirical work is raised by Naqvi (1990), who examines the effect of landlord risk aversion in Basu's model. If W_0 is the landlord's initial wealth, and u is his von Neumann–Morgenstein utility, his expected utility from innovating is

$$qu(W_0 + X - dC) + (1 - q)u(W_0 - dC). \tag{13}$$

In this case, even for a known, single quit probability q, the innovation may not occur. Naqvi shows that if the landlord is sufficiently risk averse, there will be an interval (q_1, q_2) such that for q in this interval the innovation will not occur because there is no mutually-agreeable cost share. This is unsurprising, in that when the landlord is faced with an uninsurable risk (that the tenant will stay), the social benefit, $X - C$, alone cannot govern resource allocation. The prediction of Naqvi's model is that innovation will occur if q is sufficiently small (in which case the tenant will undertake it essentially on his own) or if q is sufficiently large (in which case the landlord will undertake it). In a different sense from Basu's model, there is no monotonic relationship between mobility and innovation. As with Basu's model, the empirical relevance of Naqvi's explanation of technological stagnation remains to be ascertained.

I conclude this section with three remarks. First, note that risk aversion played a role in the incentive models described in section 3.1. In each case, risk aversion and the lack of some insurance market lead to inefficient allocation. Sometimes market institutions can be strengthened by government intervention. But risks such as the risk for the landlord of tenants staying seem hard to insure, because of moral hazard problems. The appropriate policy response may be elsewhere, which brings me to the second remark. Basu's and Naqvi's models make the assumption that the land contract cannot be adjusted after the land-improving innovation takes place. This is often realistic, and sometimes due to legal constraints. In such cases, alteration to the law may support more technological change. I take this up again in the next section. Finally, the models presented here assume that cost sharing is feasible whenever it is desirable for any party. As noted in the previous section, this may not always be true. This issue, also, is developed in the next section.

4.3 Subsistence Constraints

As noted in section 4.1, the non-availability of credit has been put forward as an explanation for lack of technological progress in agriculture. One can explicitly examine inter-temporal utility maximization with borrowing constraints, but it is simpler and perhaps more realistic to model the peasant's choice as constrained by the need to achieve subsistence consumption as well as by the lack of external credit. Furthermore, while one can look at subsistence and credit constraints without any possibility of tenant quits, the latter feature enriches the analysis and permits comparison with the models of the previous section. The following analysis is based on Singh (1991). The notation and assumption are basically those of section 4.2.

The subsistence constraint will be captured by allowing for an explicit two-period structure: the cost of the innovation, C, is incurred in period 1, while the benefit, X, accrues in period 2. The landlord and tenant receive Y_L and Y_T, respectively, if no innovation is undertaken. Also, the tenant receives Y_T if he quits—this is a simplifying assumption that is easily relaxed.

Expected incomes with the innovation are therefore:

	Landlord	Tenant
Period 1	$Y_L - dC$	$Y_T - (1-d)C$
Period 2	$Y_L + qX$	$Y_T + (1-q)X$

A further simplifying but inconsequential assumption is that the discount factor is one. Hence the landlord finds the investment acceptable if $qX - dC \geq 0$, or $d \leq qX/C$. The tenant's acceptability condition without any other constraint is

$$(1-q)X - (1-d)C \geq 0 \qquad \text{or} \qquad d \geq qX/C - (X-C)/C.$$

Clearly, for any known given q, there will be a range of cost-share values such that the innovation will occur.

However, if there is a subsistence constraint for the tenant, such that he must consume at least Y_0, then implementing the innovation through cost sharing alone requires

$$Y_T - (1-d)C \geq Y_0 \qquad \text{or} \qquad d \geq 1 - (Y_T - Y_0)/C.$$

This is independent of the quit probability. Hence, innovation is infeasible if

$$1 - (Y_T - Y_0)/C > qX/C \qquad \text{or} \qquad q < [C - (Y_T - Y_0)]/X \qquad (14)$$

In words, innovation will not occur if the quit probability is too low. In particular, if $q = 0$, the innovation will not occur. The logic is as follows: with a low quit probability, the tenant gets a higher, and the landlord a lower, expected benefit. The landlord is less willing to bear the investment cost, but a higher cost share for the tenant makes violation of the period 1 subsistence constraint more likely.

The inequality also implies that larger projects are more likely to be rejected. If C and X are increased in proportion, so that the rate of return is the same, the upper bound on q in (14) is reduced. This is, of course, what one would expect with a subsistence constraint.

If the tenant faces a subsistence constraint in period 1, it is natural to ask why the landlord does not lend to him, as in the usual interlinking case. This can occur even if no external credit is available. If the landlord can lend, and is always paid back, this relaxes the subsistence constraint, and the innovation can occur with cost sharing. However, it is plausible that a loan may not be recoverable if the tenant departs. Then the loan also tightens the landlord's acceptance constraint for cost sharing and the outcome is less clear. Suppose L is the loan, and assume for simplicity that the interest rate is zero. Expected incomes are now:

	Landlord	Tenant
Period 1	$Y_L - dC - L$	$Y_T - (1 - d)C + L$
Period 2	$Y_L + qX + (1 - q)L$	$Y_T + (1 - q)(X - L)$

In this case, the acceptability constraints are $d \leq q(X - L)/C$ and $d \geq q(X - L)/C - (X - C)/C$. Again, these can hold simultaneously, but the first will conflict with the subsistence constraint if

$$q < [C - L - (Y_T - Y_0)]/(X - L). \qquad (15)$$

If the inequality (15) holds, innovation will not occur. However, the loan does help by reducing the range of q for which this happens. In fact, if L is large enough, the upper bound on q in (15) will become zero, and innovation will always occur. The remaining problem is that such a value of L may violate a subsistence constraint for the landlord as well. Ultimately, therefore, this theory of under-innovation must rely on the poverty of both landlord and tenant.

A loan from landlord to tenant helps implement the innovation by relaxing the tenant's subsistence constraint. Alternatively, if the landlord has the flexibility to increase the rent after the innovation, this relaxes his acceptance constraint for cost sharing, and again makes innovation more likely. Hence, the predictions of the model are that more innovation will occur:

1. the more mobile are tenants,
2. the more landlords are able to lend to tenants,
3. the more flexible are rental contracts.

The third prediction is common with Basu's and Naqvi's analyses. Without a tenant subsistence constraint, landlord lending to tenants does not matter. Finally while Basu's model predicts that innovation will occur for tenants with low quit probabilities, Naqvi's analysis says that innovation will occur either for low or high quit probabilities. Hence the three explanations for agricultural stagnation: subsistence constraints, adverse selection, and risk aversion imply very different correlations between tenant mobility and likelihood of innovation. Empirical testing may help to choose among the theories. If one were to hazard a guess as to which is most relevant for Indian agriculture, however, it would seem that it would be subsistence constraints.

5. CONCLUDING REMARKS

This has been far from an exhaustive survey. In particular, I have not examined explanations of technological stagnation based on standard externalities or the public good nature of investments such as irrigation. Boyce (1987), in particular, has stressed the importance of irrigation in his study of agriculture in Bengal, and free rider problems and externalities are significant in that context.

Indeed, my sense is that straightforward coordination problems for large investments may be one of the most important factors in explaining India's relative lack of technological progress in agriculture. Public investment in irrigation fell relative to various subsidies and transfer payments, from 1974–5 to 1987–8, and fell in absolute terms from 1980–1 to 1987–8. Much of that spending was for operation and maintenance of existing installations. Hence new investment in irrigation has fallen behind. Even if one argues that irrigation investment does not embody any technological progress since the technology is well known, irrigation is a crucial complementary input for HYV seeds and new cultivation techniques.

What I have emphasized in this essay is the relative under-investment in knowledge, including research, but even more so, in general and technical education. This kind of investment builds up human capital which is important for growth (section 2.3), and also facilitates the transfer of new technology (section 3.2) even when it does not directly increase productivity. My own guess is that India's relative neglect of investment in people has been even more of a hindrance to its growth rate than insufficient investment in physical facilities. Given that the agricultural sector was India's biggest employer, this applies more strongly to agriculture, though the same criticisms could also be made of India's strategy for the industrial sector.

In looking at some of the explanations of technological stagnation based on imperfect information, I found moral hazard (section 3.1) to be less than persuasive as a significant factor. Bargaining models, too (section 3.3), seem insufficiently general to capture significant aspects of India's relative lack of agricultural growth, though I think the idea that those in power may oppose technological progress because it may erode their power over time, deserves more formal investigation.

Similarly, I argued (section 4.1) that interlinking by itself provides no explanation of insufficient agricultural change. More promising, but lacking empirical investigation, are recent theories tracing connections between innovation and mobility in the agricultural sector (sections 4.2, 4.3). These theories are of course built on other market imperfections, in particular lack of flexibility in land contracts, and lack of access to credit. These are obvious barriers to innovation, and have probably been significant in the Indian context.

In conclusion, therefore, one suspects that some of the theories outlined above are more empirically relevant than others. I have no doubt that there is considerable benefit to be gained from further empirical investigations of the causes of, and barriers to, technological change in Indian agriculture. I hope that the sifting of theories above will be somewhat of a guide to future empirical work.

REFERENCES

AHMED, I. (1981), *Technological Change and Agrarian Structure: A Study of Bangladesh,* International Labour Office, Geneva.

AKERLOF, G. (1970), The market for lemons: qualitative uncertainty and the market mechanism, *Quarterly Journal of Economics,* 89, 488–500.

AKERLOF, G. (1984), *An Economic Theorist's Book of Tales*, Cambridge University Press, Cambridge.

BANNOCK, G., et al. (1978), *The Penguin Dictionary of Economics*, Penguin, Harmondsworth.

BARDHAN, P., ed. (1989), *The Economic Theory of Agrarian Institutions*, Clarendon Press, Oxford.

BASU, K. (1984), *The Less Developed Economy*, Blackwell, Oxford.

____ (1987), Technological stagnation, tenurial laws and adverse selection, Working Paper No. 14, WIDER, Helsinki.

____ (1989), Technological stagnation, tenurial laws and adverse selection, *American Economic Review*, 79, 251–5.

BECKER, G.S., K.M. MURPHY, and R. TAMURA (1990), Human capital, fertility and economic growth, *Journal of Political Economy*, 98, 5, 512–37.

BELL, C. (1988), Credit markets and interlinked transactions, Chenery and Srinivasan, *Development Economics*, Ch. 16.

____ (1989), A comparison of principal–agent and bargaining solutions: the case of tenancy contracts, in Bardhan, ed., *Agrarian Institutions*.

BHADURI, A. (1973), A study in agricultural backwardness under semi-feudalism, *Economic Journal*, 83, 120–37 (reprinted in *Unconventional Economic Essays: Selected Papers of Amit Bhaduri*, OUP, Delhi, 1993).

BLAUG, M., R. LAYARD, and M. WOODHALL (1969), *The Causes of Graduate Unemployment in India*, Allen Lane, London.

BOYCE, J.K. (1987), *Agrarian Impasse in Bengal: Institutional Constraints to Technological Change*, Oxford University Press, Oxford.

BRAVERMAN, A. and J.E. STIGLITZ (1986), Landlords, tenants and technological innovations, *Journal of Development Economics*, 23, 313–32.

____ (1989), Credit rationing, tenancy, productivity and the dynamics of inequality, in Bardhan, ed., *Agrarian Institutions*.

BYRES, T.J. (1972), The dialectic of India's green revolution, *South Asian Review*, 2.

CHAUDHRI, D.P. (1968), Education and agricultural productivity in India, Ph.D. dissertation, University of Delhi.

CHENERY, H. and T.N. SRINIVASAN (1988), *Handbook of Development Economics*, 1, North-Holland, Amsterdam.

CHINAPPA, B.N. (1977), Adoption of the new technology in North Arcot district, in B.H. Farmer, ed., *Green Revolution? Technology and Changes in Rice-Growing Areas of Tamil Nadu and Sri Lanka*, Macmillan, London.

DAS, S.K. and M. PANT (1991), Green revolution and agricultural growth—a micro-theoretic approach, *Journal of Quantitative Economics*, 7, 115–24.

The Economist (1991), Caged: a survey of India, 4–10 May, 319.

EPSTEIN, T.S. (1967), Productive efficiency and customary system of rewards in rural South India, in R. Firth, ed., *Themes in Economic Anthropology*, Tavistock Publications, London.

GRIFFIN, K. (1974), *The Political Economy of Agrarian Change*, Macmillan, London.

GRILICHES, Z. (1964), Research expenditure, education and the aggregate agricultural production function, *American Economic Review*, 54, 961–74.

HART, G. (1986), Interlocking transactions: obstacles, precursors or instruments of agrarian capitalism? *Journal of Development Economics*, 23, 177–203.

HAYAMI, Y. and V.W. RUTTAN (1985), *Agricultural Development: An International Perspective*, Johns Hopkins University Press, Baltimore.

HICKS, J.R. (1932), *The Theory of Wages*, Macmillan, London.

JOHANSEN, L. (1972), *Production Functions*, North-Holland, Amsterdam.

JOHNSON, D.G. (1950), Resource allocation under share contracts, *Journal of Political Economy*, 58, 111–23.

KAMIEN, M.I. and N.L. SCHWARTZ (1968), Optimal induced technical change, *Econometrica*, 36, 1–17.

____ (1969), Induced factor augmenting technical progress from a microeconomic viewpoint, *Econometrica*, 37, 668–84.

____ (1983), *Market Structure and Innovation*, Cambridge University Press, Cambridge.

KENNEDY, C. (1964), Induced bias in innovation and the theory of distribution, *Economic Journal*, 74, 541–7.

NAQVI, N. (1990), Technological stagnation, tenurial laws and adverse selection: comment, *American Economic Review*, 90, 935–40.

NEWBERY, D.M.G. (1975), Tenurial obstacles to innovation, *Journal of Development Studies*, 11, 263–77.

PARTHASARATHY, G. and D.S. PRASAD (1978), Response to the impact of the new rice technology by farm size and tenure: Andhra Pradesh, India, International Rice Research Institute, Los Banos.

PIGOU, A.C. (1920), *The Economics of Welfare*, Macmillan, London.

REDDY, S.K. and J.E. KIVILIN (1968), Adoption of HYV in three Indian villages, Research Report No. 19, National Institute of Community Development, Hyderabad.

RIVERA-BATIZ, L.A. and P.M. ROMER (1991), Economic integration and endogenous growth, *Quarterly Journal of Economics*, 106, 531–56.

ROMER, P.M. (1990a), Are nonconvexities important for understanding growth? *American Economic Review*, Papers and Proceedings, 97–103.

____ (1990b), Endogenous technological change, *Journal of Political Economy*, 98, S71–S102.

ROSENZWEIG, M.R. (1982), Agricultural development, education and innovation, in M. Gersovitz et al., eds., *The Theory and Experience of Economic Development*, George Allen Unwin, London.

ROTH, A.E. (1979), *Axiomatic Models of Bargaining*, Springer-Verlag, Berlin.

SAMUELSON, P.A. (1965), A theory of induced innovation along Kennedy–Weisacker lines, *Review of Economics and Statistics*, 47, 343–56.

SAMUELSON, W. (1984), Bargaining under asymmetric information, *Econometrica*, 52, 995–1006.

SCHULTZ, T.P. (1988), Education investments and returns, in Chenery and Srinivasan, *Development Economics*, Ch. 13.

SCHULTZ, T.W. (1963), *The Economic Value of Education*, Columbia University Press, New York.

SIDHU, S. (1976), The structural value of education in agricultural development, Department of Agricultural and Applied Economics, Staff Paper 76, University of Minnesota, St. Paul.

SINGH, N. (1991), Technological stagnation, tenurial laws and subsistence constraints, processed, University of California, Santa Cruz.

STIGLITZ, J.E. (1988), Economic organization, information and development, in Chenery and Srinivasan, *Development Economics*, Ch. 5.

TIMMER, C.P. (1988), The agricultural transformation, in Chenery and Srinivasan, *Development Economics*, Ch. 8.

VYAS, V.S. (1975), India's High Yielding Varieties Program in Wheat 1966/7 to 1971/2, Working Paper, *Centro Internacional de Mejoramiento de Maiz y Trigo*, Mexico City.

ZARKOVIC, M. (1987), *Issues in Indian Agricultural Development*, Westview Press, Boulder, Colorado.

Some Issues in Interlinked Agrarian Markets

SHUBHASHIS GANGOPADHYAY

1. INTRODUCTION

The literature on agrarian contracts in less developed countries (LDCs) highlights the presence of 'interlinked' markets. Transactions in any one market are invariably linked with the nature (and amount) of transactions in the other markets. While, theoretically, interlinkages may be of various kinds, the most commonly observed ones are those involving the informal (agrarian) credit market, the labour market and the market for grains. (See, for example, Rudra, 1982; Bardhan and Rudra, 1978.) Given that agents are interested in the total outcome of all the transactions that they undertake (and not particularly of any one transaction), it is not surprising that markets in different commodities should be directly related.

What makes the problem of interlinkage interesting is the diversity of relations among the various markets in LDC agriculture. In addition, particular instances of agrarian contracts have been variously interpreted by political economists as examples of exploitation and power or, alternatively, as necessary internalization, for efficiency, of external market forces. To be able to resolve the debate, it is essential to know the major empirical facts in agrarian economies.

First, how do we identify interlinkage? Consider two markets dealing in two commodities A and B. There are agents operating on both sides (i.e. as buyers and sellers) of the two markets. Suppose there are some agents who are common to both markets. If it is observed that (even one of) such common agents transact at prices different from those operating in one of the markets only, we will say that there is interlinking of markets by the common agent(s). Consider, for example the credit–labour linkage. There is a 'market' rate of interest for various types of loans and a market wage rate for various types of labour. However, it is often found that when the lender is also a landowner and lends to a labourer who works on the landowner's land, neither the rate of interest nor the wage rate is the same as the corresponding market rates. This is a clear case, by our definition, of an interlinked contract entered into by the landowner (lender) and the labourer (borrower).[1]

The second observation deals with the credit market *per se*. Agrarian credit markets in India are characterized by (i) the high variability of interest rates (Basu, 1989; Bhaduri, 1973), and (ii) the existence of very low interest rates (Bardhan and Rudra, 1978). For an understanding of (ii), we will have to explain what is meant by low interest rates. Suppose the opportunity cost of the borrower for loans is r. If a particular lender is willing to offer this borrower a loan at interest rates less than r, we will say that a low interest has been charged. This is clearly a significant observation when we keep in mind the uncertainties of Indian agriculture and the difficulty of small farmers and landless labourers, i.e. those without much collateral, to obtain loans even from nationalized banks.

While (i) has been partially explained by the term structure of different loans (Basu, 1989), the difference in interest rates for loans of similar duration still have to be explained. High interest rates have been interpreted by many authors to reflect the imperfection of credit markets either through the monopoly (power) of the lenders (Bhaduri, 1977) or through the risk of default faced by the lender (Bottomley, 1975). This has led to an intense debate between those writing about the power structure in agriculture leading to exploitation through 'usurious' interest rates, and the others highlighting the importance of government policies to correct market imperfections.

Third, we come to the related issue of collateral and what has been termed, in particular instances, as 'bonded' labour (Srinivasan, 1980). The borrower has often been found to transfer assets to the lender as part, or full, repayment for a contracted loan. This, in itself, is not surprising; however, it has been noted that these collaterals are undervalued during the transfer. When future labour had been contracted as

---

[1]Instances of various interlinked contracts are available in the readings listed in the references.

the collateral and underpriced, this has obviously led to politically sensitive issues. The important issue in this debate is whether such collateral underpricing is due to the (political or economic) power of the lender over the borrower.

In section 2 we will discuss the interlinkage between the product and credit markets. Two types of loans will be considered—production and consumption loans. Section 3 will consider the credit–labour linkage and address the issue of bonded labour as studied by economists. Section 4 will generalize the models studied in sections 2 and 3. Section 5 concludes our exercise.

Throughout the text, lengthy proofs will be omitted, the emphasis being more on an analysis of the issues involved. Also, much of the material covered here (except in section 4) is already available in various forms. The interested reader can look at the appropriate references as they appear in the text.

2 . PRODUCT–CREDIT LINKAGE

2.1 Production loan

Much of the material in this section is in Gangopadhyay and Sengupta (1987a). Consider a farmer (i.e. owner of cultivable land) producing output Q. There is a lag between production decisions and the actual realizations of output. Production decisions entail the use of inputs which have to be paid for when such decisions are carried out. Consequently, the farmer organizing production on his land has to have liquid funds to undertake production.[2] For this, the farmer has to take a loan. The farmer is 'small' in the sense that he has no liquid funds of his own to start up the production process.

The relationship between the farmer's output and the available credit, C, is given by[3]

$$Q = f(C) \qquad (2.1)$$

---

[2]This is often referred to as working capital in economics.

[3]$f(\cdot)$ is differentiable and satisfies the following assumptions: as $C \to 0, f_C \to \infty$, and as $C \to \infty, f_C \to 0$. The interested reader can easily check that any production function, that is well-behaved, will allow itself to be written as a function of the total expenditure, provided input markets are perfectly competitive; i.e. an individual farmer's decision does not affect the relative price of various inputs. Consequently, (2.1) can be interpreted as a general production relationship with many inputs under competitive conditions.

The farmer faces a credit market where the cost of borrowing is given by $\bar{r}$. In other words, if the farmer borrows an amount C, he has to pay back $(1 + \bar{r})C$. Let there be an agent in the village who has an opportunity cost of liquid funds equal to r, with $r < \bar{r}$. Notice that such a difference between the interest rates can be due to a host of reasons. It could be because of the different wealth positions (and, hence, the ability to post different types and levels of collaterals) or differences in the availability of liquid funds. For a firm fix, these interest rates could be looked upon as the cost of loans faced by the agents when they borrow from institutional credit sources.

The interest rate differential opens up possibilities of mutually advantageous trade between the two agents with the lender being the one with the lower opportunity cost and the farmer being the borrower. One may wonder why the village lender should be able to make a positive gain by arbitrage when the institutional credit source charges the farmer $\bar{r}$. Works by Akerlof (1970) and Bottomley (1975) point out that it is possible for a village lender to have better information about other villagers than is ever possible by institutional sources. Moreover, as we will soon see, the ability of the village lender to interlink is precisely the method by which she can affect the possible arbitrage.

There is a market for the output of the farmer. The price in this market is competitively determined and is equal to q. Since q is given for both the borrower and the lender, we will normalize it to unity. This price is known with certainty at the time the farmer makes his production decisions. This market is perfectly accessible to all persons in the village; consequently, the lender, too, can operate in this market. By perfect accessibility we mean that all agents face the same product price ($q = 1$). This is a strong assumption: we know that in villages not all agents, especially small farmers, have equal access to product markets. However, as will become clear, it is a simplifying assumption. Relaxing this assumption only strengthens the major result!

If the farmer was to operate through the institutional credit market, his cost of funds would be $\bar{r}$. Thus, for any loan amount C, he would have to pay back, in terms of interest and principal, the amount $(1 + \bar{r})C$. Given output $f(C)$, this would mean a net income to the farmer equal to $f(C) - (1 + \bar{r})C$. The farmer will choose the loan amount C to maximize this income; call this maximum net income $\bar{Y}$. Then,

$$\overline{Y} = \max_{C} [f(C) - (1 + \overline{r})C] \qquad (2.2)$$

The farmer is always guaranteed this amount of income, regardless of the presence of the village lender. So, if the latter wants the farmer to enter into any deals with her, she must guarantee him at least $\overline{Y}$. This $\overline{Y}$ is a function of $\overline{r}$. The higher is $\overline{r}$, the lower is the value of $\overline{Y}$.

The major difference between the institutional credit source and the village lender is the fact that while the institutional source is restricted to operating in the credit market alone, the village lender does not face any such restrictions. Consequently, she can transact with the farmer in more than one market. The farmer in this model operates in two different markets, output and credit; both markets are accessible to the lender also. So, she has the option of contracting with the farmer in both the markets. The farmer sells output and buys credit; the lender can, therefore, sell credit to, and buy output from, the farmer. When the lender buys output from the farmer, she acts as a trader (retailer) between the farmer and the final consumer of the output. Since the output market is competitive, the selling price of output (to the consumer) is always unity regardless of who the seller is. The lender's profit from operating in the output market arises from the price difference, if any, between what she pays the farmer and unity.[4] The other source of income to the lender is of course due to the difference in the price that the farmer pays to her for credit and her opportunity cost of credit (r).

In principle, the lender can offer the farmer a contract (δ, μ), which we will interpret as follows: if the farmer takes any loan from her, he will have to pay back an amount $\mu(1 + r)$ per unit of loan and sell the crop to her at a price equal to δ. I will assume that all contracts are enforceable; thus if the farmer accepts the lender's deal, he will have to honour the two transactions specified by the lender. If the farmer accepts the contract, then he will have to now choose the amount of production loan to be taken that will maximize his payoff, Y. Y now depends on δ and μ. Let $Y(\delta, \mu)$ be the maximum income the farmer can obtain from the contract (δ, μ). Clearly, for the contract to be acceptable to the farmer, the following must be satisfied:

$$Y(\delta, \mu) \equiv \max_{C} [\delta f(C) - \mu(1 + r)C] \geq \overline{Y} \qquad (2.3)$$

---

[4]Recall that we have normalized q, the competitive price of the output, to unity.

i.e. the farmer must be at least as well off as he can be by going directly to the institutional source.

If the contract offered by the lender and accepted by the farmer is such that $\delta = 1$ and $\mu = (1 + \bar{r})/(1 + r)$, then this contract is a non-interlinked contract according to our definition. This is because, even though the farmer is selling the crop to, as well as taking loans from, the same person, the two prices in the two markets (output and credit) are the same to him as he would have faced if he had entered into the two transactions separately in the two different markets. Notice that the market price faced by the farmer for credit is $\bar{r}$, while the market price for output is unity. However, if the δ and μ are different from the above values, then we have a case of interlinking. So, now the question is: will the lender offer an interlinked contract?

The lender's income from such a contract is given as

$$D(\delta, \mu) = (1 - \delta)f(\hat{C}) - (1 - \mu)(1 + r)\hat{C} \qquad (2.4)$$

where

$$\hat{C} = \arg \max_{C} Y(\delta, \mu).$$

The lender maximizes (2.4) by a choice of (δ, μ).

Before I state the first result, we need to define one more term. Let

$$Y^* \equiv [\max_{C} \{f(C) - (1 + r)C\}] \qquad (2.5)$$

Y^* is the income that could be generated for the farmer if he could obtain loans at the interest r, or the income that could accrue to the lender if she owned the land (and the technology of production). Since Y^* is the maximum income generated at a credit cost r, less than $\bar{r}$, $Y^* > \bar{Y}$. In a sense, Y^* is the maximum surplus that could be generated in the system; it is indeed the efficient outcome.

PROPOSITION 1 *The unique optimal contract* (δ^*, μ^*) *is characterized by*

(i) $Y(\delta^*, \mu^*) = \bar{Y}$ (ii) $\delta^* = \mu^* = \bar{Y}/Y^* < 1$.

(For a proof, see Gangopadhyay and Sengupta, 1987a.)

Here, I will give a heuristic argument for the proof. First note that the second part of the proposition implies that the lender charges a rate of interest which is less than her own oppportunity cost of funds, not just less than $\bar{r}$! This is because if we look at equation (2.3), the cost of a unit of loan to the farmer is $\mu^*(1 + r)$ and $\mu^* < 1$ which means that the cost is less than $(1 + r)$. Also, the lender allows the farmer a price for the crop which is less than unity, since δ^* is less than unity. If $\delta^* = \mu^*$, then one can write equation (2.3) as

$$\delta[f(C) - (1 + r)C] \tag{A}$$

and the maximization of this is independent of the actual value of δ, as long as it is positive. The farmer, therefore, chooses C to maximize this expression. This also maximizes the total surplus available in the system and the value of δ^* determines the share of this surplus accruing to the farmer. The fraction $(1 - \delta^*)$, of course, goes to the lender. This can be seen from observing equation (2.4) and using the second part of the proposition. By choosing $\delta = \mu$, the lender is able to do away with the distortion in the credit market by allowing the farmer to choose C subject to a product price equal to unity and credit price equal to r.

This has an obvious similarity with a profit tax for industry; we know that the profit tax is non-distortionary. We say that there was an original distortion in the credit market because of the following reason. Notice, if the lender also owned the land and could organize production herself, then she would produce the surplus Y^*. The farmer, on the other hand, acting without any interlinked contract would produce $\bar{Y}$. Given our assumptions, $\bar{Y} < Y^*$. Since the lender possesses no land, the cost of land to the moneylender can be thought to be infinity. The opportunity cost of land to the farmer is, therefore, less than that of the lender's. On the other hand, the cost of credit is higher for the borrower than the lender. If the lender owned the land or the borrower faced the same opportunity cost of credit as the lender, then the total surplus could be maximized at Y^*. This would entail the optimum use of the variable factor, credit, at the level $\hat{C}$. Interlinkage allows the realization of this efficient utilization of the variable factor.

The first part of the proposition now obviously holds; if $Y(\delta^*, \mu^*) > \bar{Y}$, reduce δ^* and μ^* by the same amount such that the new $\delta(= \mu)$ gives exactly $\bar{Y}$ to the farmer. This, of course, increases the amount going to the lender. Thus the optimal (δ^*, μ^*) must satisfy the condition in Proposition 1.

Notice that here is a simple case where interlinkage takes place in the sense that the interlinked prices are different from the corresponding market prices. Also note that interlinkage is endogenously effected; after all, there is nothing in the model to prevent the lender from choosing $\delta = 1$, and the rate of interest $\mu = (1 + \bar{r})/(1 + r)$, the case of no interlinkage.

There is a further interesting result: *the rate of interest is less than the lender's own cost*. Recall the initial situation. The farmer was at a disadvantage in the credit market $(\bar{r} > r)$ but at no extra disadvantage in the product market. However, the farmer gets a lower price for his product and pays a lower price for the credit! Notice that formally this is equivalent to a system where the output is taxed and the input is subsidized.

This is a very important observation. Much of the debate in Indian agricultural economics regarding the economic disadvantages faced by small farmers has centred around the empirical observations regarding 'usurious' rates of interest. The term usurious has been used to describe interest rates higher than the market rates. A weak definition would term usurious any interest rate higher than r; a stronger definition would take $\bar{r}$ as the threshold. However, even by the weaker definition, interlinkage leads to no usurious interest rates on credit. Usurious interest rates have often been equated to exploitation of the farmer by the lender, an outcome that can be obtained whenever the credit market is discriminatory against the farmer, i.e. $\bar{r} > r$. The model presented here suggests that such a conclusion would be erroneous in the presence of interlinked contracts.

Furthermore, this analysis tells us that the worse the access of the farmer to the credit market, i.e. the greater the difference between $\bar{r}$ and r, the *lower* is the interest charged to the farmer in an interlinked contract! We show this in the next subsection.

2.2 Different farmers

We are now in a position to study why different farmers sign different contracts for similar loans from the same lender. Suppose there are two farmers, one with reservation level $\bar{Y}_1$ and the other with $\bar{Y}_2$. Such differences in the reservation levels could come about because of the different interest rates faced by the farmers when taking loans from lending institutions. The latter could, for example, be due to the marketability of different collaterals offered by the farmers. In other words, the different $\overline{Y}$'s are due to different $\overline{r}$'s (for different farmers) in equation (2.2). Our result then states that, in the presence of the village lender, farmers on identical plots of land but different credit ratings, will take identical amounts of loans, to produce the same amount of crop. This is because the loan amount to be taken by the farmer is determined completely by the maximization of the expression (A) (in the previous subsection), which is independent of the actual values of δ or μ. However, each farmer will get a return equal to his $\overline{Y}$. This can be brought about by lowering δ for the farmer with the lower $\overline{Y}$, and keeping a higher δ for the farmer with the higher $\overline{Y}$. (Recall from Proposition 1, that $\delta^* = \overline{Y}/Y^*$.) Since optimality demands that $\delta^* = \mu^*$, it is straightforward that the lower is $\overline{Y}$, the lower will be the interest charged by the lender. In other words, the *lower* are the opportunities of the farmer, the *lower* is the interest charged from him in an interlinked contract.

Our next result is a generalization. Consider farmers with different technologies, f^k, and/or different land sizes. Then for the kth farmer, one can define the following parameters, $\overline{Y}_k$ and Y_k^* as in equations (2.2) and (2.5). Define b_k as $(\overline{Y}_k)/(Y_k^*)$.

PROPOSITION 2. *Consider two farmers i and j with $b_i \geq b_j$. Then* $\delta_i^* = \mu_i^* \geq \delta_j^* = \mu_j^*$.
Observe that from Proposition 1, each farmer's optimal contract will be characterized by $\delta_k^* = \mu_k^* = b_k$! Note that for any given Y^*, the lower is $\overline{Y}$, the lower will be the explicit interest charged by the lender. In other words, the farmer whose alternative opportunities are limited (as measured by a lower $\overline{Y}$), also pays a lower interest. Consequently, it is erroneous to try and link the farmer's plight directly with the interest on loans taken from the village moneylender.

2.3 Consumption loans
We distinguish between consumption loans and production loans by the use to which they are put. Thus, while a production loan affects the

output produced and, hence, the surplus realized, a consumption loan does not affect the output produced. So now, Q, in equation (2.1), is independent of C. However, C directly affects the well-being of the farmer. Let $U(\cdot)$, the utility function, be a measure of this well-being. $U(\cdot)$ can then be written as a function of two arguments C, i.e. consumption today, and y, i.e. net income tomorrow after loans are repaid. Like $\overline{Y}$ before, define

$$\overline{U} = \max_{C} \left[U(C, \ Q - (1 + \overline{r})C) \right]. \tag{2.6}$$

Again consider (δ, μ) a contract from the lender to the farmer. Then the lender must guarantee that

$$\max_{C} \left[U(C, \ \delta Q - \mu(1 + r)C) \right] \geq \overline{U}. \tag{2.7}$$

The lender maximizes

$D(\delta, \mu) = (1 - \delta)Q - (1 - \mu)(1 + r)C$ subject to (2.7).

By a method similar to the reasoning in Proposition 1, one can derive the following result:

PROPOSITION 3. *The optimal contract on consumption loans is characterized by* $\delta^* < 1$ *and* $\mu^* = 1$.

Summarizing the results derived so far, we see that the interest rates charged on all loans are reduced from the borrower's opportunity cost if the lender is allowed to provide interlinked contracts. Furthermore, the relationship between the farmer's explicit interest charges in an interlinked loan market and his income position is an inverse one. Interlinkage results in the efficient allocation of credit as is evident from the fact that the total surplus is always equal to Y^* for a production loan. Also, the higher interest faced by the farmer in the non-interlinked market, $\overline{r}$, is reflected in an undervaluation of the product price and not in usurious interest charges. Finally, the interest charged on interlinked consumption loans is higher than that on interlinked production loans; in both types of loans the product price is less than the market price even with complete accessibility of the farmer to this market. With product–credit interlinkage we have thus demonstrated differential interests for (i) loans taken for different purposes but for the same time duration, and (ii) similar loans but taken by different types of farmers also for the same time duration.

3. COLLATERAL AND BONDED LABOUR

In this section we will study another aspect of interlinkage: collateral pricing and the possibility of bonded labour. Collateral is important in every loan transacted. It is an alternative form of payment if the borrower is unable to repay through the proceeds of the project which was financed by the loan. The collateral is usually a non-liquid asset which, however, has some value. Clearly, the value of the collateral is important to both the borrower and the lender. One such collateral could be land, another could be labour services at a future date, or any other marketable asset. (Of course, the collateral could also be a non-marketable asset like family labour. However, as long as the lender puts some valuation on the borrower's asset, it qualifies as a collateral.)

In the special case where the collateral is (marketable or family) labour, it has often been termed as 'bonded' labour. This has attracted a great deal of social and political debate. It assumes special significance when the valuation put on this 'tied' labour is less than the market price of the labour during the repayment period. In the previous section we had seen how in a product–credit interlinkage, the imperfection in the credit market was manifested in a lower-than-market price of the product even under perfect accessibility of all agents to the product market. The relevant question, therefore, is whether in a contract where labour is offered as the collateral, the imperfection of the credit market is also reflected in an undervaluation of labour even when the labourer has complete access to a labour market. (Notice that family labour is usually non-marketable and, thus, in that sense does not have complete access to the labour market. However, our result about product price undervaluation was in spite of perfect access. Again, since we are interested only in the analytical issue, we will not make this particular distinction excepting where necessary to interpret the results.)

The literature on credit markets has emphasized the role played by collaterals in agrarian economies. Its significance lies in the observation that collaterals are often found being transferred from the borrower to the lender (in the event of a default on loan) at (implicit) prices well below the market value. In the special case of the collateral being labour, this has led to an emotional debate regarding the 'bonding' of labour to credit sources. The first papers attempting an analytical model of this phenomenon are Bhaduri (1977), Srinivasan (1980), and Basu (1984). Here, I will concentrate on the analyses in Bhaduri and Basu (referred to henceforth as BB). Srinivasan deals explicitly with bonded labour and we will come to that later. In the BB models, the lender uses her monopoly power in the credit market to undervalue the collateral. Furthermore, by undervaluing the collateral, the lender is not only able to avoid any losses should there be a default, she actually gains in the event of a default!

This literature is a critique of the default rate hypothesis of Bottomley (1975). According to Bottomley, the high interest rates were due to the lender hedging against the possibility of default. Simply put, if the lender is advancing a loan equal to x, at a rate $\bar{r}$, she is likely to get back only a fraction α of the loans repayable. Consequently, r has to take this into account and the interest charged on the portion of the loan that will be recovered will be that much higher. In other words, if the default rate went down, the rate of interest on loans would go down. The Bhaduri model, on the other hand, maintains that the interest is used to encourage default so that the lender can acquire the collateral at undervalued prices. Basu's model is more general than Bhaduri's and it also comes to the same broad conclusion.

The model I will now describe departs a little from the BB models; not in the nature of the analysis but in the type of assumptions used. This will allow us to see how important are the assumptions made in model building. Much of what follows next is derived from Gangopadhyay and Sengupta (1987b).

Consider a borrower and a lender. The borrower has an asset that he values at π_B. This asset could be land or (family) labour services. He needs liquid funds today to finance his consumption needs. If he should take a loan C today, he will have to repay $(1 + i)C$ tomorrow where i is the rate of interest. The repayment of the loan will be made partly from his earning K tomorrow, which is independent of the amount of loan taken today (an assumption to be relaxed later), and partly through the transfer of asset should K fall below the level of repayment. I will make an unrealistic assumption now; there is no uncertainty in K. This is unrealistic because the major reason why collaterals are needed is precisely to ensure that in the event of a failure to repay the loan due to bad realizations of income, the lender can recover her losses through possessing the collateral offered by the

142   SHUBHASHIS GANGOPADHYAY

borrower. However, in the next section, we will consider a much more
general model with uncertainty. For the present, we are more interested
in getting the intuition behind the model, so we will continue with this
assumption.

The lender offers a contract (i, p), where i is the rate of interest and
p is the price at which the collateral is valued. The lender's own
valuation of the borrower's collateral is π. This valuation would, in
principle, be the market price of the asset. Suppose $K < (1 + i)C$. Then
the amount of *collateral* transferred to the lender, in units of the
collateral, will be $[(1 + i)C - K]/p$. It is here that our assumption differs
from the BB models. There, in the case when $K < (1 + i)C$, the amount
of default was measured as

$$C - [K/(1 + i)] = [(1 + i)C - K]/(1 + i) < (1 + i)C - K,$$

the last expression being the measurement of default by our calculations.
Consider the case where p is a market price of the asset and is also
valued the same by the lender. Whenever there is any default in the BB
case, the lender loses compared to the case of no default. In our case what
the lender does not get through K, she gets through the collateral.

The demand for loan by the borrower is given by[5]

$$C = C(i, p), \quad C_i < 0, C_p \geq 0. \tag{3.1}$$

It is easy to derive this loan-demand function from any standard utility-
maximizing behaviour of the borrower whose utility depends on the
consumption today and the amount of net asset he possesses tomorrow
after making all repayments. We are using the demand function as it
vastly simplifies the analysis. Define the rate of default β as

$$\beta = \begin{cases} \dfrac{C(1 + i) - K}{C(1 + i)} & \text{if } K < C(1 + i), \\ 0 & \text{otherwise.} \end{cases} \tag{3.2}$$

From any contract (i, p), and a valuation π by the lender of the
borrower's collateral, the lender gets an income

$$D(i, p) = \begin{cases} C(i, p)[(i - r)(1 - \beta) + \beta\{(\pi/p)(1 + i) - (1 + r)\}], & \text{if } \beta > 0, \\ C(i, p)[i - r] & \text{otherwise.} \end{cases} \tag{3.3}$$

[5]The loan-demand function will satisfy the usual assumptions. In particular, we want the
loan demand to go to zero for sufficiently large interest rates for any given non-negative price
of the collateral.

Before we go on to discuss the results it is instructive to take stock of what we have so far. First, we have not assumed anything about the relative valuations of π and π_B. In principle, $\pi < \pi_B$, since often the collateral is non-marketable like family labour. Also, the land may be fragmented being of smaller value to the lender; or the lender may not be a farmer and this may be cultivable land only; or there may be non-market 'attachments' to the asset of the borrower which may not be shared by the lender (see Bhaduri, 1977 for a discussion on this). Secondly, whatever contract the lender offers is restricted by the loan-demand function of the borrower. Thirdly, the lender is a Stackelberg leader in the sense that she knows the loan-demand function of the borrower. Finally, and most importantly, there is no uncertainty.

We will illustrate our major result with the help of Figs. 1 and 2. In Fig. 1, the vertical axis measures the perceived wealth tomorrow of the borrower. This wealth consists of two parts: the fixed income K and

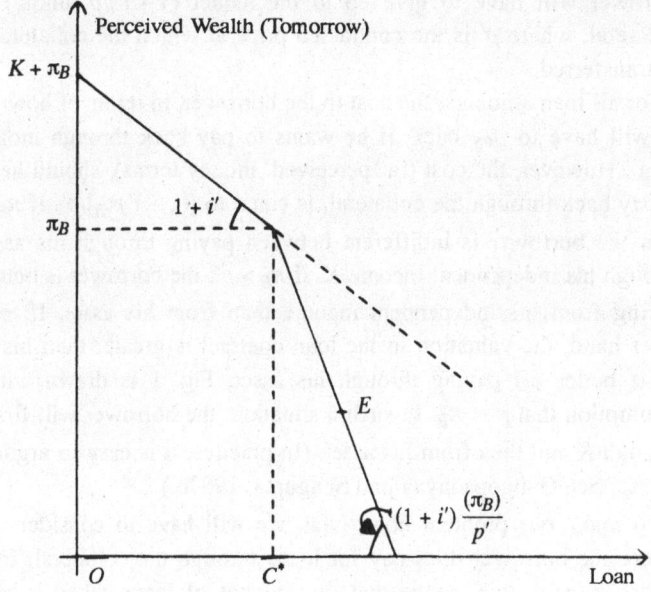

FIG. 1

the borrower's asset π_B. It is 'perceived' because part of the valuation is the borrower's own, and does not reflect the true market cost or the valuation of the lender which is π. The horizontal axis measures the loans taken by the borrower. If he takes no loans, his wealth tomorrow is $K + \pi_B$. For any positive amount of loan taken today, the amount of wealth tomorrow will be less than $K + \pi_B$ by the amount of repayments to be made. For any given interest rate i', define C^* as the amount of loan such that

$$C^* = K/(1 + i') \qquad (3.4)$$

If the borrower borrows more than C^*, he is unable to repay the loan through his independent source of income alone; part of the repayment has to be made through the transfer of collateral. The amount of collateral to be transferred in part payment will depend on the interest rate, as well as the agreed price at which the collateral will be valued by the lender. In other words, for each unit of loan above C^*, the borrower will have to give up to the lender $(1 + i')/p'$ units of the collateral, where p' is the contracted price at which the collateral will be transferred.

For all loan amounts, the cost to the borrower, in terms of how much he will have to pay back, if he wants to pay back through money is $1 + i'$. However, the cost (in 'perceived' money terms), should he have to pay back through the collateral, is equal to $[(1 + i')\pi_B]/p'$. If $\pi_B = p'$, then the borrower is indifferent between paying through his asset or through his independent income K. If $\pi_B > p'$, the borrower is better off paying from his independent income than from his asset. If, on the other hand, the valuation in the loan contract is greater than his own, he is better off paying through his asset. Fig. 1 is drawn with the assumption that $p' < \pi_B$. In such a situation, the borrower will first pay through K and then from his asset. (In practice, it is easy to argue that $p \leq \pi_B$. See Gangopadhyay and Sengupta, 1987b.)

To make our problem non-trivial, we will have to consider cases where the borrower does pay for loans through the collateral. In case where $\pi_B > p'$, this means that the amount of loans taken is greater than C^*. In Fig. 2, the kinked line is the same as in Fig. 1. This corresponds to the contract (i', p') with $p' < \pi_B$. Let E be the point chosen by the borrower under such a contract. Now consider the contract (i'', p''), where $p'' = \pi_B$ and i'' solves the equation

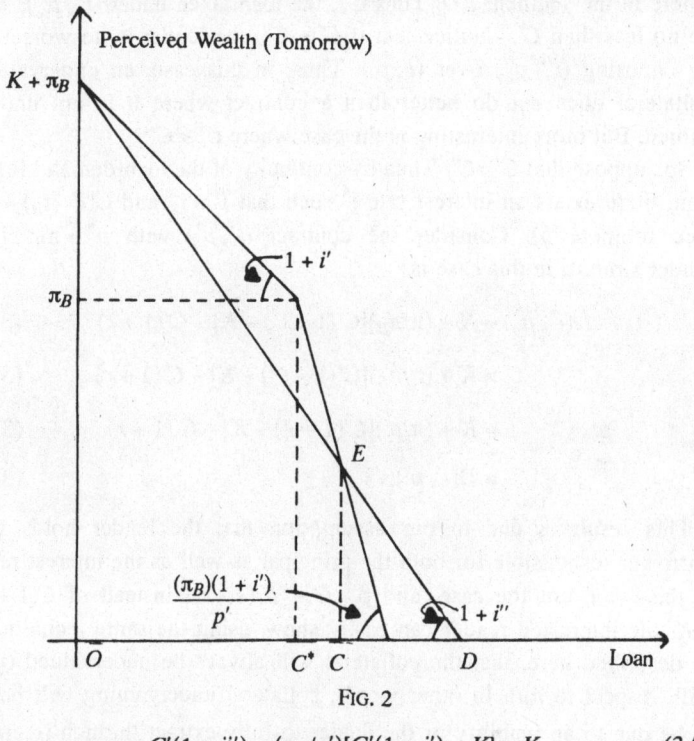

FIG. 2

$$C'(1 + i'') = (\pi_B/p')[C'(1 + i') - K] + K \qquad (3.5)$$

where C' is the loan taken by the borrower at the contract (i', p'). We will now show that any contract where the collateral is undervalued (i.e. with respect to π_B), can be bettered by one where that collateral price is exactly equal to π_B. In other words, I will argue that, given (i', p'), there exists a contract (i^*, p^*), with $p^* = \pi_B$, and the lender is better off than in the primed contract. Since the borrower decides the amount of loans to be taken, this is sufficient to show that the collateral is never underpriced.

The (i'', p'') contract is depicted in Fig. 2 by the straight line passing through E. This follows from two observations: (i) $p'' = \pi_B$, and (ii) the definition of i''. In other words, E, the previous choice of the borrower, is still available to him. Consequently, he cannot be worse off under (i'', p'') compared to (i', p'). Indeed the borrower's new equilibrium, by the theory of revealed preference, will be somewhere in the segment ED. Thus C'', the loan taken under (i'', p''), will be no less than C'. Notice that if $C' = C''$, the lender is no worse off by choosing (i'', p'') over (i', p'). Thus, in this case, an undervalued collateral does not do better than a contract where it is not undervalued. But more interesting is the case where $C' < C''$.

So suppose that $C'' > C'$. Then by continuity of the loan-demand function, there exists an interest rate i^* such that $i^* \geq i''$ and $C(i^*, \pi_B) = C'$ (see footnote 5). Consider the contract (i^*, p^*) with $p^* = \pi_B$. The lender's return in this case is

$$D(i^*, p^*) = K + (\pi/\pi_B)[C'(1 + i^*) - K] - C'(1 + r) \qquad (3.6)$$

$$> K + (\pi/\pi_B)[C'(1 + i'') - K] - C'(1 + r) \qquad (3.7)$$

$$= K + (\pi/p')[C'(1 + i') - K] - C'(1 + r) \qquad (3.8)$$

$$\equiv D(i', p'). \qquad (3.9)$$

This result is due to our assumption that the lender holds the borrower responsible for both the principal as well as the interest rate. If this were not the case, and $\beta = C - [K/(1 + i)]$ instead of $C(1 + i) - K$, the interested reader can easily show, using the same techniques as described here, that the collateral will always be undervalued (i.e. with respect to π_B). In other words, collateral undervaluing will have to be due to an inability of the lender to fully extract through interest payments the profit from lending. We will look more closely at this issue in the next section where a more general model will be developed allowing for uncertainty.

However, collateral underpricing does take place. See, for example, the references cited in Basu, 1984. What the above theoretical analysis points to is the fact that the lender should have no reason to undervalue the collateral if the borrower decides the amount of loan to be taken. A closer look suggests that, in principle, the lender is willing to offer the same valuation as that by the borrower. In Gangopadhyay and Sengupta (1987b), a detailed explanation for collateral underpricing is worked out. The major conclusion there is that the reasons for such underpricing are constraints on the types of contracts that can be agreed upon. This is something that the reader can easily verify from the above analysis. For example, if the lender is unable to extract the full amount of default (as in the BB models), or faces some other constraints like restrictions on interest rates, the lender will take recourse to collateral underpricing. One word of caution: all the above conclusions are true in a very stylized model with no uncertainty. We, therefore, move on to the next section where a more general model is developed.

4. A GENERAL MODEL

In this section we will generalize the approach taken in the last two sections. So far, we have studied two special models: one of inter-linkage between the product and credit markets, the other dealing with the pricing of collateral. These models were stylized as in neither case did we allow for any uncertainty in production. In the model with collateral pricing this is a serious shortcoming because a transfer of the borrower's asset was inevitable and not caused only by unfortunate climatic conditions. On the other hand, for credit markets, a collateral, almost by definition, is an *insurance* against the non-repayment of a loan. Consequently, to make the analysis more realistic, we are going to allow for uncertain production.

The second drawback of the collateral-pricing model studied so far was the fact that the borrower's income in the next period was independent of the amount of loans taken this period. In other words, we were looking only into instances of pure consumption loans. Is the major result of 'no collateral underpricing' true even in the case of production loans?

In this section I will build a model taking into account all these factors. Furthermore, instead of building separate models for the two cases, we will develop a single 'general' model that will have both the features of interlinkage and collateral pricing. Recall that the collateral-pricing model could have been interpreted as a model of labour-tying or bonded labour, if the asset in question was the labour services of the borrower at a future date. In other words, it is a simple case of interlinking the credit and labour markets. It, therefore, makes sense to study both the models together as interlinkage models.

We will develop a model where the repayment of the production loan is partly through incomes earned in the repayment period and, in case of default, through the collateral. Default now takes place in the event of a bad crop. In other words, we define default to be a situation when the farmer is unable to repay the loan through his income from land. In such cases, the lender extracts the payment through the collateral posted by the borrower. Our main purpose is to demonstrate that the major results in sections 2 and 3 are still valid, thereby emphasizing the robustness of the intuitions developed in the earlier sections.

Let the production relationship be denoted

$$Q = \theta f(C) \tag{4.1}$$

where θ is a random variable with distribution $F(\theta)$.[6] $f(\cdot)$, of course, satisfies the same conditions as before (see footnote 3). Let the support of θ be $[\underline{\theta}, \bar{\theta}]$, i.e. θ takes on values between $\underline{\theta}$ and $\bar{\theta}$, both inclusive. For any loan C, let r be the opportunity cost of the lender and let δ and μ be the same as in section 2. Then, for any realization of θ, the borrower will be able to pay back the loan (plus interest) from his produce if and only if $\delta\theta f(c) \geq \mu(1 + r)C$. Define $\hat{\theta}$ as the value of θ which satisfies the above expression as an equality. Thus

$$\hat{\theta} = [\mu(1 + r)C]/[\delta f(C)] \tag{4.2}$$

Clearly, $\hat{\theta}$ depends on δ, μ as well as C, all of which are to be determined in the system.

Recall from section 3 that the borrower has an asset which he values at π_B and the lender values at π. In the event that the realization of θ is such that the income from land is sufficient to pay back the loan plus interest, the farmer's asset is untouched. If, however, θ is small, then the farmer has to pay the excess of loan over production through the collateral. Define the borrower's income in any state θ, $Y(\theta)$, as follows:[7]

$$Y(\theta) = \begin{cases} [\delta\theta f(C) - \mu(1 + r)C] & \text{if } \theta \geq \hat{\theta} \\ -(\pi_B/p)[\mu(1 + r)C - \delta\theta f(C)] & \text{otherwise} \end{cases} \tag{4.3}$$

When $\theta \geq \hat{\theta}$, the borrower can pay back all his debts from his earnings. (Recall, from the previous section, that it never pays the lender to allow a collateral price greater than π_B.) When $\theta < \hat{\theta}$, then the borrower's share of production, $\delta\theta f(C)$ is not sufficient to pay back all

---

[6]This is the same equation as in (2.1) excepting the term θ. Notice that this uncertainty could also be interpreted to be one regarding the price of the product of the farmer.

[7]$Y(\theta)$ is the net change in the farmer's position in the next period. If the collateral is untouched then Y is the addition to the collateral value of π_B while, if payment has to be made through the collateral, the net value of the farmer is less than π_B by this amount.

the loans taken. Consequently, he pays the shortfall $\mu(1 + r)C - \delta\theta f(C)$ from his collateral. His collateral is, therefore, depleted by this amount. Similarly, one can define the lender's income $D(\theta)$ as:

$$D(\theta) = \begin{cases} [(1 - \delta)\theta f(C) - (1 - \mu)(1 + r)C] & \text{if } \theta \geq \hat{\theta} \\ \theta f(C) + (\pi/p)[\mu(1 + r)C - \delta\theta f(C)] - (1 + r)C & \text{otherwise} \end{cases}$$

(4.4)

Notice that when $\theta > \hat{\theta}$, $\delta\theta f(C)$ is less than $\mu(1 + r)C$. The lender, then, gets $\delta\theta f(C)$ from the borrower plus her own share of the output $(1 - \delta)\theta f(C)$ plus the shortfall of $\delta\theta f(C)$ from $\mu(1 + r)C$ through the collateral. Both agents are risk-neutral and maximize their respective expected incomes. Thus, if E is the expectations operator, the borrower maximizes

$$EY(\theta) = \int_{\hat{\theta}}^{\bar{\theta}} [\delta\theta f(C) - \mu(1 + r)C]dF(\theta)$$

$$- \int_{\underline{\theta}}^{\hat{\theta}} [(\pi_B/p)[\mu(1 + r)C - \delta\theta f(C)]]dF(\theta) \qquad (4.5)$$

The lender, similarly, maximizes her expected income which is

$$ED(\theta) = \int_{\hat{\theta}}^{\bar{\theta}} [(1 - \delta)\theta f(C) - (1 - \mu)(1 + r)C]dF(\theta)$$

$$+ \int_{\underline{\theta}}^{\hat{\theta}} [\theta f(C) + \frac{\pi}{p}[\mu(1 + r)C - \delta\theta f(C)] - (1 + r)C]dF(\theta) \quad (4.6)$$

The algebra will be less cumbersome, if a few more terms are defined.

$$H(\hat{\theta}) \equiv \int_{\underline{\theta}}^{\hat{\theta}} \theta dF(\theta) \qquad (4.7)$$

$$\theta^e \equiv \int_{\underline{\theta}}^{\bar{\theta}} \theta dF(\theta) \qquad (4.8)$$

Then it is easy to show that

$$EY(\cdot) = \delta\theta^e f(C)\left[1 + \left(\frac{\pi_B}{p} - 1\right)\frac{H(\hat{\theta})}{\theta^e}\right]$$

$$- \mu(1 + r)C\left[1 + \left(\frac{\pi_B}{p} - 1\right)F(\hat{\theta})\right] \qquad (4.9)$$

It then follows that one can rewrite $ED(\cdot)$ as

$$ED(\,\cdot\,) = [\theta^e f(C) - (1 + r)C]$$
$$+ \delta\theta f(C)\left[1 + \left(\frac{\pi}{p} - 1\right)\frac{H(\hat{\theta})}{\theta^e}\right]$$
$$+ \mu(1 + r)C\left[1 + \left(\frac{\pi}{p} - 1\right)F(\hat{\theta})\right] \qquad (4.10)$$

In keeping with the previous sections' analyses, we will continue to assume that the lender uses the borrower's response to maximize her income. In other words, the lender chooses δ, μ, and a collateral price p, knowing how the borrower will respond in terms of the amount of loan taken. The borrower, of course, chooses the amount of loan C, and this choice is dependent on the contract (δ, μ, p) offered by the lender. For the borrower to accept the contract offered by the lender, the contract must guarantee the borrower's reservation level of income, which we denote $\overline{Y}$. Thus,

$$\max_{C \geq 0} EY(\,\cdot\,) \geq \overline{Y} \qquad (4.11)$$

As in section 2, this reservation level can be defined as the income that the borrower gets when borrowing from the institutional source. The institutional credit market deals in credit alone; since default is always possible in case θ is small, the institutional credit market will always charge a higher rate of interest than the lender who will take payments through the borrower's collateral in the event of default. As in Bottomley (1975), the institutional rate of interest will, therefore, be higher. $\overline{Y}$ is calculated using this higher rate of institutional credit.

Assuming an interior solution for the borrower's problem, i.e. the farmer (borrower) takes a positive loan, the following condition must be satisfied:[8]

$$\delta\theta^e f'(C)\left[1 + (\frac{\pi_B}{p} - 1)\frac{H(\hat{\theta})}{\theta^e}\right]$$
$$= \mu(1 + r)\left[1 + \left(\frac{\pi_B}{p} - 1\right)F(\hat{\theta})\right] \qquad (4.12)$$

From equations (4.5) to (4.10), it is evident that

---

[8]We will assume that relevant second-order conditions are always met.

$$ED = [\theta^e f(C) - (1 + r)C] - EY$$

$$- \frac{\pi_B - \pi}{p} \int_{\underline{\theta}}^{\hat{\theta}} [\mu(1 + r)C - \delta\theta f(C)]dF(\theta) \quad (4.13)$$

Note that when $\pi_B = \pi$, then (4.13) reduces to

$$ED = [\theta^e f(C) - (1 + r)C] - EY \quad (4.14)$$

For our purposes, we will assume that $\pi_B = \pi$. This vastly simplifies the analysis. The more interested reader can get similar results even for the case when $\pi_B \neq \pi$. Since π can be interpreted to be the true market value, π_B is purely a perceived phenomenon on the part of the borrower. Since in the very stylized case (in Section 3), we have already given the basic intuition for the suboptimality of collateral underpricing, here we refrain from getting into too many hairy algebraic details. In the case where $\pi_B = \pi$, the result is straightforward and we quote it here.

PROPOSITION 4. *If $\pi = \pi_B$, then $\delta = \mu$ and $p = \pi$ is a solution, and $EY(\cdot) = \overline{Y}$.*

Proof: Notice that the lender is interested in maximizing (4.14) subject to (4.11). In other words, the maximum the lender can *ever* get is obtained when $EY = \overline{Y}$ and

$$\theta^e f(C) - (1 + r)C$$

is maximized. Now, choose $p = \pi_B = \pi$. Then (4.12) reduces to

$$\delta\theta^e f'(C) = \mu(1 + r) \quad (4.15)$$

If we now choose $\delta = \mu$, then for (4.14) to be maximum, we must have

$$(4.16) \quad \theta^e f'(C) = (1 + r)C$$

which would also maximize $[\delta\theta f(C) - \mu(1 + r)C]$. If we can now show that by suitably manipulating δ and μ, $EY(\cdot)$ can always be kept at $\overline{Y}$, then we are through. But this is easy. Suppose, instead, $EY \neq \overline{Y}$. Then, as long as we vary δ and μ simultaneously without making them unequal to each other, then we can always reduce (or increase) $EY(\cdot)$

to $\bar{Y}$. This observation follows directly from an inspection of (4.9), using $\pi_B = \pi = p$, and $\delta = \mu$.

5. CONCLUSION

In this paper we have dealt with interlinkage and its economic issues. Interlinkage is an endogenous outcome in the model(s) studied here. The paper uses the imperfections in the credit market as the major cause for interlinked contracts. It may appear that we have taken this imperfection as a datum and not tried to explain how this may have developed. This is, however, true only for sections 2 and 3. As we have suggested in section 4, one can develop the interest rate differentials (in the institutional sources) for the farmer and the village lender by observing that the lender has better marketable collateral than the farmer, whose only collaterals, often, are the land he works on or the labour he possesses, both of which are unacceptable to an institutional credit source. In a more general sense, we have worked out the economic connections between interlinkage and imperfect credit markets. Our major result is that the inherent economic inefficiencies due to such imperfections can be eliminated by interlinked markets. However, if one looks at the incomes accruing to the borrower, an interlinked contract allows the lender to extract the full surplus attributable to the interlinking of markets. It is possible to come up with situations where the farmer may be better off without interlinking. E.g. if the village lender did not interlink in section 2, then she would maximize $(r' - r)C$ where r' is the rate of interest charged and C is the loan demand by the farmer. Clearly, there is no reason why the maximum r' should be equal to $\bar{r}$. (It can never be larger than $\bar{r}$, for then the farmer will go to the institutional source.) Whenever $r' < \bar{r}$, the farmer gets more than $\bar{Y}$, the income when markets are not interlinked. In other words, interlinkage does not immediately mean more 'exploitation' of the borrower.

This exercise, therefore, also points to another important issue. In rural markets, it is erroneous to consider the plight of small farmers (or landless labourers) by looking at individual markets in which they operate. Given that interlinking is a (economic) fact of life, one should consider *all* the markets together. E.g. as we show in section 2, the (small) farmer earning a higher income *also pays a higher interest on loans taken,* while the *poorer* farmer pays a *lower* interest.

REFERENCES

AKERLOF, G. (1970), The market for lemons: qualitative uncertainty and market mechanism, *Quarterly Journal of Economics*, 89, 488–500.

BARDHAN, P.K. (1980), Interlocking factor markets and agrarian development: a review of the issues, *Oxford Economic Papers*, 32, 82–98.

_____ (1984), *Land, Labour and Rural Poverty: Essays in Development Economics*, Oxford University Press, New Delhi.

BARDHAN, P.K. ed. (1989), *The Economic Theory of Agrarian Institutions*, Oxford University Press, New York.

BARDHAN, P.K. and A. RUDRA (1978), Interlinkage of land, labour and credit relations: an analysis of village survey data in East India, *Economic and Political Weekly*, 13, 367–84.

BASU, K. (1983), The emergence of isolation and interlinkage in rural markets, *Oxford Economic Papers*, 35, 262–80.

_____ (1984), The Less Developed Economy, Blackwell, Oxford.

_____ (1989), Rural credit markets: the structure of interest rates, exploitation and efficiency, in Bardhan, ed., *Agrarian Institutions*.

BELL, C. and T.N. SRINIVASAN (1989), Some aspects of linked product and credit market contracts among risk-neutral agents, in Bardhan, ed., *Agrarian Institutions*.

BHADURI, A. (1973), A study in agricultural backwardness under semi-feudalism, *Economic Journal*, 83, 120–37 (reprinted in *Unconventional Economic Essays: Selected Papers of Amit Bhaduri*, OUP, Delhi, 1993).

_____ (1977), On the formation of usurious interest rates in backward agriculture, *Cambridge Journal of Economics*, 1, 341–52 (reprinted in *Unconventional Economic Essays: Selected Papers of Amit Bhaduri*, OUP, Delhi, 1993).

BHARADWAJ, K. (1974), *Production Conditions in Indian Agriculture*, Cambridge University Press, Cambridge.

BOTTOMLEY, A. (1975), Interest rate determination in underdeveloped rural areas, *American Journal of Agricultural Economics*, 57, 271–91.

BRAVERMAN, A. and T.N. SRINIVASAN (1981), Credit and sharecropping in agrarian societies, *Journal of Development Economics*, 9, 289–312.

BRAVERMAN, A. and J. STIGLITZ (1982), Sharecropping and the interlinking of agrarian markets, *American Economic Review*, 72, 695–715.

GANGOPADHYAY, S. and K. SENGUPTA (1987a), Small farmers, moneylenders and trading activity, *Oxford Economic Papers*, 39, 333–42.

_____ (1987b), Usury and collateral pricing: towards an alternative explanation, *Cambridge Journal of Economics*, 11, 47–56.

MITRA, P.K. (1983), A theory of interlinked transactions, *Journal of Public Economics*, 20, 167–92.

RUDRA, A. (1982), *Indian Agricultural Economics: Myths and Realities*, Allied Publishers.

SRINIVASAN, T.N. (1980), Bonded labour contracts and incentives to adopt yield-raising innovation in 'semifeudal' agriculture, *Indian Economic Review*, 14, 165–9.

_____ (1989), On the choice among credit and bonded labour contracts, in Bardhan, ed., *Agrarian Institutions*.

Tenancy and Accumulation

UTSA PATNAIK

1. INTRODUCTION

The domain of peasant studies is an extensive one spanned by a number of academic disciplines including history, sociology, political science, and economics. A varied and rich literature in this domain has developed during the past half-century. There is little doubt that a substantial impetus to scholarly studies in this area was provided by the upsurge of revolutionary peasant movements in the Third World from the 1930s, and sustained by the continuing importance of the agrarian question in relation to industrialization strategies in developing economies. The influence of Marxist theory on scholars has been considerable, including on those who do not necessarily use overtly Marxist categories. This is not surprising since the major agrarian and peasant movements of this century have been informed by some variety of Marxist thought, while in the realm of theoretical discourse, dynamic questions of transition from one social formation to another are addressed pre-eminently by Marxists.

The discipline of economics has remained however on the whole quite remarkably impervious to the influence of Marxist theory. There has been an efflorescence in recent years of a literature on tenancy which is firmly located within the framework of neo-classical concepts. If there is one key concept of neo-classical theory applied to agriculture which demarcates it sharply from Marxist theory, it is perhaps that of 'the peasant' representing a homogeneous economic type to the exclusion of all other types—somewhat akin to the old notion of the 'representative firm' in industry. The extension of the concept of 'the peasant', leads to the use of the concepts of 'the owner' and 'the tenant' as categories of analysis. Such use either presupposes an absence of economic differentiation amongst owners and tenants, or implicitly assumes that such differences as do exist are unimportant for the issues being discussed. Only on such implicit presuppositions and assumptions can these categories be used as the central or crucial categories for the explanation of variations in input use and output performance (as in formulating the question: Are tenants more or less efficient than owners?).

The very use of these categories rules out the concepts of class differentiation and class formation within the peasantry, which are so central to the Marxist framework. In the latter the starting point is the historically-evolved, existing inequality in the distribution of land and other resources, which implies, at any given point of time, wide variations in the effective per capita resource endowment across rural households. This is what generates relations of labour hiring, land leasing, and credit relations between these households. The idea of 'the peasant' as a central analytical category (applied to contemporary societies with large peasantries) is antithetical to the recognition of peasant economic differentiation. There is not one representative type of the producing and consuming unit called 'the peasant', but rather very different types defined by varying effective resource endowments per head, ranging from the labour-hiring capitalists and rich peasants, through the primarily self-employed middle and small peasants, to the poor-and-hired peasants. It also follows from this that the categories of 'owner-peasant' and 'tenant-peasant' do not, in any way, constitute useful categories from the perspective of the Marxist framework, which recognizes that in reality there are very different kinds of owners ranging from the capitalists/rich peasants to the semi-proletarians, and as many different types of tenants, quite apart from the landlords. Posing the question of owner versus tenant efficiency from the beginning assumes away the possibility that factors other than the tenurial relation may have a substantial impact on each household's decision-making.

The second important respect in which neo-classical theory differs from Marxist theory is with regard to the theory of rent. A modified version of Ricardian rent theory is accepted, that is, differential rent arising from variations in land fertility and capital application, while the theory of absolute ground rent, first put forward by Adam Smith and developed by Marx, is ignored completely. This becomes particularly significant when the terrain of discussion is agrarian relations in the less developed countries, in many of which land concentration, and rent as the main form of surplus appropriation continue to be of economic importance.

Marxists do of course accept and operate with the concept of the peasantry, but it is not conceptualized as an internally homogeneous category. To the question of whether the peasantry constituted a 'class' or not , the answer given in Lenin (1972 and 1972a) encapsulated the contradictory character of twentieth-century peasantries: the peasantry did once constitute a class in an estate sense, of feudal society; but it ceases to constitute a class in all contemporary transition-to-capitalism societies, for it is in the process of differentiation into 'the classes' of capitalist society. This process of class formation might be relatively rapid under favourable conditions or be prolonged over a long duration. During this process, at any given point of time, all sections of the peasantry might come together to act concertedly on particular occasions (against a centralized State, especially a colonial State), and at the same time the component factions might act on the basis of particular class interests in relation to other issues like rent reduction.

This key neo-classical concept of the peasant defined as a family-labour based producing and consuming unit goes back to A.V. Chayanov[1] who was perhaps the first to give a systematic exposition of the equilibrium arrived at by the family-labour farm, using the marginal calculus. In his central model Chayanov puts forward the proposition that a family farm's objective is not profit maximization but the satisfaction of the consumption requirements of the family out of the farm income. The question of what determines the level of desired consumption is, however, not analytically tackled by Chayanov, for to say that it is 'the pressure of consumer demand' which in turn depends on the size of the farm family and the consumer–worker ratio, still leaves unanswered the question of what level of consumption per head is the objective. This indeterminacy leads, as we argued elsewhere,[2] to a tautological interpretation of every observed income/consumption level including those far below imputed wages, as the outcome of a utility-maximization process and as representing an equilibrium. Since no lower bound is placed to acceptable income/con-

---

[1]Chayanov, first published 1915, translation 1966.
[2]See Patnaik, 1979.

sumption, we can have the strange result of a starving or dead peasant household which has successfully maximized utility.

The family farm in Chayanov's model usually succeeds in meeting the changing consumption requirements of the family which is changing in size, by suitably adjusting its command over land and other resources through purchase, lease etc. The idea that farm size always adjusts to family size, rejects the basic Marxist approach of looking at the historically-evolved and existing inequality in the distribution of landed property and capital. The observed variations in farm size across households are sought to be explained not in terms of the concentration of property but only in terms of variations in family size; all questions of class differentiation and class formation are thereby assumed away. However Chayanov also employed a subsidiary model[3] in which land shortage leads producers to put in more labour per unit area than they would have done otherwise; but this land shortage, again, does not arise from property concentration in a few hands but from generalized factors affecting all households; hence the classless model of demographic differentiation remains intact.

Contemporary neo-classical or 'mainstream' literature has developed the basic Chayanovian model, usually with no reference to its originator.[4] The important modification in the modern models is the acceptance of the market wage rate as the opportunity cost of peasant labour. The modern models do not, unlike Chayanov, seek to situate the micro theory of peasant equilibrium within the context of the macro functioning of the agrarian economy and in this respect they remain partial theories. Some modern models do try to incorporate differentiation (in a manner analytically similar to Chayanov's 'demographic differentiation') by deriving it not from property concentration but from other factors.[5]

In this paper we would like to take up for discussion one important issue from the range of issues addressed by the received theory, namely the question of tenant versus owner efficiency, briefly referred to earlier. From the Marxist perspective the very posing of the question

[3]Also referred to as a 'deviant' model, cf. Harrison, 1975.
[4]An exception is Sen, 1966.
[5]Eswaran and Kotwal (1989) derive the difference between a household being self-employed and one hiring labour, on the basis of each household's varying access to credit without specifying what determines this varying access to credit in the first place.

in these terms appears as something of a *non sequitur*. It is arguable
that a realistic analysis of the determinants of decision-making for
agricultural producers requires not only cognizing, but also integrating
into such analysis the organizational and motivational differences
amongst production/consumption units which coexist (and do so not
passively but in a relational way) within a given matrix of agrarian
relations. The received theory by ignoring these real-life variations in
production objectives and constraints, on the other hand, provides at
best a very partial and at worst a misleading conceptualization of the
determinants of decision-making. In particular, it fails to locate these
determinants within any theory of historically-formed institutions;
paradoxically, those neo-classical theorists who do talk of institutions
do not identify these historically, in any way, but in terms of particular forms of contract like sharecropping without apparently
realizing that the economic substance of a given type of contract
can vary greatly depending on the particular set of socio-economic
relations—which constitute the real institutions—within which it is
located. In much the same way, the economic content of the
employer–labourer contract can vary greatly depending on the
specific socio-economic matrix within which it is embedded. It
would be difficult to maintain that the Indian *bandhua mazdoor* of
the early decades of this century or the Japanese *hokonin* of the late
Tokugawa represented the same 'institution' as the hired labourer on
the capitalist farm today. Yet, sharecropping tenancy from antiquity
two thousand years ago to modern Taiwan is referred to as an
'institution' in the standard literature.

As an illustration of these propositions we will take up for discussion the two related questions of the 'efficiency' of owner versus
tenant cultivation and that of tenancy and accumulation.

2. THE IMPLICATIONS OF A DIFFERENTIATED PEASANTRY FOR 'EFFICIENCY'

In the standard literature it is customary to enquire into the relative
productive efficiency of the owner and the tenant, the analysis being in
terms of static resource allocation, and efficiency being defined in
terms of output per unit area alone. A further development is to
enquire into the efficiency, so defined, of various contractual forms of

tenancy—fixed rent versus sharecropping, for example. Comparison of
the efficiency of tenant cultivation versus hired-labour based cultivation is also undertaken, and various types of costs of entering into the
alternative arrangements—'transaction costs' for tenants compared to
'supervision costs' for labourers, have also figured as assumed determinants of choice between the two types of operation. The 'interlinking of markets' has been taken up for analysis as well, in terms of this
framework.

The very terms in which the discussion is carried on appear highly
unrealistic as soon as it is recognized that large inter-unit variations
exist in scale, objective function, organization and labour process both
within the category of owner as well as within the category of tenant.
The difference between owner and tenant is after all a juridical one
and tells the investigator nothing about the economic status of either
owner or tenant. Within the category of owner can be found—in South
Asia at least—households which run the entire gamut of scale of
ownership from big landowners owning vast areas of land to the
poor-and-hired peasant with, say, a quarter acre of land; within the
category of tenant are found households which run, similarly, the
entire gamut of scale of production, from large-scale capitalist holdings producing for profit to the small-scale petty tenants struggling for
subsistence.

What is true of South Asia is generally true also of most large
developing countries. The matrix of agrarian relations in such
developing countries is, of course, complex and country or region-
specific, but certain common features are observable. There is generally a high degree of concentration of landed property, not mitigated
very much by the pattern of leasing owing to a substantial concentration of even the leased area with well-to-do producers. In India, for
example, about 55 per cent of the total area under lease is with the top
three pentiles of holdings ranked by operated area. In fact most of the
area under lease is with a minority of well-to-do cultivators who
dominate the lease market in economic terms while most tenants are
poor cultivators, who predominate only in numbers. The really big
property owners, known by different names (*latifundist, zamindar* etc.)
operate with a combination of tenants and labourers, while the
peasantry proper shows a fairly high degree of economic differentiation, with a minority of rich peasants developing in a capitalist direc-

tion, i.e. producing with hired labour for profit, a majority struggling for subsistence as poor and small peasants hiring out their labour or paying rent partly to the landlords and partly to rich peasants, with the entirely family-labour based, reasonably viable holdings in-between.[6]

It is observed that the tenancy contract is not confined to any one type of holding. The fact that a household enters into a tenancy contract obviously implies a desire to expand the scale of direct operation in the case of the lessee, and to reduce the scale of direct operation in the case of the lessor. The motivation for the reduction or the expansion of the scale of direct operation can be very different, however, and is related to the economic status, in short, the class status, of the agent concerned. If the lessee is a landless or poor peasant with insufficient land, his objective in leasing-in land is to obtain a large enough net output for the family's subsistence and reproduction of the cycle of small-scale production. If the lessee is a rich peasant or capitalist however the objective is quite different—namely to expand the scale of profitable production on the basis of hired labour. The first type of leasing has been referred to often in the Marxist literature as 'hunger leasing' and we will retain this evocative term. The second type of leasing, while it has always existed, is becoming a visibly growing phenomenon in many countries, and is usually referred to as 'commercial leasing' because the objective is the sale of the product for profit rather than family consumption alone. However, since the hunger-leasing petty tenant may also be highly 'commercialized'—if for example he specializes in industrial crops like cotton or jute which cannot be directly consumed but must be sold—we would prefer the more accurate term 'capitalist leasing' for the well-to-do cultivators leasing-in land.

In the case of lessors, similarly, the motivation for reducing the scale of direct operation by leasing-out owned land will be quite different for the large owners of landed property compared to the medium and petty owners. A big landlord will lease-out rather than cultivate direct-ly with hired labour if he can get more by way of rent and income on capital saved, than by investing that capital in the direct cultivation of

[6]On the basis of Indian reality we have earlier used a taxonomy, which is an empirical approximation based on a labour-use index, to the analytical concept of class among cultivating households which has proved useful; it is given briefly in the Appendix. It is on the basis of this taxonomy that terms such as rich peasant, middle peasant etc. are being used here.

land.[7] A petty owner may be obliged to lease-out, for example owing
to loss of ploughing cattle; or might lease-out because a larger income
may be made if he is free to move in search of rural wage-paid work.[8]

Apart from these major objectives of leasing there may be subsidiary, 'convenience' reasons—such as the inconvenient location of
inherited plots, perhaps in a different village altogether, specialization
in cropping plus the desire to obtain a particular crop which is not
grown, etc., which need not detain us.

Schematically, we may depict the different types of lessor/lessee
relationships, in the sense of 'who leases to whom', in terms of a
matrix of agrarian classes as in Table 1. Positive elements may be
expected in every cell of the matrix, though for some the number of
observations may be quite small.

TABLE 1

Tenant in each row leasing in from —	Landlord	Rich Peasant	Middle Peasant	Small Peasant	Poor Peasant	Labourer
Landlord	t_{11}	t_{12}	t_{13}	t_{14}	t_{15}	t_{16}
Rich Peasant	t_{21}	t_{22}	t_{23}	t_{24}	t_{25}	t_{26}
Middle Peasant	t_{31}	t_{32}	t_{33}	t_{34}	t_{35}	t_{36}
Small Peasant	t_{41}	t_{42}	t_{43}	t_{44}	t_{45}	t_{46}
Poor Peasant	t_{51}	t_{52}	t_{53}	t_{54}	t_{55}	t_{56}
Labourer	t_{61}	t_{62}	t_{63}	t_{64}	t_{65}	t_{66}

Note: The categories used here are defined in Chart 1 in the Appendix.

It is clear that—given our classification of the population connected
with land ownership and operation—there are thirty-six possible pairs
of relations between lessors and lessees. In six of these the parties are
of the same or similar economic-class status, namely those relations
comprising the diagonal elements (t_{11} through to t_{66}). These relations
are not generally considered to be of any great theoretical interest and
arise probably for reasons of convenience. Where the lessor is of

[7]This is discussed in some detail further on.
[8]The Indian Census returns several thousand rural labourers reporting land rent as a
secondary source of income after wages.

superior economic status compared to the lessee, these relations appear in the cells below the diagonal. The received theory has been concerned with only one or two of these relations, namely those between the landlords and the small peasant or the poor peasant. (Of course, there is also the problem that in the standard analysis, sometimes every type of lessor is referred to as landlord, adding to the theoretical confusion.)

There exist another set of relations, however, in which the lessor is of inferior economic status compared to the lessee, captured in the cells above the diagonal in the matrix; this is almost entirely ignored in the literature. Even when it is nominally recognized that the economic status of lessors and lessees may vary, this fact is not theoretically integrated into the analysis of tenancy, in any substantive way, because no cognizance is taken of the differing objective functions and the differing constraints faced by the various categories of lessor and lessee. This in turn is because no categories are systematically defined, i.e. no class differentiation is recognized.

The production objective and constraints faced by a small peasant-tenant, say, will be quite different from the objective and constraints of a rich peasant-tenant. It will be generally accepted that the small peasant operating exclusively or primarily with family labour, without perhaps an adequate endowment of land and other resources, has the objective of obtaining a large enough income to meet the necessary consumption needs of the family (to which, it is reasonable to assume, the farm labourer's income constitutes a lower bound) and thus reproduce the cycle of petty production. The constraint of inadequate land and/or other resources means that family labour is likely to be underemployed and a low-level interaction with the labour market is often resorted to, in order to supplement insufficient cultivation-income with wage-income.

The objective of the capitalist, or the rich peasant-turning-capitalist, is to make and maximize profit. The constraint is of meeting an outlay for hired labour out of net output, at a market wage rate which is given. This crucial difference—obtaining a target level of family labour income in one case and maximization of profit in the other case—has important implications which we will take up later. First let us consider owner and tenant within a given class, such as the small peasant-owner and the small peasant-tenant.

Let us assume that there are two small peasant households of identical family size, composition, and consumption requirements. Figs. 1a and 1b depict the standard marginal value productivity of labour curve against input of labour time, but in this case defined over one standardized unit area (standardized for fertility, irrigation etc.). The size of farm can be expressed as multiples of the unit area.

Let us suppose, to begin with, that the owner household has a large enough holding, i.e. a sufficient number of units n such that it can obtain its desired net output (income) at a labour input which gives a daily reward to its labour no lower than the wage rate for hired workers. In Fig. 1a, this household pushes its labour input to OB where net output per unit area is $OBCD$, equal to the imputed wages of family labour $OBC'E$. The total net output of the farm is $n \cdot OBCD$. Note that there is no surplus here; the entire net output is used up in the family's economic reproduction. The family could restrict its labour input to OB' where there would be a notional surplus over imputed wages, but it would not do so because the total net output summed over the n units it has $(n \cdot OB'E'D)$ would then be insufficient for its subsistence.

The second small peasant household, let us assume, is a pure tenant household and has to pay a fraction r of its net output as crop-share rent. Clearly, it cannot maintain the same total income and consumption of the family as the owner, call this x, as well as pay rent, unless it produces an output larger than that of the small peasant-owner given by the multiplier $1/(1 - r)$. Only then will it be able to have the same net income as the owner does without lowering the rate of reward to its labour. To take a numerical example, if total net output per unit area is 100 and this is the small peasant-owner's income, for the tenant who has to pay 60 per cent, say of net output, and retain 40 per cent, total output should be larger than 100 by the the multiple $(1/0.40) = 2.50$. Provided the household can lease-in a suitably larger area, in Fig. 1b it applies labour units to OB, produces $OBCD$ net output, and retains $OBC'D'$ as its income which equals imputed wages. Although $OBC'D'$ is less than the owner's income per unit area in Fig. 1a, which was $OBCD$, the pure tenant obtains the same total income which is $[1/(1 - r)] \, OBC'D' = x$. In short, the tenant must produce a surplus product payable as rent whereas the small peasant-owner need not; and this is possible without depressing the average reward to family labour below the wage rate, only if larger resources are operated by the small peasant-tenant.

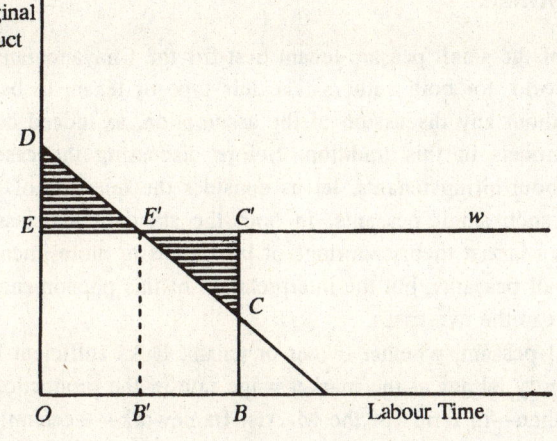

FIG. 1a

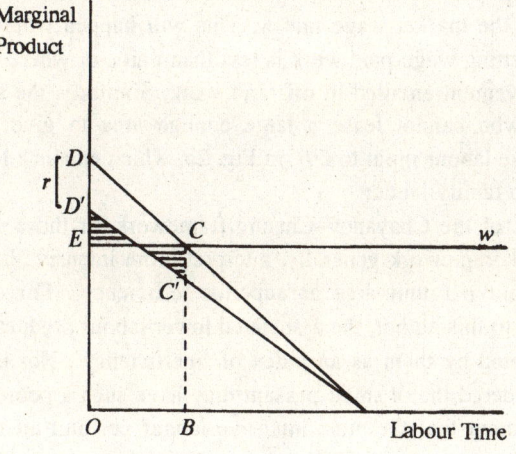

FIG. 1b

This case of the small peasant-tenant best fits the Chayanovian and Cheungian world, for both authors take this type of tenant to be the only type without any discussion of the assumption, as indeed do all subsequent models in this tradition. Before discussing the case of well-to-do labour-hiring tenants, let us consider the question of land shortage for such small peasants. In both the standard neoclassical theory and in Marxist theory shortage of land leads to more intensive labour by small peasants, but the interpretation of this phenomenon is quite different in the two cases.

If the small peasant, whether owner or tenant, lacks sufficient land to reward family labour at the market wage rate in the production of subsistence, then—in terms of the Marxist framework—the family is forced to work the available land area more intensively at the cost of lowering its labour productivity, which is identical with lowering its daily reward to labour. Thus if the available land area is less than n units for the small peasant-owner, then (see Fig. 2a) it will push its labour input to OB' per unit area where it gets a higher net output $OB'CD$ but at the cost of lowering the reward to family labour to w' which is below the market wage rate w. This will happen where the probability of getting wage-paid work is less than unity, or where there are costs of movement entailed in off-farm work. Similarly, the small peasant-tenant who cannot lease a large enough area to give x, is forced to increase labour input to OB' in Fig. 2b, which entails a lower rate of reward to family labour.

The adherents of the Chayanov–Cheung framework, or those using the neo-classical framework generally, interpret more intensive labour and higher output per unit area as superior 'efficiency'. For some reason not clear to this author, the associated lower labour productivity is never interpreted by them as an index of 'inefficiency'. Nor is the possibility considered that a small peasant may have such a poor *total* resource endowment that the most intensive labour per unit area and the highest possible output at the lowest possible labour productivity, may still leave the family with a consumption deficit. If for example a small owner or tenant has only half a unit area, $n/2$, then the highest possible output it could obtain by pushing the marginal product of labour to zero would be around half of $OBCD$. The small tenant would obtain in turn only around half of $(1 - r) \cdot OB'CD$, in both cases insufficient for subsistence. A semi-starving peasant household, very

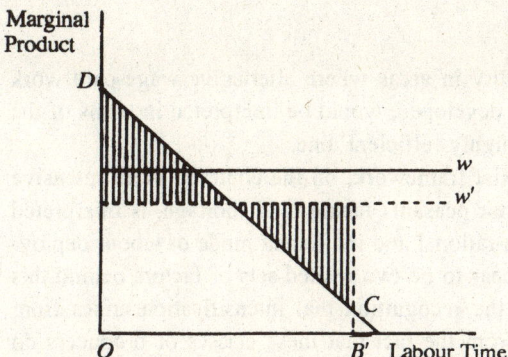

Fig. 2c

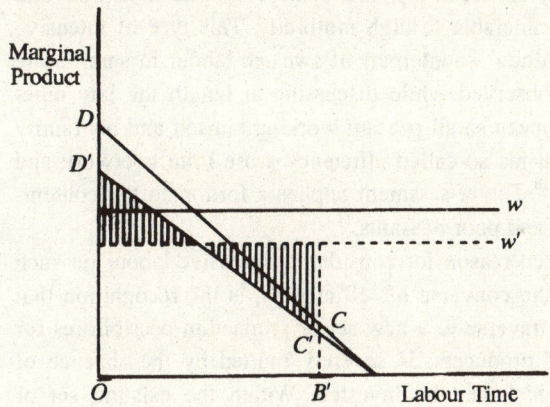

Fig. 2b

much an empirical reality in areas where alternative wage-paid work possibilities are poorly developed, would be interpreted in terms of the standard analysis as a highly 'efficient' one.

In terms of the Marxist framework, on the contrary, more intensive labour by small and poor peasants facing land shortage, is interpreted as a fundamentally non-rational and inefficient mode of labour deployment. There would appear to be two related sets of factors behind this interpretation. First is the recognition that intensification arises from economic duress, i.e. from the fact that these classes of producers do not have enough resources: not primarily because resources are scarce in any absolute sense (though this element too may be present) but primarily because resources are concentrated in the hands of a few.[9] Under South Asian conditions small and poor peasants, putting in intensive labour on inadequate land, do not reach or barely reach poverty level incomes, are often worse off than full-time labourers (owing to absence of mobility), are subject to undernutrition and malnutrition, and vulnerable to high morbidity. This type of intensive labour is the agricultural counterpart of sweated labour in small-scale industry. Kautsky observed while discussing at length the late nineteenth century European small peasant working himself and his family extremely hard, that his so-called efficiency arose from overwork and underconsumption.[10] This assessment applies a fortiori to the contemporary Asian small and poor peasants.[11]

The second, related reason for considering intensive labour on such holdings as being the converse of 'efficiency', is the recognition that the feasibility of a traverse to a new set of production possibilities for these categories of producers, is severely limited by the absence of retained surplus which can be invested. Within the existing set of techniques and organization the petty producers may indeed be forced to work very hard at the expense of lowering labour productivity, but

[9] For this reason the Chayanovian use of the term 'self-exploitation' of labour is considered to be inaccurate from the Marxist point of view, for it carries the inference that harder work is voluntarily chosen rather than being the outcome of duress imposed by the property structure. In any case, whether 'exploitation' can be used as a reflexive relation—self-exploitation—or necessarily as a relation between two parties, is a matter for explicit discussion rather than unquestioning assumption.

[10] See Kautsky, 1988, 110–20.

[11] For some data on labour input and income levels of small and poor peasants as well as labourers relative to poverty-level incomes in a green-revolution area in India see Patnaik, 1987.

the highest possible output per unit area thus obtained can be well below that secured by the well-to-do cultivators monopolizing resources and retaining surplus, who have been able to invest in productivity-raising techniques and have thereby raised output without lowering labour productivity. In short, the petty producers are usually in no financial position to push outward the production possibility frontier through new investment in technical and/or organizational change, even when the know-how is available. If they are able to borrow to invest, this can only be on terms which allow the creditor to appropriate, by way of interest, the additional income arising from the new investment.

This element is generally ignored completely in analysis employing neo-classical concepts. Within a static-allocative framework the small peasant's efficiency—defined in the partial sense of output per unit area alone—is much discussed, but dynamic questions of accumulation and transition to new sets of production possibilities are seldom, if ever, mentioned.[12] Authors like Schultz (1964) who do talk in terms of 'traditional argriculture' and the transition to 'modern agriculture' through applying green revolution technology, appear to make the implicit assumption that there is no problem of investible funds for any peasants, that traditional agriculture can be 'transformed' simply by disseminating the know-how.

The classical economists on the other hand were quite consistently concerned with the question of agricultural accumulation and 'improvement', and specifically with the barriers which might be raised to such 'improvement' by the existence of tenancy.

3. AGRICULTURAL 'IMPROVEMENT' AND TENANCY

In his *Theory of Share Tenancy* (1969), S.N.S. Cheung claims to have difficulty in understanding the concept of agricultural 'improvement' used by the classical economists. There was a long tradition in British classical political economy, of discussion regarding disincentives to long-term investment (especially that involving permanent asset creation or embodying productivity improvements), thought to be inherent in the separation of landed property ownership and cultivation, which

---

[12]See Martinez-Alier (1983) for a typical static-allocative exposition of the 'effficiency' argument, and Caballero (1983) for its extension.

was such a marked feature of the English agrarian social structure from the eighteenth century onwards. The classical economists thought that the Continental system of metayage was even less desirable than the English system, for reasons we will discuss a little later. Referring to Richard Jones' argument that the European metayerie system 'mars almost every attempt at improvement', Cheung says that

By improvement or what they called 'stock' in the land (sic) classical economists seem to mean 'investment' in land, but exactly what they did mean is not clear. According to our convention, investment is the balancing of consumption over time; that is, present sacrifice for future benefit. A man is investing when he tills the soil today for corn tomorrow, pulls a weed, or removes a rock. The various time-lengths of the investment returns are treated in a general framework. And it is conceptually the same whether the work is done by a man or a horse, or through the use of more fertilisers, better irrigation, or other assets ... Under our convention, therefore, to say both that the intensity of labour input (which can be used to improve land) can be freely adjusted and also that 'the divided interest mars almost every attempt at improvement', is contradictory indeed (Cheung, 1969, 37).

Cheung's puzzlement appears to arise from the fact that within the neo-classical framework of ideas to which he adheres and refers to as 'our convention', there is no role for the concepts of economic reproduction and economic surplus generated during a given period of production, which are conceptual cornerstones of the classical system. The classical economists were perfectly clear about what they meant when they talked of the investment of a given value of stock, i.e. a given outlay of money-capital embodied in equipment, livestock, current material inputs, and labour on a unit of land to secure a given level of output over a given production period, and the need for new forms of investment embodying technical change ('improvements') in either the same or in a larger total stock in order to raise the output per unit area. Cheung is not quite correct in the passage quoted above in thinking that 'stock' and 'improvement' were interchangeable concepts. 'Stock' referred to the capital outlay in money terms required over a given production period to secure a given level of output.[13] 'Improvement' referred to rise in productivity, which in principle could be achieved even with the same total money-capital or stock per unit area provided it was

[13]See Smith (1986, 150–2, 167–9); Ricardo (1986, 1, 30–8).

embodied in new forms; but in practice improvements on any scale required accumulation, i.e. addition to stock.

Cheung's condemnation of both the classical economists and the post-Ricardians (37–8) is quite severe:

> to Jones and his contemporaries and even to Mill and others after him, the concept of 'improvement' or 'investment' was ambiguous on two counts. First, they failed to distinguish farming inputs at one moment of time from farm investments over time. Second, instead of viewing labour and non-labour inputs as different physical entities performing different functions in production, they viewed them as different conceptually. To them labour is short and non-labour is long, and 'improvements' were made only by 'capital' and not by 'labour'.

Cheung's charge that there was a failure to distinguish between farm inputs at one moment in time and investment over time, is surely quite baseless. Farm inputs are in any case applied over a discrete period of production and not at 'one moment of time'; no one has as yet invented a way of obtaining instantaneous output from inputs in crop or livestock production. The classical framework using the period-of-production idea applied to agriculture has been well explicated in the introductory volume by Robinson and Eatwell (1973, 61–88) and we need not further expand on it.

Secondly, it is important to bear in mind that the classical economists, including Marx, were talking of *capitalist* production in agriculture (unless they explicitly specified otherwise) where labour is always wage-paid labour hired by a capitalist farmer who is himself the tenant of a landlord. 'Capital' in their conception was not fixed equipment and material inputs alone but included the wages advanced during the production period before the harvest is realized.[14] Capital, therefore, included the wages advanced to labour as part of what Smith and Ricardo called circulating capital; while Marx considered the role of labour to be qualitatively so distinct that he preferred to separate wages advanced into the category of 'variable capital' while both fixed equipment and raw materials were subsumed under 'constant capital'. Within the classical framework, increasing labour input *ipso facto* meant increasing the corresponding part of capital outlay.

It is difficult to see what Cheung could mean when he alleges that

---

[14]See Smith (1986, 167–9), Ricardo (1986, 1, 30–8).

the classical economists 'viewed labour as short and capital as long' or that for them 'improvements were made only by capital and not by labour'. Quite the contrary was in fact the case; because capital, in their conception, comprised outlays on both labour and non-labour, any 'improvements' when undertaken as part of accumulation required an increase in both components of such capital outlays. It would appear that while reviewing the classical theorists' propositions, Cheung consistently imputes to them the neo-classical concept of capital which of course refers to non-labour alone. This can hardly be termed a valid procedure.

In order to secure an increase in the output level of a given capitalist enterprise, it was generally necessary to increase the stock, i.e. undertake additional investment over and above that required for producing the previous level of output. Now, it seems to have been taken for granted that 'additional investment' per unit of area could not consist in doing more of the same things as before. In the example Marshall gives, of ploughing land more often, weeding more often, and so on, he points out that diminishing returns will set in;[15] and if static allocative efficiency is assumed it is reasonable to suppose that in producing a given output level per unit of area capitalists were already using the profit-maximizing combination of farm operations in disbursing their capital outlay over operations. Thus, making the traverse to a higher level of profit-maximizing output was viewed as requiring investment in doing qualitatively new things, i.e. in 'improvements'.

The historical background to the classical discussions was the improvements actually taking place especially in British agriculture after the mid-eighteenth century enclosures, which added up to a veritable agricultural revolution according to the economic historians.[16] These included new systems of crop rotation permitting 'convertible husbandry', floating of water meadows, drainage of low-lying land, and improvements in animal breeds and in farm implements and machinery.[17] All this required considerable additional investments or accumulation for the farmers adopting them. The classical economists and those who followed them were greatly interested in the incentive to invest in such improvements for capitalist tenants; and they com-

[15]See Marshall (1961, 155, fn. 1a).
[16]See Mantoux (1970, 136–85); Deane (1965).
[17]See Chambers and Mingay (1970, 34–72).

pared the English system of capitalist tenancies with European metayage from the point of view of long-run accumulation.

It was recognized, as corroborated by the economic historians, that Britain had seen more improvements and a greater rise in productivity than the continental countries; the advantages of the English system of capitalist tenancy on fixed rents were contrasted, perhaps rather complacently with the demerits of metayage with regard to the incentive to invest. Marshall followed in a long tradition when he compared the English system with European metayage, except that he had somewhat more favourable things to say about the latter. It is worth devoting a little time to the conception of the 'farmer' under the English system and that of the *metayer*, for in modern writing on tenancy by economists much confusion appears to prevail on this.

Marx explicates the classical conception of the typical agricultural producer, which always used the English model as the reference point:

the actual tillers of the soil are wage labourers employed by . . . the capitalist farmer who is engaged in agriculture merely as a particular field of exploitation for capital . . . this capitalist farmer pays the land-owner, the owner of the land exploited by him, a sum of money at definite periods fixed by contract, for instance annually (just as the borrower of money capital pays a fixed interest) for the right to invest his capital in this specific sphere of production. This sum of money is called ground rent, no matter whether it is paid for agricultural land, building lots, mines, fishing grounds or forests etc. . . . Ground rent therefore is here that form in which property in land is realised economically, that is, produces value. Here, then, we have all the three classes—wage labourers, industrial capitalists, and landowners constituting together in their mutual opposition the framework of modern society (Marx, *Capital*, 3, 618).

A close reading of the relevant chapters in Adam Smith (1986, 247–65) and Ricardo (1986, 1, 67–92) would indicate that this is indeed the conception of the 'farmer' which they employed; subsequently Marshall too takes for granted that the English system comprised capitalist cultivation based on hired labour for profit, by large-scale producers who were tenants paying a money rent fixed for the duration of the contract to the landlord. Before discussing the difference between this system and continental metayage, let us dispose of the important question of how we may expect the capitalist owner and tenant to decide on labour input and output compared to the small peasant owner and tenant. The answer to this question is important for analysing the character of metayage as well.

Maximum profit versus target family-labour income

The basic and crucial difference between the family-labour based small peasant producer and the capitalist producer is that the objective of the former is to attain a target family-labour income (net output) whereas the objective of the latter is to maximize profit (surplus of net output over the wage bill). In effect, 'labour cost' plays a qualitatively different role in the two cases. For the small peasant, the labour 'cost' involved in production is simultaneously his income, for he is directly engaged in labour; so in the process of reaching a target total income (to which a lower bound, set by the farm labourer's income, may be assumed) the reward to labour per unit of time is sought to be maintained whenever possible.

In the case of the capitalist the converse holds: the reward to labour is the wage bill which is always a cost alone, and this is inversely related to the capitalist's income (profit) for a given level of net output. The capitalist farm necessarily has to produce a surplus of net output over the wage bill in order to make a profit while the petty family-labour farm need not since its net output is equal to the return to its own family labour. We may assume that for a capitalist the price of labour, like other prices, is given.

By extension of the argument, if the small peasant must produce a surplus payable as rent because he leases-in land (as in Fig. 1b) then *a fortiori* the capitalist-tenant must produce a larger surplus than this in order to both pay rent at the same rate per unit area and retain a profit. The capitalist cannot produce a sufficiently large output and surplus per unit area, however, if he operates on the same production possibility frontier as the small peasant-tenant. The latter, by all accounts, is already producing a larger net output and some are, in that process, even obliged to lower the reward to family labour below the market wage rate, which constitutes a binding constraint for the capitalist farms hiring labour.

There is thus a fundamental contradiction involved in postulating the coexistence of profit-making capitalist farms and small peasant farms based on family labour, with identical production functions for the two types of production units. Yet, identical production functions are routinely assumed in the neo-classical models. The problem of the logical contradiction inherent in this assumption cannot be resolved by arguing that the capitalist pays out a smaller amount as wage bill than family workers obtain as net output, for an equivalent number of days worked; and that the capitalist therefore manages to squeeze out a surplus from similar levels of net output as peasants produce. For as long as there is a reasonable degree of mobility between small peasant cultivation and wage-paid work, the market wage rate cannot be substantially lower than the net product per labour-day worked on small peasant farms. Indeed the literature is full of the converse proposition: the market wage rate is higher than the average return that some family workers are prepared to accept for their labour, owing to uncertainty of finding wage-paid work and other factors. Even if this strong condition of a 'wage-gap' does not hold and family workers never accept a level lower than the market wage as the daily return to their labour, then too capitalist farmers with identical production functions as small peasants, will always make a loss after paying the wage bill than if small peasants obtain a family-labour income equal to imputed wages.

Let us see how this will occur. In Fig. 3, according to the standard analysis, the family-labour based farm will put in $OB(P)$ labour input and produce $OB(P)C'D$ output, to obtain at least imputed wage income (at this point $DEC = CE'C'$). If the same labour productivity curve is applicable for the capitalist, he will put in a smaller input of $OB(C)$ hired labour days, produce a smaller output $OB(C)CD$, paying out $OB(C)CE$ as the wage bill and retaining DEC as profit.

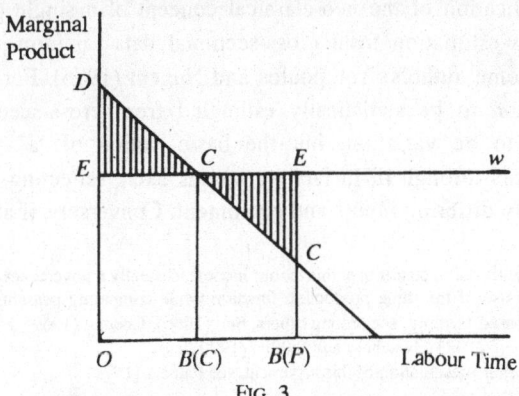

FIG. 3

It may be noted that given the assumption of identical production functions, the capitalist's profit DEC is only a fraction of the small peasant's labour income $OB(P)C'D$. It does not appear to strike the theorists putting forward the above argument, as an unrealistic and indeed quite absurd proposition, that their 'capitalist' would accept a 'profit' income which is only a fraction of the small peasant's labour income, equal to imputed wages.[18] With only a fraction of the labour income of the small peasant, the putative 'capitalist' would not even succeed in meeting the consumption requirements of his own family, leave alone obtain a return on capital invested, for a similar size of standardized area.[19]

The standard argument could be rescued, perhaps, by saying that for every n units of land that a small peasant operates, the capitalist always operates a multiple $k \cdot n$ where k is a large integer. But we find that no such stipulation is advanced by the authors of the models in question. What is indeed being argued by them is that for a given area in operation, peasant farming is more efficient than capitalist farming. As we have just demonstrated, the logical implication of this is that the capitalist gets an income which is a fraction of the imputed wages of the small peasant. In short, the capitalist cannot be a capitalist at all on any sensible definition of a capitalist farmer.[20]

In reality capitalist farmers coexist with family farmers because they operate more productive techniques. Empirically observed large variations in productivity across farms, taking a cross-sectional sample at a point of time, reflect precisely the operation of varying 'production functions' all together. At a statistical level the contradiction involved in the application of the neo-classical concept of a single production function to estimation from cross-sectional data on farms, has been noted by some authors: Yotopoulos and Nugent (1976). For a production function to be statistically estimated from cross-sectional data there has to be variation; but the basic notion of 'a' production function falls through if, in fact, variations exist, reflecting the use of qualitatively differing inputs and equipment. Conversely, if all farms in

---

[18]Under South Asian conditions, this labour income is usually a poverty-level income.

[19]For such use of the same production function while comparing peasant farming and hired-labour based farming, see among others, Sen (1966), Cheung (1969), Martinez-Alier (1983), Caballero (1983), Newbery and Stiglitz (1979), etc.

[20]For an earlier presentation of this argument, see Patnaik (1979).

fact did operate with identical functions as the neo-classical theory assumes, there would be no variation from which 'a' production function could be estimated.[21]

The above-mentioned contradiction has not been related analytically, by the authors concerned, to the structural reasons for the observed variations in productivity: our argument is precisely that 'a' production function cannot be validly assumed because 'a' single type of 'representative peasant' does not exist. What we do have are peasant classes in the process of formation, characterized by the use of qualitatively quite distinct technical complexes comprising equipment and inputs. This gives rise in turn to the variations in productivity.[22]

The upshot is that we find that genuinely profit-making capitalist farms and subsistence-oriented small peasant farms did coexist in history and continue to coexist today, despite the impossibility of their coexistence given the neo-classical assumption of identical production functions. The reason is that the assumption itself is untenable. The capitalist farms are those which have been able to shift to a new production possibility frontier through investment in technical change, or better organization, or both, permitting a higher output and surplus per unit area without any necessary lowering of labour productivity.

This situation is depicted in Fig. 4 which shows an outward shifting of the marginal value productivity of labour curve on the capitalist farm; in this case the shift is depicted as a parallel one, but the exact nature of the shift will depend on the type of technical or organizational change and may affect the slope of the curve as well. The small peasant owner in Fig. 4 produces a net output equal to imputed wages, as in Fig. 3. The capitalist owner must obtain a profit on capital, which realistically speaking must be substantially larger than the entire family-labour income $OB(P)C'D'$ of the small peasant, in order to maintain the capitalist's family at least at the same poverty-level income as the peasant, as well as give a return on capital invested. This is only possible with a corresponding substantial outward shifting of the productivity of labour curves. The capitalist hires more labour per unit

[21]On this, also see Ellis, (1988, 72–4).

[22]See Da Silva (1984) and Patnaik (1987a) for the application of Fisher's discriminant function analysis, employing several indices of intensive cultivation, to ascertain the statistical distance between classes approximated by the labour-use dex using, respectively, cross-sectional data from north-east Brazil and Haryana, India.

178   UTSA PATNAIK

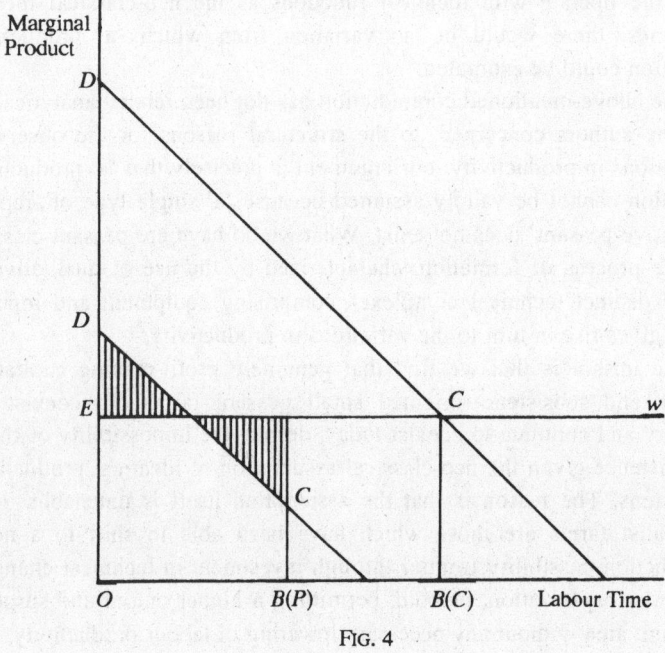

FIG. 4

area (in this case, since labour-displacing technical change is not being
assumed), produces a much larger output *OB(C)CD* per unit area and a
surplus over the wage bill equal to *DEC*, which has to be sufficiently
larger than total net output *OB(P)C'D'* on the small peasant holding to
give a profit at the going rate on capital invested per unit area after
meeting the capitalist's consumption requirements.

As has been demonstrated at length elsewhere, it is fallacious to
interpret the observed inverse relation between farms grouped by size
and average output per unit area in each group, at least in the case of
South Asia, as reflecting high-productivity family-labour based cultivation versus low-productivity hired-labour based cultivation. This interpretation relies on identifying the small-sized farms (size in acres
unadjusted for irrigation, fertility, family size, etc.) with family-labour
based ones, and large-sized farms with hired-labour based ones. A
direct separation of family-labour farms from hired-labour ones using
the same but ungrouped data, however, gives a direct relation between

yield and class status i.e. with the hired-labour based farms registering the highest yields.[23]

Although our concern is with theory, in order to avoid possible misunderstanding, it should be mentioned at this point that the consistent emphasis we are placing on the technical and productivity advantages of large-scale production compared to small-scale production does imply in our view, that the Kautsky–Lenin propositions are applicable to Asian agriculture as well and are likely to be borne out by empirical analysis which transcends the categories of preconception. This does not imply however that the tendency for capitalist production which has been in operation now for some decades in South Asia, is capable of providing a solution to the most pressing rural problems of underemployment and poverty. On the contrary, there is mounting evidence that this tendency is likely to aggravate the problems, given the private profitability of mechanization as multiple cropping grows on large-scale farms and given the inadequate expansion of non-agricultural employment (itself constrained by effective demand or market problems arising from the high concentration of assets and of income flows). Furthermore, private capitalist investment by its very logic of ignoring social costs is proving to be instrumental in rapid environmental degradation.

Let us now return to the question of tenancy. Consider the small peasant-tenant paying rent as share of crop as in Fig. 1b. As we have argued elsewhere, assuming competition, the rich peasant or capitalist farmer paying crop-share rent, must pay at least the same absolute level of rent per unit of area as this small peasant, and still retain a profit.[24] This is possible only if a larger surplus per unit area is produced by the capitalist, of which the rent is only a part, the remainder constituting profit.

In Fig. 5a we have the small peasant-tenant pushing labour input to OB in order to retain an income $OBFG$ equal to imputed wage income $OBCE$, after paying a share of crop rent of $GFCD$ out of the output $OBCD$. In Fig. 5b, the capitalist or rich peasant is able to pay the same absolute rent $GFCD$ (equal to $GFCD$ of Fig. 5a) and still retain a larger profit GEF than the labour income of the small peasant-tenant,

[23]See Rao and Brahme (1973), Patnaik (1987 b).

[24]See Patnaik (1983).

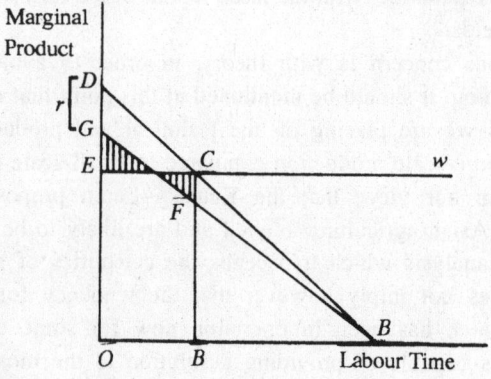

FIG. 5a

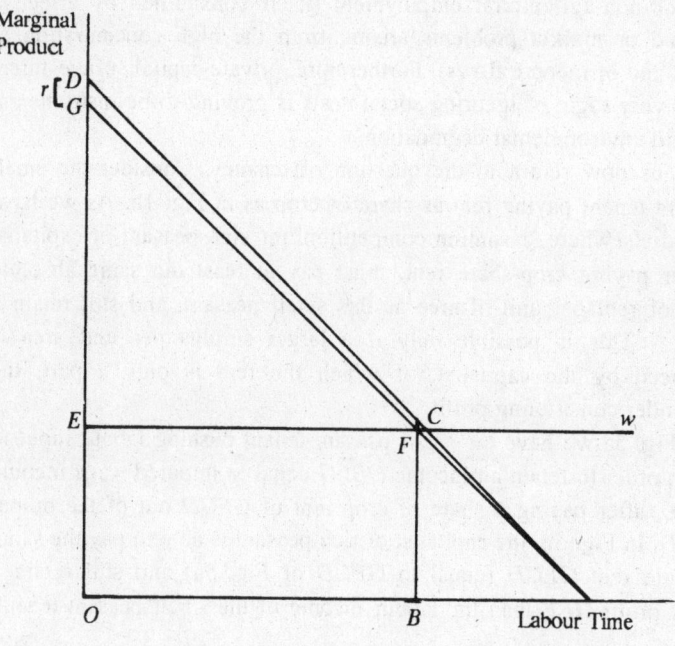

FIG. 5b

only through a rightward shift of the marginal value product of labour curve to the requisite extent. This implies that the same rent per unit area that the small peasant farmer pays, will be a smaller proportion of the higher total output on the capitalist farm. Even if the small peasant-tenant was forced by inadequate holding size to push labour input to OB' and maximize output, the output and surplus per unit area would still be less than that obtained by the capitalist.[25]

Those theorists who routinely use Fig. 3 and its variants to argue that small peasant production is equally or more 'efficient' than capitalist production, are able to do so only by using terms like 'peasant' and 'capitalist' as virtually empty categories—empty, that is, of any economic, social, or historical content. The economic and social content is drained out of the concept of capitalist by making him a producer who is content with a smaller income than is acceptable to a small peasant struggling for subsistence; the historical content is drained out of the concept by ignoring the fact that petty production existed long before capitalist production did. Why profit-making capitalist production should have emerged at all or how it could have developed if indeed it was inefficient relative to petty production, is a question which does not appear to occur to the theorists concerned.

Looking at the matter from the viewpoint of the contemporary landlord who has a choice between leasing-out land to tenants and cultivating directly with hired labour, it is often argued in standard analysis that small tenant cultivation is at least as efficient as hired-labour cultivation, to which combinations of tenant labour and hired labour are counterposed.[26]

Now for economic analysis of this type to have any validity, a minimum condition is that like must be compared with like, i.e. *ceteris paribus* conditions must hold. The basic conceptual problem is that tenant labour and hired labour are thought of by these authors as symmetrical and interchangeable categories, whereas it is doubtful whether the economic consequences of an elementary but very important difference between the use of these two types of labour can be ignored. Leasing-out land and cultivating directly with hired labour are

---

[25] For data showing falling ratio of rent paid out to output as output rises on the better-off farms with adoption of high-yielding varieties, see Bharadwaj and Das (1975).

[26] See Cheung (1969), Martinez Alier (1983), Caballero (1983), Eswaran and Kotwal (1989), Newbery and Stiglitz (1979), etc.

two qualitatively different ways of organizing production; the quantitative dimension of this difference lies in the fact that cultivating with
hired labour requires *capital* to be invested by the landowner whereas
cultivation with tenant labour does not necessarily involve any capital
outlay by the landowner. With direct cultivation the landowner must
necessarily undertake a certain amount of capital outlay (in the classical sense) by way of draught cattle or machinery, irrigation equipment,
current material outlays, and wage advances to hired labour. With
tenant cultivation all this is typically provided by the tenant; under
South Asian conditions the landowner is not even under any obligation
to provide farm buildings, fencing or any permanent improvements.
Under prevalent conditions of land-hunger there are petty tenants
vying to bid up rents of even unimproved land. More than anywhere
else in the world, perhaps, in South Asia it may be said that land rent
represents almost pure 'absolute ground rent', an income the landowner gets by virtue of legal title of ownership to a piece of a resource
which cannot be augmented in the short run and is in monopolized
ownership, with little or no element in this rent of a return to previously invested capital in the land, on his part.[27]

The investible surpluses (obtained by way of such high ground rent)
that such a landlord gets are substantial even after allowing for high
levels of consumption by customary standards. These surpluses are not
any longer, if they ever were, converted to gold and buried under-
ground, or held as banknotes sewn inside mattresses. These surpluses
are put into moneylending at interest, term deposits in banks, shares in
industry, or used to finance trade in commodities. The landowner,
therefore, obtains a profit, say Rs P, at the going average rate of p per
cent, on his money capital Rs M disbursed over one or more such uses.
Assuming that direct cultivation of a unit of land requires at least
Rs M of capital advanced (by way of equipment, input costs, and
pre-harvest wage payments) it follows that the landowner will have an
economic incentive to go in for such direct cultivation with hired
labour only if he obtains a total profit of Rs $(P + R)$, for this was his
income in the alternative situation of leasing-out to petty tenants at

[27]For an early exposition of the concept of what Marx was to call 'absolute ground rent'
see Adam Smith (1961, 56, 162, 180–97); Ricardo's misconceived criticism of Smith in
Ricardo (1986, 67–8), and Marx's defence of Smith's concept against Ricardo in Marx (1969,
240–50). See also Patnaik (1983).

Rs *R* rent per unit area and investing his money capital (which was "free" and not tied up in land) for Rs *P* profit.

Now since it is reasonable to assume that Rs *R* per unit area is the entire surplus that small peasant-tenants are capable of producing at existing levels of technique, a quantum jump in surplus produced per unit area is required, by the proportion *P/R*. For a given *R*, the higher is *P*, the higher the proportion by which surplus per unit area must increase. Such a quantum jump in surplus per unit area, however, would not be technically possible unless direct investment embodies new methods of cultivation which entail an outward shifting of the production possibility frontier. To sum up, the choice between cultivating with the labour of tenants (who take production decisions and use their own equipment, livestock, etc.) and cultivation with hired labour, is not a choice determined by the so-called efficiency of the two types of labour, but by considerations of the relative profitability of investment of the landowner's money capital, which is free for alternative use in tenant cultivation but must be invested directly in agricultural production in direct cultivation.[28] Given the prevalence of high levels of absolute ground rent paid by the petty tenants, this profitability requirement imposes rather stringent conditions for the switch from petty-tenant cultivation to hired-labour cultivation to take place: not only must direct investment produce the equivalent of this rent per unit area, but also a profit at the going rate. To put the same thing in slightly different words, capital in direct cultivation must produce a surplus profit equal to rent over and above an average profit.

This argument, which was advanced some years earlier by the author in terms of the barrier posed to capitalist investment by ground rent, can be viewed as a generalization of the Bhaduri model (1973) in one sense, while going beyond that model in seeking to understand not only the conditions giving rise to stagnation but also those giving rise to dynamism. It will be recalled that in his model Bhaduri postulated an interlinking of rent extraction and interest extraction by a landlord from an indebted petty tenant. There was therefore a disincentive to undertake productivity-raising investment, which would raise the tenant's income (given a crucial assumption of institutionally-fixed

---

[28]The case of input-sharing is taken up a little later, which leads to the 'tenant' ceasing to be an independent petty producer and his reduction to the status of a piece-rate labourer as the landlord takes investment and production decisions.

rental share) and reduce his indebtedness and hence the interest income of the landlord. Under certain conditions this fall in interest income might outweigh the increase in rental income. The basic thrust of the model was to explore the conditions giving rise to a failure to undertake productivity-raising investment by landlords, with empirical reference to rural West Bengal.

The specific assumptions of the model were easily criticized, however (if, indeed, the landlord was powerful, what prevented him from raising the rental share as output rose with investment regardless of legal maxima; empirically, interlinking of rent and credit by the same landlord was a small fraction of all such landlord–small tenant relations, etc.). These criticisms detracted from the validity of the basic thrust of the model, which sought to explore the conditions promoting stagnation which were inherent in particular types of agrarian relations. From one point of view the author's 'model' of the barrier of rent to investment, can be seen as a jettisoning of the unduly restrictive assumptions of the Bhaduri model in the interests of valid generalization; at the same time, it also permits an exploration of not only the conditions giving rise to stagnation, but also—perhaps as important— the conditions under which stagnation is overcome. Thus, it is being argued in the present 'model' of rent as barrier-to-investment, that such a barrier operates regardless of whether there is interlinking of leasing and credit by the same landlord, or not; all that is required is that the landlord does invest his money capital in one or more uses, not necessarily in the form of interest-bearing loans alone and even if he does lend, not necessarily to the same tenant to whom he leases land. Provided the landlord gets a generalized average return on his money-capital, he will not invest it in direct cultivation unless it is technically feasible through such investment to obtain a discrete, large rise in surplus per unit area such that a surplus profit equal to rent can be obtained.[29]

Landlords will not invest productively and there will be a perpetuation of stagnation in productivity as long as the total profitability of direct investment is not sufficiently high to overcome the rent barrier. If the rather stringent conditions of technical change and rise in

---

[29]For stable input and output prices, this is equivalent to raising the physical yield per unit area by the required proportion. If output prices are rising relative to prices of new inputs, this would reduce the requirement of physical yield rise, and conversely.

physical productivity can be met, however, then the rent barrier can be overcome and it will be profitable for landlords to switch to direct investment in agricultural production rather than remaining pure rentiers. We suggest that both the specific type of technical change South Asian agriculture is undergoing as well as its spatial concentration can be understood in terms of this hypothesis.[30]

The trajectory of landlords-turning-capitalist can take two forms. The landlords may evict tenants and go in for direct cultivation with hired labour: this appears to have taken place in today's green-revolution areas in India like Punjab and Haryana, which saw major spates of tenant eviction in the sixties and seventies. But there can also be an alternative trajectory in which the landlord retains his petty tenants and over time reduces them to the status of piece-rate labourers, as he himself turns capitalist. This happens typically when the landlord finds it paying to 'share inputs', or more accurately, advance capital embodying green-revolution type technology (irrigation machinery, fuels, fertilizers, HYVs, etc.). Once this starts happening on any scale at all, involving not merely the traditional *beej–khad* loan (literally, seed–manure loan) but new technology, typically the landlord starts taking decisions regarding input application, cropping pattern, and the labour process. The tenants who continue to provide a falling share of the new higher working-capital requirements, remain tenants only in name since production decisions are no longer taken by them, nor is the labour process under their control: they become providers of mainly labour (supplemented by hiring of casual labour and farming-out of operations to contract labour by the landlord-turned-capitalist). As output per unit area rises the tenant's share of it falls drastically for this share now represents the reward to labour paid in kind, much as the permanent farm servant on long-term contract is remunerated in a share of the harvest, i.e. on an output basis rather than at time rates.

In Fig. 6a, the petty tenant who initially provides all the equipment, draught cattle, and inputs, puts in OB units of labour time per unit area and obtains $OBCD$ total output of which he retains say $(1 - r) = 1/2$, or

---

[30]Green revolution technology had a chance of being adopted by landlords in areas of endemic tenancy because it involved land-augmenting technical progress, raising output and surplus per unit area. However, the proportion by which surplus per unit area could be raised was by no means uniform across crops and regions, being influenced by a complex set of factors. The crops and regions where it was feasible to achieve a large rise in yields have seen a spate of evictions of petty tenants and a switch to direct capitalist cultivation.

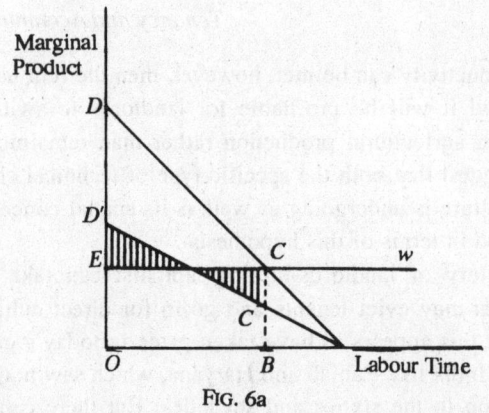

FIG. 6a

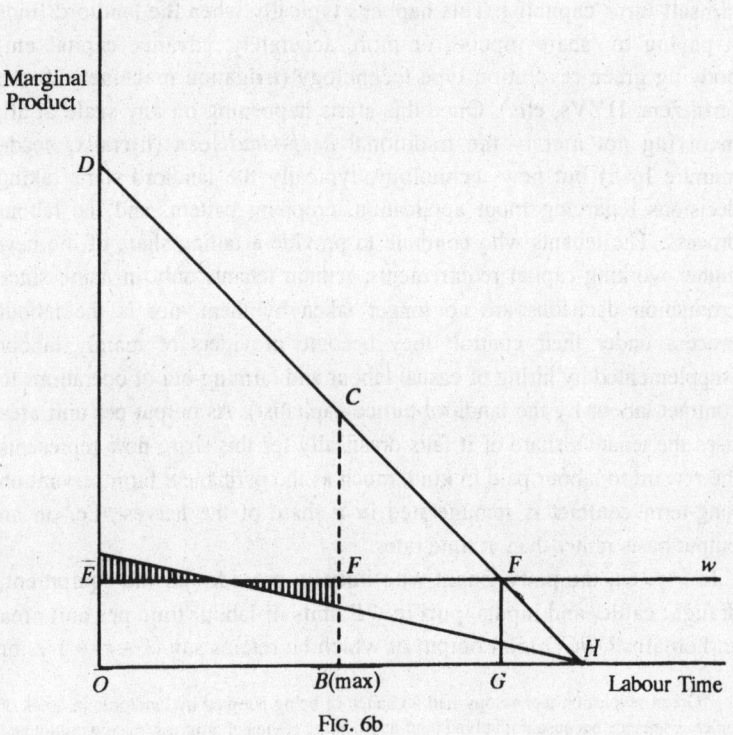

FIG. 6b

OBC'D' which equals imputed wages *OBCE*. In Fig. 6b the landlord has invested in the fixed and working capital embodying new technology and shifted the marginal value productivity of labour curve to *DH*. Suppose that tenant labour had been earlier underemployed and is now fully employed with *OB*(max) labour input per unit area, being rewarded as before with output equal to imputed wages, which though a larger sum in absolute terms constitutes a lower proportion than before, of the new higher output *OBCD*. At this point, however, the landlord can profitably expand output further and will do so to *OGFD* by hiring-in additional labour *BG* at a wage payment of *BGFF'*. The landlord-turned-capitalist's total profits will be *EFD* and the transition will only be undertaken by him if this total profit per unit area is sufficiently higher than his earlier rental income *DCC'D'* (the entire surplus of the tenant in the former situation) to yield a profit on the capital invested at the going rate.

Without entering into the question in detail we may mention that the weighing of supervision-cost and transaction-cost considerations are likely to prove of peripheral importance on any empirical test, because of the growing importance of contract labour in South Asia for large-scale production. The labour-intensive operations of irrigated cultivation such as weeding, transplanting, and harvesting are often contracted to peripatetic labour groups for fixed payment per unit area, and it is up to the group how it allocates the work and shares payment amongst its members. Such systems of payment to hired labour at piece rates eliminates direct supervision. Even if costs of supervision are zero, however, there will be no switch to direct cultivation by landlords unless the minimum profitability conditions specified above are satisfied, i.e. the latter are of far greater relevance for the choice between direct and indirect cultivation.

We will now return to the question of metayage in Latin Europe in the nineteenth century, particularly in the aspect of its relation to Asian forms of sharecropping.

Metayage in European and Asian sharecropping: the same, or differing conditions?

An obligatory and cursory reference is often made to the theoretical analysis of European metayage, in contemporary writing on tenancy, particularly the sharecropping form of tenancy. The conclusion reached by the classical economists that the system of metayage was not conducive to investment in agricultural improvement; and Marshall's argument that the metayer would cultivate less intensively than the capitalist farmer on fixed money rent are both sought to be criticized on the basis of the argument of equal or superior 'efficiency' of sharecropping, taking the small peasant using family labour as the typical sharecropper.[31] This raises the question of whether the eighteenth and nineteenth century European metayer as an economic and social type was indeed sufficiently similar to the contemporary small peasant sharecroppers, to warrant this kind of theoretical comparison and criticism. On the basis of a close reading of the discussion of metayage, it is difficult to escape the conclusion that—whatever the typical metayer might in fact have been—the conceptualization of the metayer by the classical economists was in terms very distant from the type of the contemporary small peasant sharecropper in Asia or Latin America. The latter type of sharecropping tenant, as is clear from the analysis in Cheung (1969), Caballero (1983), Bhaduri (1983), Stiglitz (1989) and so on, is thought of as a family-labour based producer whose objective is to obtain a subsistence income equal to imputed wages, and who may also accept a lower daily reward than the wage rate if the land area leased is deliberately restricted by the landlord.[32] In short, the present-day small peasant sharecropper engages in hunger leasing, and his family's labour supply function reflects this, with more labour being supplied at a falling daily reward in order to maximize output where the land resource is inadequate, the situation depicted earlier in Fig. 2.

The metayer in Europe, in the late eighteenth and through the nineteenth century, was conceptualized on the other hand as a transitional type to the capitalist farmer. He was thought of, typically, as a rather well-to-do farmer who might occasionally hire labour himself though mainly cultivating with family labour. He was also thought of as a producer who retained surplus which, in principle, could be invested in 'improvement' if the incentive to invest was not weakened by the form of the lease contract which entailed sharing every increment to output as a consequence of new investment, with the landlord.

[31] For example, see Cheung (1969), Stiglitz (1989).

[32] See, in particular, Bhaduri (1983).

The metayer was not thought of as a small peasant content only with an income equal to imputed wages, but as a proper farmer representing a transititional type to the fully-fledged capitalist-tenant. It seems to us that to impute the type of the contemporary small peasant sharecropper and his labour supply function to the European metayer, and then to criticize the classical economists as well as Marshall on that basis (as, for example, is done by Cheung, 1969), represents a fallacy of misplaced application. This in turn arises from a failure to appreciate the fact that the economic content of any given type of lease contract can vary widely depending on the class status of the producer and the nature of the matrix of production relations in which his production enterprise is embedded. A poor peasant who has a sharecropping lease will have quite different objectives and constraints compared to a capitalist with a sharecropping lease. Indeed 'the sharecropper' as an analytical category is nearly as useless as 'the peasant' or 'the tenant' if the determinants of decision-making are sought to be understood.[33]

Let us substantiate our proposition. Marshall describes the metayer thus:

In the greater part of Latin Europe the land is divided into holdings, which the tenant cultivates by the labour of himself and his family, and sometimes, though rarely, that of a few hired labourers, and for which the landlord supplies buildings, cattle and sometimes even farm implements (Marshall, 1961, 643).

Marshall thought that the advantage of the system was to provide the farmer, with insufficient capital of his own, access to capital provided by the landlord. He evidently thought of the difference with the English system (of fully capitalist tenancies on rents fixed for the duration of the contract) as one of degree and not a deeper difference, for the fully capitalist-tenant too was viewed as partly using capital provided by the landlord; speaking of the English tenancy system and the capital required for cultivation, Marshall says:

His (the landlord's) part consists of land, buildings and permanent improvements, and averages in England five times that which the farmer has to supply himself; and he (the landlord) is willing to supply his part in the enterprise with this great capital at a net rent which

[33]For empirical examples from India of small and poor peasant sharecroppers versus the capitalist sharecropper, see Patnaik (1983).

seldom gives interest at as much as three per cent on its cost. There is no other business in which a man can borrow what capital he wants at so low a rate, or can often borrow at all. The metayer may indeed be said to borrow an even larger amount, but at a much higher rate (Marshall, 1961, 648–9).

Marshall is much more sympathetic to the English landlords here in treating not only fixed capital but all land as 'capital' and not, as the classical economists did, as representing primarily inherited and undeserved (because it was not the outcome of any investment) monopoly control over landed property. Marx surely articulates the view of Anderson, Jones, and Smith on this, more accurately, when he says that landlordism inhibited long-gestation investments on the part of even capitalist-tenants under the English system:

the more permanent fixed capital investments which are incorporated in the soil and used up over a longer period of time, are also in the main . . . made by the capitalist farmer. But as soon as the time stipulated by the contract has expired . . . the improvements incorporated in the soil become the property of the landowner . . .
Thus they pocket a product of social development created without their help—*fruges consumere nati*. But this is at the same time one of the greatest obstacles to a rational development of agriculture, for the tenant farmer avoids all improvements and outlays for which he cannot expect complete returns during the term of his lease. We find this situation denounced again and again, not only in the eighteenth century by James Anderson but also in our own day by opponents of the present constitution of landed property in England (Marx, 1974, 619–20).

If 'tenancy as an obstacle to improvement' applied to the fully capitalist-tenant paying money rent fixed for the duration of the contract, then it applied *a fortiori* to the metayer paying cropshare rent, where every addition to output owing to productivity-raising investment had to be shared with the landlord.

Marshall phrased the formal argument differently—not in terms of the inducement to invest in improvement, but in terms of a restriction of current labour input and output on the part of the metayer, below the level of the fully capitalist-tenant operating with similar levels of technique. Fig. 7 can be used to explicate Marshall's argument regarding the metayer, who restricts labour input to *OB* and produces *OBCD* output per unit area at which his share of the marginal product of labour equals the wage rate. In short, the principle of determination of equilibrium is no

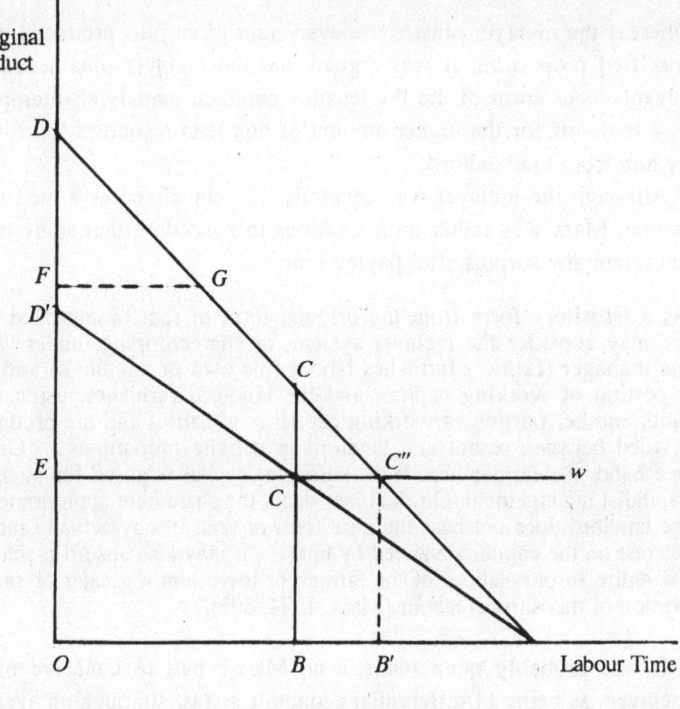

FIG. 7

different compared to the case of fully capitalist operation. Of this output *OBCD*, the reward to labour is *OBC'E*, where labour comprises the family labour of the metayer or might include hired labour as well, both rewarded at the market wage rate, *w*. The total surplus is *EC'CD*, of which *DD'C'C* is paid as cropshare rent and *D'EC'* retained as profit by the metayer.

The fully capitalist-tenant, who pays a money rent fixed for the duration of the contract, puts in a larger dose of (hired) labour *OB'* per unit area in Fig. 7, produces a larger output *OB'C"D*, determined by the equality of the marginal product of hired labour to the wage rate. The difference of equilibrium in the case of the metayer and the capitalist tenant in Marshall arises not from any difference in objective function or constraint, but solely from the difference in the form of the lease contract, which entails that the capitalist-tenant retains every unit of the larger surplus produced over and above the fixed cash rent DFG, whereas the metayer must share every unit of surplus produced in the specified proportion. It was argued that the metayer obtained a less advantageous form of the the tenancy contract, namely sharecropping as a trade-off for the higher amount of non-land resources 'borrowed' by him from the landlord.

Although the metayer was generally conceptualized as a well-to-do farmer, Marx was rather more cautious in conceding that some might not retain any surplus after paying rent:

As a transitory form from the original form of rent to capitalist rent, we may consider the metayer system, or sharecropping, under which the manager (farmer) furnishes labour (his own or another's) and also a portion of working capital, and the landlord furnishes, aside from land, another portion of working capital (e.g. cattle) and the product is divided between tenant and landlord in definite proportions ... On the one hand, the farmer here lacks sufficient capital required for complete capitalist management. On the other hand, the share here appropriated by the landlord does not bear the pure form of rent. It may actually include interest on the capital advanced by him ... It may also absorb practically the entire surplus-labour of the farmer, or leave him a greater or smaller portion of this surplus labour (Marx, 1974, 803).

It was probably quite realistic on Marx's part to conceive of the metayers as being of differential economic status, although on average, as a modal type, they were substantial cultivators. Because the metayer was conceptualized as a well-to-do farmer, himself employing hired labour sometimes, Marshall was perhaps quite justified in attributing to this metayer a labour supply function such that the family would definitely not work at a lower daily reward to its labour than the market wage rate and would additionally expect to retain some surplus. The implicit assumption behind Marshall's formulation is that the metayer's total resources (in terms of our diagrams, the number of land units n) is large enough such that the restriction of output per unit area to below the level of the capitalist-tenant, poses no problems for the subsistence and reproduction of the family, which has $n \cdot OBC'D$ total output compared to $n \cdot OBCD$ in the case of the capitalist.

In making this assumption, Marshall was simply following the conceptualization of the classical authors who viewed metayage as a transitional system to capitalism, i.e. to the well-to-do metayer becoming a capitalist-tenant systematically hiring labour. This is very different indeed from the situation of the hunger-leasing small peasant and poor peasant Asian sharecroppers. It would be one thing to argue that the classical authors' conceptualization itself might have been an inaccurate reflection of the economic situation of the majority of European metayers of that time: this empirical question is not the issue however for Cheung et al. who criticized Marshall. It is taken for granted that it is valid to talk of the Taiwanese small peasant sharecropper and his labour supply function as a counter-example to Marshall's analysis.[34] This procedure amounts to a *non sequitur*, for the near-capitalist classical and Marshallian metayer cannot, with any validity, be imputed the labour supply function of a hunger-leasing peasant prepared to accept imputed wages alone as his income. The latter cannot by any stretch of the imagination be likened to near-capitalist producers; on the contrary, the majority are semi-proletarians already, with one foot in the casual labour market.

4. CONCLUDING REMARKS

In this paper we have sought to illustrate the basic methodological difference between the Marxist (to some extent the classical analytical framework as well) and the neo-classical framework with reference to a specific question, namely the analysis of tenancy and accumulation. The Marxist approach proceeds from the recognition, and substantive integration into analysis, of class differentiation within agricultural producers. Owing to an unequal distribution of resources, peasant production units are recognized to vary greatly in effective resource endowment per head of the family, and hence in objective function and labour process, leading to relations of labour-hiring and land-leasing between a subset of all households. The neo-classical theory, on the other hand, considers one type of peasant producer alone somewhat on the lines of the representative firm in competitive industry, and builds models of peasant equilibrium using the microeconomic theory of consumer choice in the two commodity case, with leisure and income as the two commodities. It derives basically two alternative types of labour supply function, depending on whether 'the peasant' is assumed to seek imputed wages or is prepared to let the average return to its labour fall below the wage rate. The models which introduce peasant

[34]See Cheung (1969).

'differentiation' do so in the Chayanov tradition of ignoring land concentration. Marxist theory, on the other hand, not only locates the economic behaviour of individual agents in their specific class status, but also seeks to understand dynamic processes of economic class differentiation associated with accumulation and technical change (including the absence of dynamism in certain cases).

The Marxist framework employing the concept of absolute ground rent, leads to a recognition of the barrier constituted by absolute ground rent to capitalist investment, both in a fully capitalist agriculture as discussed by the classical economists, and also by extension of the argument, to a predominantly peasant agriculture with landlordism. This theory leads to the proposition that capitalist producers and petty producers cannot coexist with identical production functions as is routinely assumed in the mainstream neo-classical literature; for the capitalist owner/tenant must earn a profit (profit plus surplus profit) whereas a small peasant owner/tenant need earn only imputed wages (imputed wages plus surplus payable as rent). The neo-classical theory thus operates with an assumption which is internally contradictory in its logic, when it routinely assumes identical production functions for small peasant farms and capitalist farms.

Similarly while analysing the big landowner's choice between (a) leasing out to small peasant-tenants versus (b) operating with hired labour, we find that in standard theory tenant labour and hired labour are treated as commensurable. The fact that the tenant provides fixed and working capital while the labourer does not, is ignored. Hence the question of absolute ground rent obtainable gratis in the first case is ignored, consequently the question of capital investment in the second case is also ignored. In reality, however, direct cultivation by the landowner always necessarily requires capital outlay on his part whereas indirect cultivation does not, and releases his available money capital for use elsewhere. The alternative theory, integrating these facts, postulates that in South Asian conditions the choice for the big landowner between (a) and (b) is determined primarily by the relative profitability of the two; for a given rent per unit area being paid by petty tenants, profitable direct cultivation employing hired labour requires a quantum jump in the surplus per unit area by the minimum proportion. Where this condition is met, technical change accompanying a transition to direct production may be expected whereas stagnation and absence of a transition would characterize the inability to surmount the rent barrier. Other than in South Asia, wherever there exist both concentration of land ownership and petty tenancy, we would expect the above argument to retain its applicability. Questions of 'transaction cost', 'supervision cost', and so on are of peripheral importance compared to the basic question of relative profitability: and this is especially the case because in reality hired labour for large landowners is often contract labour paid at piece rates and not time rates.

RERERENCES

BHADURI, A. (1973), Agricultural backwardness under semi-feudalism, *Economic Journal*, 83, 120–37 (reprinted in *Unconventional Economic Essays: Selected Papers of Amit Bhaduri*, OUP, Delhi, 1993).

_____ (1983), Cropsharing as a Labour Process, in T.J. Byres, ed., *Sharecropping and Sharecroppers*.

BHARADWAJ, K. (1973), *Production Conditions in Indian Agriculture*, Cambridge University Press, Cambridge.

BHARADWAJ, K. and P. K. DAS (1975), Tenurial conditions and mode of exploitation: a study of some villages in Orissa, *Economic and Political Weekly*, Annual Number, Feb., and Nos. 25–6, June.

BYRES, T.J., ed. (1983), *Sharecropping and Sharecroppers*, Cass, London.

CABALLERO, J.M. (1983), Sharecropping as an efficient system: further answers to an old puzzle, in Byres, ed., *Sharecropping and Sharecroppers*.

CHAMBERS, J.D. and G.E. MINGAY (1970), *The Agricultural Revolution 1750–1880*, Batsford, London.

CHAYANOV, A.V. (1966), in D. Thorner, D. Kerblay, and R.E.F. Smith, eds., *Theory of Peasant Economy*, R.D. Irwin, Homewood, Illinois.

CHEUNG, S.N.S. (1969), *The Theory of Share Tenancy*, University of Chicago Press, Chicago.

DA SILVA, E. ARAQUEM (1984), Measuring the incidence of rural capitalism: an analysis of survey data from north-east Brazil, *Journal of Peasant Studies*, October.

DEANE, P. (1965), *The First Industrial Revolution*, Cambridge University Press, Cambridge.

ELLIS, F. (1988), *Peasant Economics*, Cambridge University Press, Cambridge.

ESWARAN M. and A. KOTWAL (1989), Credit and agrarian class structure, in P. Bardhan, ed., *The Economic Theory of Agrarian Institutions*, Clarendon Press, Oxford.

HARRISON, R.M. (1975), Chayanov and the economics of the Russian peasantry, *Journal of Peasant Studies*, 2, 2.

JONES, R. (1831), *An Essay on the Distribution of Wealth and the Sources of Taxation*, J. Murray, London.

KAUTSKY, K. (1988), *The Agrarian Question*, 1, Zwan, London.

LENIN, V.I. (1963), Preliminary draft theses on the agrarian question, *Selected Works*, 1, Progress Publishers, Moscow.

⸺ (1972), *The Development of Capitalism in Russia*, Collected Works, 3, Progress Publishers, Moscow.

⸺ (1972a), *The Agrarian Programme of Social Democracy in the First Russian Revolution*, Collected Works, 13, Progress Publishers, Moscow.

MANTOUX, P. (1970), *The Industrial Revolution in the Eighteenth Century*, Methuen, London.

MAO ZEDONG (1967), How to differentiate the classes in the rural areas, *Selected Works*, Foreign Languages Publishing House, Beijing.

MARSHALL, A. (1961), *Principles of Economics* (annotated by C.W. Guillebaud), Macmillan, London.

MARTINEZ-ALIER, J. (1983), Sharecropping: some illustrations, in T.J. Byres, ed., *Sharecropping and Sharecroppers*.

MARX, K. (1969), *Theories of Surplus Value*, 3, Lawrence and Wishart, London.

⸺ (1974), *Capital: A Critique of Political Economy*, 3, in F. Engels, ed., Progress Publishers, Moscow.

NEWBERY, D.M.G. and J.E. STIGLITZ (1979), Sharecropping, risk-sharing and the importance of imperfect information, in J.A. Roumasset, J.M. Boussard, and I. Singh, eds., *Risk, Uncertainty and Agricultural Development*, New York Agricultural Development Council.

PATNAIK, U. (1979), Neo-populism and Marxism: the Chayanovian view of the agrarian question and its fundamental fallacy, *Journal of Peasant Studies*.

⸺ (1983), Classical theory of rent and its application to India, with some thoughts on sharecropping, in Byres, ed., *Sharecropping and Sharecroppers*.

⸺ (1987a), *Peasant Class Differentiation: A Study in Method with reference to Haryana*, Oxford University Press, Delhi.

⸺ (1987b), Ascertaining the economic characteristics of peasant classes-in-themselves in rural India, *Journal of Peasant Studies*.

RAO, R.S. and S. BRAHME (1973), Capitalism in agriculture: an inquiry, Paper presented to seminar on Political Economy of Indian Agriculture, Calcutta, 1973 (results quoted in Patnaik, 1987).

RICARDO, D. (1986), *On The Principles of Political Economy and Taxation*, in Vol. 1 of the Works and Correspondence of David Ricardo, edited by Piero Sraffa with the collaboration of M.H.Dobb, Cambridge University Press, Cambridge.

ROBINSON, J. and J. EATWELL (1973), *An Introduction to Modern Economics*, McGraw-Hill.

SCHULTZ, T.W. (1964), *Transforming Traditional Agriculture*, Yale University Press, New Haven, Connecticut.

SEN, A.K. (1966), Peasants and dualism with and without surplus labour, *Journal of Political Economy*.

SMITH, A. (1961), *The Wealth of Nations*, in E. Cannan, ed., Methuen, London.

____ (1986), *The Wealth of Nations*, Penguin Books.

STIGLITZ, J.E. (1989), A theory of rural organisation, in P. Bardhan (ed.), *The Economic Theory of Agrarian Institutions*, Clarendon Press, Oxford.

YOTOPOULOS, P.A. and J.B. NUGENT (1976), *Economics of Development: Empirical Investigations*, Harper & Row, New York.

APPENDIX

The categories used in Table 1 are based on the concept of agrarian classes in Lenin (1963) and Mao Zedong (1967). As an empirical approximation we have found it useful to formulate a labour-use index (E) to classify farming households. This index is defined as the net use of outside labour through hire or lease (or the net extent of working for others by the family) expressed as a ratio of the extent of self-employment. The limits set to the index for defining the categories is given below, followed by the relation of the index to the discussion in the guiding texts. For a more detailed explanation, see Patnaik (1987).

CHART 1

Class	Defining Characteristic	Value of $E = X/F$	Reason	
1. Landlord	No manual labour in self-employment, large employment of others' labour	$E \to \infty$	$F = 0$, $X > 0$, and large	Primarily exploiting labour of others
2. Rich peasant	At least as large an employment of others' labour as self-employment	$E > 1$	$F > 0$, $X > 0$, $X \geq F$	
3. Middle peasant	Smaller employment of others' labour than self-employment	$1 > E > 0$	$F > 0$, $X \geq 0$, $X < F$	Primarily self-employed
4. Small peasant	Zero employment of others or working for others; and working for others to smaller extent than self-employment	$0 \geq E > -1$	$F > 0$, $X \leq 0$, $|X| < F$	
5. Poor peasant (poor tenant and labourer with land)	Working for others to a greater extent than self-employment	$E \leq -1$	$F > 0$, $X < 0$, $|X| \geq F$	Primarily exploited by others
6. Landless labourer	No self-employment; working entirely for others	$E \to -\infty$	$F = 0$, $X < 0$ and large	

Note: See also Chart 2.

Labour-use index E is defined as X/F where F is the family labour days used and $X = (H_i - H_o) + (L_o - L_i)$, where H_i and H_o are the outside labour days hired in and family labour days hired out, L_o and L_i are the labour days used on land leased out and land leased in.

CHART 2

A 'Preliminary Draft Theses'	B 'How to Differentiate Classes'	C Empirical Labour Exploitation Index Corresponding to A & B respectively
1. 'The agricultural proletariat, wage-labourers (by the year, season or day) who obtain their livelihood by working for hire at capitalist agricultural enterprises.'	'The worker (including the farm labourer) as a rule owns no land or farm implements, though some own a very small amount of land and very few farm implements. Workers make their living wholly or mainly by selling their labour power.'	A: Full-time labourers: $E \to -\infty$ B: Above plus labourers with land: $E \le -1, |X| \ge F$, and $a > b$
2. 'The semi-proletarians or peasants who till tiny plots of land, i.e., those who obtain their livelihood partly as wage labourers ... and partly by working their own or rented plots of land, which provide their families only with part of their means of subsistence.'	'The poor peasant: Among the poor peasants some own part of their land ... Others own no land at all but only a few odd farm implements. As a rule poor peasants have to rent the land they work on and are subject to exploitation, having to pay land rent and interest on loans and hire themselves out to some extent.'	A: Poor peasants, either mainly petty tenants or mainly labourers: $E \le -1, |X| \ge F, a \gtrless b$ B: The petty tenant-cum-labourer section of poor peasants: $E \le -1, |X| \ge F, a \le b$
3. 'The small peasantry, i.e., the small-scale tillers who, either as owners or tenants, hold small plots of land which enable them to satisfy the needs of their families and their farms, and do not hire outside labour.'	(i) 'The middle peasant: Many middle peasants own land. Some own part of their land and rent the rest ... Others rent all their land. A middle peasant derives his income wholly or mainly from his own labour. As a rule he does not exploit others and in many cases he himself is exploited by others.'	A: Small peasant: $0 \ge E > -1$ B: Lower middle peasant: (i) $0 \ge E > -1$

CHART 2 (contd.)

A	B	C
'Preliminary Draft Theses'	*'How to Differentiae Classes'*	*Empirical Labour Exploitation Index Corresponding to A & B respectively*
4. 'In the economic sense, one should understand by "middle peasants" those small farmers who (i) either as owners or tenants hold plots of land that are also small, but under capitalism are sufficient not only to provide as a general rule a meagre subsistence for the family and the bare minimum needed to maintain the farm, but also produce a certain surplus which may in good years at least be converted into capital; (ii) quite frequently . . . resort to the employment of hired labour.'	(ii) 'Some middle peasants (*the well-to-do middle peasants*) do practice exploitation to a small extent, but this is not their regular or main source of income.'	A: Middle peasant $1 > E > 0$ B: Upper middle peasant (ii) $1 > E > 0$
5. 'The big peasant (*Grossbauern*) are capitalist entrepreneurs in agriculture, who as a rule employ several hired labourers and are connected with the "peasantry" only in their low cultural level, habits of life, and the manual labour they themselves perform on their farms.'	'The rich peasant: The rich peasant as a rule owns land. But some rich peasants own only part of their land and rent the remainder. Others . . rent all their land. His main form of exploitation is the hiring of labour . . . A person, who owns a fair amount of good land, farms some of it himself without hiring labour but exploits the peasants by means of land rent, loan interest and in other ways, shall also be treated as rich peasant.'	A: Rich peasant of proto-bourgeois type alone $E \gtrless +1$ and $a > b$ B: Rich peasant of both types. $E \gtrless +1$ and $a \gtrless b$

CHART 2 (contd.)

A 'Preliminary Draft Theses'	B 'How to Differentiate Classes'	C Empirical Labour Exploitation Index Corresponding to A & B respectively
6. 'The big landowners, who in capitalist countries—directly or through their tenant farmers—systematically exploit wage labour and the neighbouring small (and, not infrequently, part of the middle) peasantry, do not themselves engage in manual labour, and are in the main descended from the feudal lords.'	'The landlord: The landlord is a person who owns land, does not engage in labour himself or does so only to a very small extent, and lives by exploiting the peasants. The collection of land rent is main form of exploitation.'	A: Landlords of both feudal and capitalist types: $E \rightarrow \infty$ and $a \gtreqless b$ B: Landlord of feudal type only $E \rightarrow \infty$ and $a \leq b$

Note: $a = (H_i - H_0)s$; $b = (L_0 - L_i)s$ and $(a + b) = X$

A: 'Preliminary Draft Theses': abstracted from Lenin (1963).

B: 'How to Differentiate Classes': abstracted from Mao Zedong (1967).

Agriculture in Economic Growth: Handmaiden or Equal Partner?

J. MOHAN RAO

1. INTRODUCTION

What is the appropriate 'role' of the agricultural sector in the process of economic development? By what criteria can one identify sectoral balance or imbalance between agriculture and industry? This paper addresses these questions using a judicious mix of theoretical argument and empirical evidence, paying special attention to the neo-classical and structuralist perspectives.

In considering the role of agriculture in economic growth, development economists have until recently confined their attention primarily to what may be called supply-side factors. Notwithstanding the nuances and qualifications, early development economists took the view that agriculture could not serve as a major, independent source of growth but only as a handmaiden to industry. By supplying surpluses of labour, food, and/or foreign exchange, and possibly also a saving and a budgetary transfer, agriculture might be expected to hasten the industrial transition. However, the primary source of dynamic growth—whether through accumulation of capital or through the dynamic process of learning and technical change—would be provided by industry. Thus, sectoral balance consisted, at the most, in providing for a modicum of agricultural growth to ensure adequate food supplies, a low product wage, and adequate profitability in industry. On the demand side, low elasticities—in both domestic and international markets—of food demand were emphasized.

More recent neo-classical and structuralist arguments depart in different ways from this set of views. Neo-classical economists focus on the costs of deviating from optimal resource allocation as dictated by comparative advantage in international markets. This implies a readily applicable notion of sectoral balance based on border prices, measured by the rate of effective protection (or implicit taxation) of agriculture. Clearly, demand constraints—whether in the home or world markets— are completely wished away in this conception of sectoral balance. But even on the supply side, it reduces the problem of transforming agriculture to the problem of generating and diffusing new technologies. The neo-classical policy literature on agriculture is devoted mainly to documenting the claim that most governments in developing countries have systematically taxed their agricultural sectors, and to raising alarms about the damaging effects of such 'urban bias' on both growth performance and distributive equity.

The essential building blocks of the alternative structuralist approach to this question span both the demand and supply sides. While recognizing the limitations of remaining locked into the traditional pattern of international specialization, this approach also acknowledges the problem of generating demand to induce investments. This has further implications for sectoral balance between agriculture and industry which are significant. The balance between agriculture and industry is an important determinant of growth because it affects (a) profitability and private investment and (b) government revenues and the accumulation of overhead capital. But the resolution of supply problems in agriculture is not just a matter of technology and investments alone; agricultural expansion hinges, in important ways, on the structure and organization of agricultural production. Underlying these propositions is the critical role that the distribution of the means of production and of incomes plays in shaping both supply and demand.

The paper is organized as follows. Section 2 lays out the more traditional view of industrialization and the role of agriculture in that process. Section 3 suggests some alternative measures or norms by which sectoral balance (or imbalance) may be reckoned. Section 4 summarizes available evidence for and against the view that agriculture has been neglected and growth biased towards the urban/industrial sectors. Sections 5 and 6 elucidate the theoretical framework and policy implications of the neo-classical and structuralist positions. The final section raises a number of considerations, from the viewpoint of agriculture/industry balance and agricultural policies, relevant to an assessment of the Indian growth experience.

2.   AGRICULTURE AS A HANDMAIDEN TO GROWTH

Early development thinking was influenced both by the particular global context in the mid-twentieth century facing late-arriving nations, and by the general lessons derived from the historical experience of the developed countries. While increasing the overall rate of saving and capital accumulation stood out as the fundamental condition for economic growth, sectoral state policies were also deemed instrumental in accomplishing this task: specifically, in moving labour from low-productivity, low-saving traditional sectors to high-productivity, high-saving modern *industry*.

It was felt industrialization would be facilitated by the advantages of exploiting readily available technologies imported from the advanced countries. These supply-side arguments for favouring industry were reinforced by a judgment that the prospects for raising incomes by pushing traditional primary exports were strictly limited. Raising industrial output to meet the requirements of the home market would not encounter similar demand barriers.

Agriculture could not, in this vision of economic development, serve as a major, independent source of growth but only as a *handmaiden to industry* and this for three reasons. First, the growth of home demand for the food and raw materials originating in agriculture would be progressively limited by the operation of Engel's law. Second, low income and price elasticities facing export agriculture also blocked external sources of agricultural growth; besides, productivity growth in primary exports was liable to be lost through adverse shifts in the terms of trade. Finally, agriculture was in any case a major part of the low-productivity, low-saving sector so that gains in investable surplus from raising its output would be severely restricted. Instead, it was expected to provide a low-cost supply of labour to get industry moving. In export-restrained economies, a growing surplus of food would be provided for the growing non-agricultural population through *balanced but unequal growth* of industry and agriculture.

An especially remarkable aspect of this approach to development is its relegation of international trade to an ancillary position in the growth process. Sectoral priorities are not markedly sensitive as between open and closed economies.[1] The observed positive relationship between per capita income and the share of industry provided forceful support for industry-led growth. No country had grown rich through agricultural specialization; so the free trade doctrine was rejected and a pro-industry policy justified. Industry had to be protected or subsidized to permit real economic growth. Agriculture was accordingly to be taxed, either implicitly or explicitly, the choice depending on fiscal feasibility. Since industry required complementary imports in the initial learning/protected phase, agricultural exports would fulfil this additional function as well. This completed the *surplus-extraction* view of the agricultural transition: agriculture had to provide surpluses of labour, food and/or foreign exchange, and possibly also a saving and a budgetary transfer.

Variations around this pattern were to be expected both over time and across countries; the role of agriculture was also expected to vary accordingly. In the early stages of growth, primary exports are used to finance the import of capital goods and raw materials to fuel 'easy' import substitution, i.e. the domestic production of non-durable consumer goods. In this phase, some authors emphasize balanced agriculture/industry growth as essential to ensure adequate food supplies, a low product wage, and adequate profitability in industry. This derives from the expectation that the industrializing open economy is likely to run an import surplus. The protection and subsidy policies for industry are designed to promote growth but the neglect of agriculture, though not necessary, becomes probable.

Beyond the easy phase of import substitution, patterns of growth could diverge across countries due to considerations of size and resource endowments (Ranis, 1988).

1. In large economies such as India or China, the balance between agriculture and industry remains important due to the relative insignificance of export enclaves. The failure to transform agriculture can therefore prove very costly to growth: balanced growth of agriculture and industry imposes itself almost as a necessity.

2. Resource-rich small economies may continue to substitute for

---

[1]Note that in open economies, agriculture is not constrained by the domestic demand for food (Engel's law in a free trade world only applies at the global level). In principle, then, agriculture could be an independent source of growth.

industrial imports while relying on resource-based exports to pay
their food imports. Balanced growth is thus eluded and agricultural
surpluses become less significant. This process may be strengthened
where the line of least resistance, politically, is the avoidance of the
difficult problems of agrarian change, and to rely on imports of foods
(as in the case of many Latin American countries). Thus, the agricultural transition is hastened without an agrarian transformation. To be
sure this requires resource bonanzas and/or foreign capital imports
(and attendant debt problems). While the export substitution phase is
skipped, capital intensity rises and both growth and equity are
sacrificed.

3. In resource-poor countries, a shift to export market production of
the same non-durable consumer goods becomes a necessity. But the
challenge also proves to be a valuable opportunity as human resources
are developed and sectoral balance achieved through both trade and
rapid domestic growth (as in the East Asian pattern).

3. SECTORAL BALANCE: NORMS AND MEASURES

Except for short periods of time, agriculture cannot sustain a growth
rate much in excess of 2 or 3 per cent per annum above the growth
rate of population.[2] The large size of the sector, coupled with decentralized decision-making, uneven access to resources, and low ability
and willingness to invest limits the rate of technological diffusion.
Even where agriculture grows rapidly, this inevitably raises non-
agricultural growth with two consequences: incomes are more unevenly distributed, which accentuates the demand restriction arising from
Engel's law, and resources tend to shift away into the more profitable
non-agricultural sectors. High rates of population growth and, by
historical standards, the low rates of labour absorption in non-agriculture seem also to guarantee that the eventual decline in the absolute
size of the agricultural labour force will be much delayed in late-
developing countries.

With respect to production technology and resources, these countries

[2]The exceptions prove the rule. The Indian Punjab, for example, achieved 13.9 per cent
annual growth for wheat output and 10.2 per cent for foodgrains from 1967–8 to 1971–2, the
high point of the Green Revolution period. From 1967–8 to 1981–2, the foodgrain growth
rate has been a high 6 per cent.

face both new opportunities and constraints in transforming agriculture. In comparison with the nineteenth century when the land frontiers of the New World provided a very substantial safety valve for extensive growth, contemporary developing countries, like Japan earlier, are generally developing against a rather inelastic land constraint. Few countries have recorded rates of land extension in excess of population growth or of outmigration sufficient to reduce the absolute population in agriculture. Hence, the land-per-worker tends to fall rather steadily.[3] This is not to say that land extension has ceased to be an important source of growth. Globally, the additional amount of land that is potentially cultivable is nearly as large as the area presently under cultivation. But among developing countries, its distribution is highly uneven being concentrated in Africa and Latin America (Scrimshaw and Taylor, 1980). Moreover, their exploitation requires substantial investments in reclamation, irrigation, and infrastructure for settlement, and there are important environmental limits.

At any rate, the empirical relation between agricultural growth and population growth is positive and fairly robust (Timmer, 1988). So a declining land–man ratio or rapid population growth is not cause for Malthusian pessimism. Quite clearly, the development of new high-yielding biological varieties used with fertilizers, which augment the effective supply of land, has been a crucial necessary condition of this development. But experience has also shown that without massive investments in irrigation, roads, extension services, rural education, etc. significant increases in HYV adoption rates or in cropping intensity would not have come about.

A stock-taking of agriculture at the end of the eighties shows that while average agricultural performance in the past two decades has not been low by historical standards, it has also been seriously deficient in relation to population growth and in meeting the minimum needs of a large mass of the population, especially in the poorer regions of south Asia and sub-Saharan Africa. Past trends, if maintained, will raise food imports to developing countries fairly rapidly. The stabilization and structural adjustment programs of the eighties have not, on balance,

[3]Available data show that the relative contribution of area expansion to output growth of major food crops in developing countries has declined over the past two decades. While land-scarce Asia continues to grow mainly by augmenting land yields, a similar tendency is also evident in the seventies for other regions.

laid the foundations for resumed agricultural growth, much less for a big agricultural push of the type some economists have called for.[4]

Can the historical record be used to argue that developing countries have systematically pursued policies that are anti-agriculture or pro-urban, that economic growth has been markedly *unbalanced* and, for that reason, lower than it might have been? Before considering the evidence (in the following section), it is useful to clarify certain conceptual issues involved in the measurement of bias or imbalance.

Discriminatory effects may be measured by means of several inter-related indicators of the effect of government interventions. These include (1) agriculture's terms of trade; (2) the net resource flow out of agriculture; and (3) net resource transfers to agriculture from government. These measures capture the impact of government price, tax/subsidy, and other policies related to agriculture. Prices received and paid by farmers, for example, are subject to a wide array of government interventions. These include interventions in international trade such as tariffs and domestic measures such as food and fertilizer subsidies. Quantitative restrictions in both external and internal trade (such as import quotas and compulsory grain purchases from farmers) are also important. With *optimality* in resource allocation as the criterion, social rates of return from marginal allocations of resources between sectors (including agriculture, industry, and public expenditures) must be equalized.

It is customary to measure the intersectoral (or barter) *terms of trade* as the ratio of price indices of agriculture and non-agriculture with an arbitrarily chosen base year. However, the movement in the barter terms of trade reflects changes not only in government policy but also in technological and other economic parameters. While it describes levels or trends in prices that actually face farmers, its policy significance is less salient. The alternative to using historical prices is to use border prices as the standard, i.e. to relate the domestic terms of trade for agriculture to its border terms of trade.[5] In contrast to the measure based on a historical base, this alternative has no behavioural relevance but its relevance for evaluating policy is arguably unique. This follows from the *neo-classi-*

---

[4]See Rao and Caballero (1990) for an elaboration of these points.
[5]This requires comparing the value-weighted average of domestic-to-border price relatives for agriculture, and the similar average for non-agriculture. If traded inputs into agriculture are important, the measure should be calculated in terms of value added.

cal proposition that, given a perfectly competitive market economy, world prices signal opportunity costs and earnings. Hence, equating domestic with border prices assures optimality.[6]

The *flow of resources between the sectors* is simply an accounting measure which includes both voluntary net transfers and net transfers through the tax and expenditure sides of the governement budget. In national accounts terminology, the net total transfer from agriculture equals gross saving in agriculture *less* agricultural investment *plus* net transfers (taxes *less* direct expenditure) from agriculture to government. Thus, the transfer is composed of net private lending to the non-agricultural sectors and net government receipts from agriculture.

Resource flows may also be divided into 'visible' and 'invisible' components (Sharpley, 1979). If agriculture's barter terms of trade relative to some base period fall, the additional real resource transfer induced thereby is called the 'invisible flow'. This can be seen from the following.

$$NCF = O - I$$

Net capital outflow equals outflows less inflows. When these are expressed in real terms using their respective price indices, the real net capital outflow is obtained.

$$RNCF = \frac{O}{P_a} - \frac{I}{P_n}$$

which can be rewritten as

$$RNCF = \frac{NCF}{P_a} + \frac{I}{P_a}\left[1 - \frac{P_a}{P_n}\right]$$

$P_a < P_n$ signifies an adverse shift in the terms of trade so that the second term is positive and represents the invisible outflow due to the price squeeze.

This measure of terms-of-trade losses/gains however does not separately account for policy-induced losses/gain and, therefore, has no direct policy significance (Lewis, 1973). Agricultural prices may have fallen faster, for example, because agricultural productivity grew differentially faster than demand as compared with non-agriculture. The choice of any base year is arbitrary unless the effects of what are

---

[6]We set aside for later consideration the serious limitations of this criterion of optimality.

essentially exogenous changes can be eliminated, and the change in the terms of trade due to government policies thus isolated.

Once again, an alternative measure of visible and invisible flows is obtained by casting the accounting in both domestic and border prices. Each element of the resource flow is measured at both sets of prices.[7] The difference in the aggregate flow, NCF_b and NCF_d, measured at border and domestic prices respectively, is a measure of the invisible flow or *implicit taxation*.

4. UNBALANCED GROWTH: SOME EVIDENCE

Differences in the objectives, constraints, and opportunities across countries notwithstanding, certain general observations at least suggest an anti-agriculture bias. First, agricultural productivity levels (particularly in low-income Asia and Africa) on the eve of industrialization (in the sixties) were only 45 per cent of that of the advanced countries at a similar stage in their development (Timmer, 1988). This would suggest a failure to create a prior agricultural revolution. Second, developing countries (particularly the middle-income group) have seen a 'premature' rise in relative manufacturing labour productivity.[8] This may be viewed as a failure to pursue productive opportunities in agriculture and labour absorption in non-agriculture. Third, the gap between agriculture's economic potential and performance is believed to be substantial. For the Indian case, it has ben estimated that the potential growth rate for the 1969–84 period was 4.9 per cent; the actual rate was less than 3 per cent (Mellor and Johnston, 1984, p. 539).

Available evidence on the aforementioned accounting measures of intersectoral transactions may also be summarized in order to establish prevalent patterns in agricultural pricing and resource transfers. The only attempt to estimate a relative price for agriculture as a whole used a wheat-equivalent domestic price of aggregate agricultural output deflated by the domestic price of fertilizers.[9] For a sample of 53

---

[7]To be comparable, these should be at the same point in the marketing chain so as to fully account for transport, distribution, and processing margins.

[8]See Rao and Caballero (1990) for relevant evidence on this point.

[9]See Peterson (1979). The use of fertilizer prices as the deflator is unsatisfactory since fertilizer costs tend to be a much smaller share of costs in LDCs.

developed and developing countries, the study found that this price relative was 3.7 times larger in the top 10 (mostly developed) countries than in the bottom 10 (all developing) countries for the late sixties. This implies that relative agricultural prices are significantly below border prices in less developed countries. The conclusion is broadly supported by other studies which measure the extent of nominal protection afforded to particular agricultural commodities by relating effective domestic producer prices and border prices. Most of these establish that agricultural commodities receive negative protection and that the magnitudes are frequently large.[10] The negative protection is systematically greater for export crops than for cereals although there is some positive protection in the case of import-competing commodities in a few countries. By the border price standard, the evidence clearly suggests that the degree of *implicit* taxation of agriculture is substantial. The conclusion is unlikely to be reversed with more refined measures or with data for other time periods.

Nonetheless, it is also the case that the share of agriculture in total *government* revenues is significantly smaller than its share in national income. For a sample of 69 LDCs, one study found that agriculture-based taxes contributed less than 10 per cent of total taxes in half the countries and less than 20 per cent in 58 of the 69 countries. In almost all the countries, this share was *substantially less* than the agricultural share in GDP (Bird, 1974). If government expenditures are distributed across sectors roughly in proportion to value added, this would imply that agriculture is generally a net recipient of resources from the government budget.

How much capital does agriculture contribute to the rest of the economy? And how much of this, in turn, is due to an unfavourable policy regime? In the Soviet debate, it was Preobrazhenski's position that keeping food prices low would help finance industrialization. This proposition is not supported by evidence about early Soviet industrialization (Ellman, 1975) or by more recent LDC experience—although agricultural exporters and East Asian countries are exceptions. A recent study of intersectoral resource flows across a sample of 18

---

[10]See, for example, Bale and Lutz (1981), Binswanger and Scandizzo (1983), and Food and Agriculture Organization (1985). The required adjustments in these calculations for processing, transport, and distribution costs, for quality differentials, and for the shadow price of foreign exchange is problematic due to data and methodological limitations.

countries found that private resource outflow (measured at domestic prices) though positive is not appreciably large, barring agricultural exporters, either relative to agricultural GDP or relative to non-agricultural investment (Quisumbing and Taylor, 1985). A comparative study of Japan and India concluded that while resource flows from agriculture contributed significantly to industrialization in Japan during 1888–1937, in the corresponding phase of Indian development (1950–70) agriculture made no such contribution and may even have been a net recipient of resources (Mody, Mundle, and Raj, 1982). In Taiwan's case, agriculture was a major source of net saving for the rest of the economy during the first half of this century. The terms of trade were turned against agriculture throughout this period (Lee, 1971). It would appear from these findings that agriculture is not, as a rule, a significant source of capital for the rest of the economy; Japan, Taiwan, and a few agricultural exporters being the exceptions.

A rather different inference could be that agricultural taxation has assumed a predominantly implicit or invisible form as governments have sought to hasten the process of industrialization by erecting significant trade barriers. This was sought to be established in a study of the Philippines which accounted for resource flows using both domestic and border price valuations of outflows and inflows (David, 1984). With an agricultural share in GDP of 33 per cent, agricultural taxes constituted only 7 per cent of its value added whereas the corresponding figure for non-agriculture was 18 per cent. However, agriculture also contributed 20 per cent of its value added in the form of invisible outflows evaluated at border prices. The author concluded that the overall effect of government policy, contrary to appearance, was to deprive agriculture of a much larger share of its income than was the case for non-agriculture. But the author fails to note that since government expenditures on agriculture amounted to 29 per cent of its value added, the net effect of the explicit and implicit outflows attributable to government policies was not unfavourable to agriculture.

This review suggests the following main points: first, in so far as governments have any control over prices, they keep agriculture's terms of trade low relative to border prices. Second, the explicit contribution of agriculture to government revenues is notably small. Third, and this flows from the first point, the implicit taxation of agriculture is large. However, there is little evidence to permit inferences on the net effects of policy on resource transfers from agriculture. The chief difficulty lies in identifying the sectoral distribution of the benefits from public expenditures. The high degree of implicit taxation by itself does not establish a policy bias against agriculture because agriculture may also derive substantial benefits from public expenditures as in the case of the Philippines.

Finally, we may consider the share of investment allocated to agriculture. Using stylized facts about agricultural growth at different stages of economic growth, Krishna (1982) established norms for that share. He then found that the actual allocations in developing countries have persistently been below these norms. While for the typical low-income and lower-middle-income country, the norm established is 22 per cent of national investment, not even one of 20 countries allocated 20 per cent in 1966–8, only 3 allocated as much as 15 per cent while about half the countries allocated less than 10 per cent. To quote Krishna,

Agriculture does not need . . . a major share of total national investment; 20 to 22 per cent would suffice in most low-income situations as direct investment, but much less than this is provided in many countries. In this sense agriculture is neglected (p. 232).

The thesis of missed agricultural opportunities appears, therefore, to be a plausible one. Neither is there much controversy about it at the present juncture. But the policy ingredients required for successful agricultural transformation involve much more than getting the prices or investment share allocated to agriculture 'right' and, on this score, there is deep disagreement. These disagreements are part of the wider disputes over development strategies that have occurred over the past fifteen years. To put the matter in perspective, we present below the sharply contrasting positions of the neo-classical and structuralist schools which have become clearly articulated and influential during the eighties. Their points of departure from the traditional paradigm outlined above should also be evident in what follows.

5. NEO-CLASSICAL DIAGNOSES AND PRESCRIPTIONS: A CRITIQUE

The presumption that the market mechanism produces beneficial economic outcomes while administrative interventions are generally harmful is the hallmark of neo-classical theorizing. Rural markets in land, labour, credit, and agricultural products are thought to be efficient, if second-best, responses to the constraints of a backward economy (the efficiency of traditional agriculture). The pursuit of free international trade and openness is similarly seen as a source of important gains (comparative advantage). Government interventions in markets have generally depressed production incentives and contributed to surplus extraction out of agriculture. Import-substitution in industry was pushed along inefficient, capital-intensive lines and little was done to provide incentives for exports, including agricultural exports. Government controls and public sector activities overburdened their political processes with economic functions that governments are not capable of performing efficiently (Schultz, 1978, p. 2). The consequence was both slow growth and the perpetuation of poverty and inequities.

The neo-classical case arguing policy discrimination against agriculture in developing countries is built around the effects of tariff and exchange rate policies. It is held that high rates of nominal protection to industry reduce the effective rate of protection to agriculture, often making the latter negative. Exchange rate overvaluation also works in the same direction on the presumption that most agricultural goods are tradable commodities.

Thus, discriminatory price policies lie at the heart of the neo-classical claim that agriculture has been neglected. Employment growth and rural welfare, it is asserted, have been sacrificed in the process. These assertions involve numerous inter-related propositions that need to be critically examined. Without attempting to be exhaustive, we shall focus on several key ones.

From a neo-classical standpoint, the invisible transfer of resources out of agriculture, whether deemed inequitable or not, is evidence prima facie of inefficiency. Accepting the neo-classical premises for now, one may ask how much of a loss is thus imposed. Disagreements arise over the magnitude both of the price 'distortion' from world levels and of the supply elasticity. Reliable empirical estimates of the long-run supply elasticity of aggregate agricultural output in developing countries are in the 0.1–0.5 range. For plausible assumptions on price distortion levels and other parameters, the efficiency loss works out to about 3 per cent of national income.[11] This is clearly a small number for a one-shot loss suffered from the distortion. But it is also atypically large for a measure of allocative inefficiency; this reflects the relatively large price distortion (50 per cent) assumed in the calculation and the size of the agricultural sector.

That such calculations have been used to buttress the view that low agricultural prices cause low agricultural *growth* is a puzzle. Problems of poverty, malnutrition, balance-of-payments disequilibrium, and slow overall growth are also blamed on wrong prices (Peterson, 1979). But the calculation takes account of long-run supply responses; so it is difficult to see how even large price distortions can produce a *cumulative* loss in efficiency. The neo-classical enthusiasm for getting prices right cannot be sustained by the logic of the case.

Besides, world prices may be misleading as efficiency indicators even on neo-classical premises. Several points may be noted in this connection. (1) Current world prices may be poor predictors of *future* world prices and it is the latter that are relevant for allocative decisions. For agricultural exports, there is evidence suggesting a downward long-run trend of prices at least for the period since World War II (Spraos, 1980). This dictates some diversification out of agricultural exports. (2) World prices and markets for agricultural commodities are subject to considerable volatility. Stable but lower average domestic prices are consistent with increasing national well-being.[12] (3) Deviations may be justified by national monopoly or monopsony power in the world market. This argument includes cases where trade-restricting policy is pursued jointly by a group of nations as with coordinated export taxes or commodity agreements. (4) A significant part of agricultural production may be non-tradable in the sense that transport costs preclude price equalization. The wedge between c.i.f. and f.o.b. prices may be large enough that the 'law of

---

[11]This is derived on the basis of the following parameter values: domestic agricultural prices equal to half of their border levels; demand and supply elasticities equal to –0.5 and 0.25 respectively; agricultural exports one-fourth of domestic agricultural production; and agriculture's share in national value added equal to 0.4.

[12]Jabara and Thompson (1980), using an extended concept of comparative advantage which recognizes world price uncertainty and risk aversion, found that national welfare will be higher if the country (Senegal) diversified more than would be dictated by the usual domestic resource cost criterion of comparative advantage.

one price' fails to hold. These considerations may seem obvious but most proponents of the world price criterion pay little attention to them.

What does a low measured aggregate elasticity of agricultural output—in the range 0.1 to 0.5—for developing countries signify? The elasticity is a reduced form measure of the long-run responsiveness to prices of all inputs used in production. Assuming profit or utility-maximizing behaviour of private agents, this would certainly include all *private* inputs including private investments in land and capital. If there are fixed factors and if the production function is Cobb–Douglas, the observed range for the supply elasticity implies an imputed output share for the fixed factors ranging between 2/3 and 10/11. Even if some factors such as land are fixed for private agents, their effective supply may be augmentable by public investments. And even if the supply of these inputs does not rise with prices, the range for their imputed share is implausibly high. A plausible explanation for the observed low elasticity is that when prices are higher, public inputs into agricultural production actually *decline*.

We shall develop economic reasons for such behaviour in the following section. Here we take up the contrary view that not only private inputs but also public inputs into agriculture respond positively to price signals. According to this view, public investments in land-augmenting infrastructure such as irrigation, in rural electricity and transport networks, and in supply-shifting factors such as agricultural research and extension services are *induced* by price increases. If food prices are rising, so the argument goes, this will serve as a signal to government policy-makers and public agencies to increase public efforts for food production and to stabilize prices. Conversely, if prices are low so that the payoffs from such public investments are undervalued, there will be underinvestment in agriculture. Setting domestic prices equal to border prices is therefore important for efficiency in resource allocation in both the private and public sectors. In particular, this line of reasoning generates the hypothesis that low agricultural prices not only create static inefficiency but also *reduce the growth rate* of agriculture in so far as public investments are a vehicle for technological progress.

Space limits us from considering the evidence relevant to this argument. Most of the evidence, however, contradicts this view and we shall indicate here only the general nature of the contradiction between evidence and hypothesis.[13] The idea that underpricing results in research underinvestment may be illustrated with respect to India. According to Schultz, the overpricing of wheat, relative to rice, restricted rice research. As a result, the growth of wheat production was twice as high as that of rice between 1948 and 1972. The argument can be faulted on several counts: First, in many cases, technology is available but not applied in the field. This implies that the generation of new technologies and their use in practice have been driven by *different* forces. Low prices cannot be responsible for both low rates of adoption and low rates of technical advance. Second, in so far as low agricultural prices and low growth are correlated, this may reflect powerful political forces shaping agricultural policy. The correlation is spurious and does not permit the inference that underpricing is the cause of restricted yield-raising research. The relatively low levels of output in rice research and of investment in infrastructure in the rice-growing regions of eastern India may reflect political/structural conditions within those regions and their political weight in the country rather than the influence of the relatively low price of rice. It has been suggested that the highly favourable price policy for wheat is part of a policy of regional discrimination by the government (Mitra, 1977). Third, the Schultz hypothesis can be challenged on the ground that, for whatever reasons, public research investment in developing countries is significantly below optimum levels even at *prevailing* prices for agriculture. While prices do enter into the valuation of returns to research, the pertinent question is to what extent social returns guide policy. If returns are already high relative to other alternatives, the hypothesis that low prices are to blame for low growth in research input is seriously in error.

Among agricultural infrastructural investments, the most direct impact on production is associated with water-control and distribution networks. In the Asian context, an important question concerns the importance of price policies *versus* public infrastructure measures in explaining observed gaps in yields across countries. Cross-country studies suggest that the returns to private inputs such as fertilizer may be constricted not so much by low price incentives as by underinvestment in complementary public inputs such as irrigation. Nevertheless,

---

[13]The interested reader may consult Rao (1989) for a more detailed consideration of the issue.

irrigation investments in the Philippines have been responses to food supply crises rather than planned according to their long-run social profitability (Hayami and Kikuchi, 1978).

To conclude, neither the low agregate elasticity of agricultural supply nor more specific evidence pertaining to public investments in land-augmenting or supply-shifting factors supports the argument that agricultural prices play a powerful role in promoting or retarding agricultural growth. 'Getting prices right' does not translate itself into faster agricultural growth.

What, in the neo-classical view, accounts for the pursuit of discriminatory policies? The neglect of agriculture, as with faulty industrialization policies, is sometimes attributed simply to policy mistakes: thus, planners underestimated the social returns to investments in agricultural growth. An alternative view blames (undifferentiated) rural/urban or producer/consumer conflicts over policy:

The balance of interests between producers and consumers is the central issue of agricultural policy, and one governed by pricing structures. In the pursuit of goals other than agriculture's development, developing-country planners have often tilted their pricing policy against agriculture—and paid a heavy price in lost agricultural growth (*World Development Report*, 1982, p. 4).

The pattern of growth reflects the politically-determined neglect of agriculture. The state, being dominated by the urban classes, acts to protect their interests. These actions consist of a wide array of *urban-biased* policies including underinvestment in agriculture; under-provision of health, education, and other services in rural areas; industrial protection and cheap food policies that serve to raise the prices received and lower the prices paid by rural producers. Such a strategy sacrifices major growth and employment opportunities that lie in the rural and agricultural sectors.

This view must be rejected on several grounds. First, the rural elite are scarcely impotent as the urban-bias thesis assumes. Nor are they merely junior partners of a political coalition dominated by urban interests. Second, rural and urban 'classes' are not homogeneous interest groups: rather, there are exploitative class relations and fundamental conflicts of interest within each of these economic sectors. Third, in view of the preceding points, it is not urban bias or rural bias that underlies the problems of slow growth and inequity but class bias favouring the interests of the rural and urban elite at the expense of peasants and workers.

The urban-bias hypothesis does not account for the fact that governments find ways to protect the interests of both the urban and rural elite simultaneously. Food subsidies and controlled food distribution by governments are used to control money wages of urban workers in the formal sector—thus, such subsidies benefit employers in the formal sector by keeping their money costs down and profits up. They do little to raise the food purchasing power of rural and urban workers in the informal sector, or of poor peasants and the landless, not to mention the unemployed. At the same time, government subsidies and expenditures on the agricultural sector benefit larger landowners and rich peasants disproportionately.

It is instructive to pursue the distributional implications of urban bias within the standard Hekscher–Ohlin model. Although the efficiency loss from low agricultural prices is small, the income-distributive effects of negative protection to agriculture can be expected to be large. In the hypothetical numerical example noted previously, agricultural consumers' gain from low agricultural prices amounts to 13 per cent of national income and government revenue rises 5 per cent while producers lose as much as 21 per cent of national income or 50 per cent of agricultural value added. In terms of the functional distribution of income, the reduction in agriculture's terms of trade can be expected to reduce the share of the specific factor—agricultural land, here—in national income. The effects on capital and labour are, in general, ambiguous. If capital is used predominantly in the non-agricultural sectors, its share will be higher when agricultural prices are reduced. Reduced agricultural prices will also tend to raise the real wage of labour to the extent that agricultural (food and raw material) goods figure heavily in labour's consumption bundle even though agriculture is labour-intensive. Peasants lose as owners of land but may gain as food consumers or labour suppliers. Within a neo-classical world, therefore, there is reason to believe that raising agricultural prices to world levels will transfer income *from capital to land* but no presumption that workers and peasants will benefit. Hence, there is little warrant within neo-classical theory for the sweeping assertion that discriminatory policies against agriculture are necessarily *inegalitarian*.

6.   SECTORAL BALANCE: STRUCTURALIST VIEWS

The neo-classical approach is founded on several key (often implicit) assumptions about agriculture and the rest of the economy. These assumptions relate to agrarian structure and markets, technological possibilities, the determinants of demand and intersectoral relationships: (1) rural inequalities in developing countries are either negligible or do not give rise to fundamental conflicts of interest over market outcomes and government policies; (2) rural market structures and institutions governing access to the means of employment and production do not adversely affect productivity, employment, new technology adoption, or distribution; (3) rural poverty is a result of the low level of technology and the neglect of agriculture; (4) governments can finance investment for agricultural modernization without 'distorting' market signals; (5) accelerating agricultural growth will necessarily reduce hunger and poverty; (6) increasing agricultural output can be readily sold either domestically or abroad; (7) the rate of saving is determined by the return to investment but unaffected by income distribution; (8) industrial output and the inducement to invest is independent of the level of aggregate demand or of distribution.

To lay out the alternative structuralist views is mostly to question every one of the above assumptions. Rural inequalities in land-ownership and access to capital give rise to important conflicts of interest between the rich and the poor. These show up in part in private resource use and income distribution. Land and capital are inefficiently utilized on large farms and employment is thereby restricted. Inequality in accumulation coupled with rural market failures impart a strong labour-saving bias in production and technical change. Governments have played an important role in programmes of technology development and diffusion in developing countries. Their role in infrastructure investment is also crucial. But where inequalities are large, as in many parts of Asia and Latin America and in some parts of Africa, governments have reinforced the market bias favouring the rich in the way these growth programmes have been designed and administered. Peasant producers have become increasingly marginalized and their poverty perpetuated. Thus, supply-side restrictions imposed by structure have limited the speed and spread of agricultural growth.

Prevailing rural inequalities are also an important barrier to agricultural modernization from the demand-side. Accelerating food and agricultural growth, if its benefits are spread wide and if initial income levels are low, tends to generate rapid growth of food demand. Supply and demand can then equilibrate at high levels without unduly depressing agriculture's terms of trade. But where the above-mentioned supply-side biases are strong so that the purchasing power of the poor remains limited, output growth may well reduce land rents and agricultural profits by reducing the terms of trade. Hence, failures to effectively distribute the benefits of growth constitute a serious threat to the implementation of an accelerated growth strategy for agriculture as the rural rich organize against it. Growth may then be accompanied by stock accumulation or subsidized exports; alternatively growth policies will be reined in to keep pace with demand growth. Thus, the neglect of agriculture is not a consequence of urban bias but of the imperative to protect the interests of rentiers. Supply and demand then equilibrate at low levels.[14] This supports the structuralist view that 'hunger is not caused primarily by inadequate production of food, nor can it be cured except in the long run merely by increasing production further' (Griffin, 1987, p. 4).

Structuralists also stress the tension between agriculture's role as a source of surplus for industry versus its role as a source of effective demand (Adelman, 1984, p. 919). In traditional development theory, an agriculture-oriented strategy is faulted as antithetical to raising accumulation. However, at low levels of income, agriculture provides a potential mass *market* for industrial growth both in the form of intermediate goods and consumer goods. Investing in agricultural modernization is therefore complementary to raising industrial investment rates via the demand factor. This too requires that agricultural growth be broad-based.

Equally important is the consideration that governments provide large subsidies to agriculture through the aforementioned programmes of public investment. Few governments manage to finance more than a small fraction of these expenditures through direct taxes on agriculture. The limited responsiveness of agricultural supply to prices noted earlier cannot be understood without due recognition of the role of public investment in promoting production and of the problems of

[14]A formal model of mutually complementary growth of agriculture and industry is developed in Rao (1987) which yields conclusions along these lines.

financing it. Even in the absence of obvious market imperfections, major initiatives in agricultural development often depend on government action. Indivisibilities, externalities, and inappropriabilities tend to be very important in developing agriculture. Investment in irrigation, water control, and land improvement systems involves indivisibilities and scale economies. Agricultural extension and water supply regulation entail externalities. Important products of agricultural research cannot be privately appropriated. Without improved transportation or electrification, the incentive content of prices is substantially weakened. Public investment can thus augment the supply of land, be an important vehicle for supply-shifting technologies, and enhance the incentive content of prices facing farmers. The weak output effect of agricultural prices reflects either the non-responsiveness of such investment or even a negative relation between farm prices and public investment as argued below.

Where markets function reasonably well, they may be relied upon to equalize returns to private investment in alternative uses. Moreover, even if private agents fail to make certain investments, as in the aforementioned cases, this does not necessarily entail extra-market action. In a sufficiently idealized system of markets, with no information, enforcement, or transaction costs, such market failures can be remedied by the systematic use of taxes and subsidies which work through the market system. In the neo-classical view, much (though not all) of the problem of providing collective inputs into agriculture and their financing effectively breaks down into the problem of getting prices right.

In reality, however, ensuring that socially profitable investments are undertaken is considerably more complex than setting corrective taxes and subsidies in the hope that private agents will be led to socially optimal choices. The ease with which such investments can be *decentralized through the market* is affected by agrarian structure and associated conflicts among private agents, and by pervasive market imperfections. Since many of these investments give rise to free rider problems, large transactions costs, and disputes over the distribution of their benefits, market solutions will be either *infeasible or inefficient*. For example, collecting water charges is notoriously difficult and costly.

Whether such investment is owned and operated by private or public agents, its financing involves a large element of public subsidy. Since agriculture is a major sector, governments have to (and do) raise resources from that sector one way or another. To the extent that surpluses need to be mobilized from agriculture, the method of doing so will have an obvious influence on the social yield from public investment. The usual forms of taxation impose economic costs since costless lump-sum taxes are simply unavailable to most governments. Raising revenues by means of direct taxes on agricultural income, land, and, more generally, wealth rather than by indirect taxes is both more efficient, if administrative costs are not prohibitive, and more equitable. The former produce few distortions because they do not adversely affect output and input price relatives. But these relatively more efficient forms of taxation are also usually unavailable because of administrative or political constraints. As noted earlier, taxes on agricultural land, capital, and labour incomes contribute very little to the public finances of most developing countries. Therefore, viewing prices merely as private incentives is apt to be highly misleading. Agricultural prices have a *necessary fiscal function*.

Tax revenues are raised predominantly by means of imposts on international trade and domestic taxes on the non-agricultural, primarily industrial, sectors. The connection between trade policy and (implicit) agricultural taxation is a prominent one in developing countries. Even as agriculture features mainly on the subsidy side and is conspicuously absent on the tax side as regards domestic interventions, this is largely reversed in the case of trade taxes and subsidies. Export taxes (subsidies) are generally agricultural (industrial) whereas import taxes tend to be predominantly on import-substituting manufactures. But while import protection for non-agriculture transfers resources from agriculture to non-agriculture, domestic taxes on non-agriculture in turn transfer resources from non-agriculture to the government. The tariff protection of industry, in other words, may reflect the need to raise government revenues indirectly, not necessarily to lower agriculture's terms of trade. The two sets of tax interventions work together to raise revenues from agriculture. If revenues are a binding constraint on public investment, it is possible that this method of raising revenues may be better than not investing in agriculture at all even though it distorts resource allocation.

In such a context, it is inevitable that the terms of trade for agriculture are viewed as a fiscal instrument by governments, not merely as prices that direct private resource use. A *ceteris paribus* increase in the terms of trade of agriculture will, in this view, constrict public finances. While this may induce a rise in private investment in agriculture, it will also reduce government's ability to finance public inputs into agriculture. Hence, agricultural output will rise to the extent that *private inputs increase* but fall to the extent that *public inputs decline.* The reduced form estimate of aggregate agricultural supply-elasticity reflects the fiscal and incentive effects of agricultural prices. This is a possible explanation for the low observed elasticity noted earlier. It also explains why governments persistently underprice agricultural output and simultaneously subsidize public inputs into agriculture. To an extent which can only be determined by empirical case studies, both are inevitable. This seemingly contradictory policy package that many observers have noted reflects the large weight of public investment and the ubiquitous constraint on direct agricultural taxation or pricing of public inputs.

Structuralists also allow that governments may not always be able to control relative prices. Developing countries trying to industrialize face endemic disproportions both internally and externally: internally, industrial demand runs ahead of agricultural supply; externally, import demand and export earnings are similarly out of balance. In flexible economies, textbook-style relative price adjustments are supposed to resolve such imbalances. Thus, a realignment of the internal terms of trade can cut back the excess demand for food arising from industrialization. Similarly, an adjustment of the exchange rate (devaluation) can restore the balance of payments. But such price adjustments usually mean substantial income redistribution and they may be successfully resisted. Thus, rising food prices may be met by demands for higher money wages. Oligopolistic industries—which are more the rule than the exception in developing countries—are then likely to pass on these cost increases into higher industral prices. Persistent inflation rather than any significant realignment of the terms of trade may be the result. Similarly, devaluations can work by inducing real wage reductions and/or a fall in national income and employment: they are apt, therefore, to be resisted but with inflationary consequences. The macroeconomic conditions required to bring about significant reductions in agricultural taxation—even when this is desirable—may not be obtained; to talk of faulty government 'policy' may not, therefore, be very meaningful.

When unemployment and aggregate demand constraints prevail, terms-of-trade changes will alter non-agricultural output through changes in aggregate demand. If there are sufficiently strong Engel effects in demand, a rise in food prices will raise the level of non-agricultural output and employment by increasing the demand from agriculture. Such situations are propitious for agriculture as both farmers and industrialists are likely to favour a reduction in the tax burden on agriculture. On the other hand, if the demand for non-agriculture is dominated by the effect of the reduction in the sector's real income following a rise in food prices, its output will fall. In this ('Ricardian') case, cheap food policies will be strongly favoured by industrialists and, of course, opposed by farmers.[15] Evidently, neither output nor distributive impacts of policy changes can be judged independently of the structure of the economy.

It is evident, therefore, that structuralist and neo-classical evaluations of the constraints on agricultural growth put forth mostly during the seventies contrast sharply and differ also from the strategic assumptions of the early fifties. Hindsight may account at least for some of the differences. Conditions for an agricultural revolution in the earlier period were less propitious than they are today. And even now, the differences in available technologies across regions remain impressive. Many countries now have the skeletons of administrative, infrastructural, and technology-delivering systems without which a modern agricultural revolution would not take off.[16]

Governments were also properly concerned about diversifying their economies out of colonial patterns of dependence. That many have yet to succeed is in part testimony to the problems of making the transition. At the turn of the eighties two sharply contrasting reports appeared on the plight of African agriculture. The OAU's Lagos Plan faulted the world recession, unfavourable commodity prices, and declining terms of trade for the stagnation. It recommended an inward-looking strategy to promote regional cooperation and integration. The

[15]The analytical basis for these results is in Taylor (1983).

[16]The achievements in education in Tanzania and Somalia have been impressive (Eicher, 1982, p. 156) just as Nigeria, Kenya, and the Ivory Coast have vastly improved their ability to organize, plan, and manage their economies.

World Bank's Berg Report, by contrast, blamed poor economic management, inefficient parastatals, low prices, and the failure to exploit Africa's comparative advantage in export agriculture. Since these reports appeared, the crisis has deepened and world commodity prices have fallen further.[17]

However, such problems of agricultural transition also arise in large economies which are not obliged to specialize in export production for accelerating growth (India and China, though in different ways). As de Janvry and Sadoulet (1987) have noted, the success of India, and to a lesser extent that of China, was limited only to making them self-sufficient in food. In the case of India, this success has been achieved at a low-level equilibrium between domestic demand and domestic supply. The problems of neglect can thus be acute, not necessarily because non-agricultural options are thoughtlessly pursued. The problem of agricultural mobilization will not go away: the problem of food demand remains a serious issue for the same reason that the problem of agricultural supply has not been resolved. Growth is also stalled on that account. The structuralist diagnoses seem especially apposite.

The basic points of this and the preceding sections may be reinforced by contrasting the East Asian experience with the experience of late-developing Asian countries. Prior to, or along with, industrialization, the East Asian economies experienced sustained growth in agricultural productivity. This provided major sources of saving and consumption demand for non-agricultural growth. Developing Asian countries have failed to register a similar record of agricultural success, especially when measured in terms of labour productivity. Second, egalitarian land reform in East Asia was crucial in three respects: (1) it facilitated the absorption of new technologies and the absorption of labour within agriculture; (2) the problem of extracting a surplus from agriculture, via the terms of trade or directly, was eased; (3) the egalitarian income base also provided significant demand stimulus for industry, both modern urban and rural. Lacking such an egalitarian distributive base, developing Asian economies find that neither agricultural growth nor the growth of industry, rural or urban,

<hr />

[17]For example, Sudan raised cotton output by 35 per cent in 1981 and 20 per cent in 1982, both as a result of macro policy changes accompanying World Bank-assisted structural adjustment, but the fall in world prices left no gains in export earnings at all (Eicher, 1983, p. 10). Can countries like Sudan afford to persist with such policies over the coming years?

makes significant dents into the problems of labour absorption or poverty. Finally, the early and rapid development of rural infrastructure in the form of transport, electricity, and education contributed significantly to both rural growth and labour absorption. Not only is the supply of such infrastructure in developing Asia low but its benefits are also very unevenly distributed—recalling again the role of prevailing rural structures. Hence, the further growth of infrastructure reproduces inequality, unemployment, and rural poverty.

In effect, the East Asian path exploited both the supply-side and, especially, the demand-side complementarity between agricultural and non-agricultural growth. Rising rural incomes and employment fuelled continued investment growth. Radical redistribution of rural assets coupled with the judicious use of fiscal instruments to raise savings considerably blunted the tradeoff between growth and employment. The result was that agricultural and rural industrial growth proceeded complementarily. In contrast, developing Asia has relied on trickle-down from urban-based industrial development with attendant tradeoffs between growth and equity. Significantly, this tradeoff has not been eased with the passage of time. The failure of trickle-down growth has generated strong pressures for ameliorative doles, created large pools of urban unemployment, and frustrated government programmes to directly reduce poverty. The resolution of this impasse requires not merely asset redistribution but complementary policies that ensure growth with equity.

7. APPRAISAL OF THE INDIAN EXPERIENCE

This section raises a number of considerations, from the viewpoint of agriculture/industry balance and agricultural policies, relevant to an assessment of the Indian growth experience. No comprehensive evaluation is feasible within the confines of the present paper; only a selective appraisal is therefore attempted. In subsection A, we deal with the overall balance between food supply and demand and the trend in the agricultural terms of trade. It is argued that both price and distributional shifts have been responsible for sustaining a low-level equilibrium between demand and supply. Subsection B considers the main policy instruments by which the food market has been influenced by the government. It suggests that while the food price has become increasingly subject to administrative interventions, there is no bias—whether based on domestic price trends or with border prices as benchmark—to suppose that they have been biased against producers. In subsection C, we examine resource flows into and out of agriculture via the fiscal mechanism. While indicating the main forms and extent of taxing and subsidizing agricultural production, it is contended that the failure to adequately mobilize rural resources seriously constricts the availability of public finance for agricultural *investment* as has become evident during the eighties. The final subsection considers the macroeconomic links between growth and inequality, especially the mutually reinforcing process in which agricultural growth and industrial growth interact. The implications of this argument about sectoral balance are briefly examined in relation to the political economy of the Indian growth experience.

A. Demand, Supply and the Terms of Trade

Over the four decades of planned economic development in India beginning in 1950, the rate of growth of food production has been modestly greater than the growth rate of population. Yet, *consumption* (however measured) per capita has essentially stagnated over this period, i.e. apart from transient changes in supplies and prices.[18] The difference is explained partly by the decline in the food-imports/gross-consumption ratio from 6.8 per cent in 1959–67, to 3 per cent in 1968–75 and then to virtually 0 per cent during 1976–83. Another explanatory factor is the rapid accumulation of stocks relative to availability from the mid seventies onwards. The deficiency relative to nutritional norms in *per capita* availability of calories from grains, vegetable fats, and sugar for 1985 was of the order of 11 per cent; in terms of availability from all foods, the norm was just satisfied in per capita terms. The most remarkable fact, however, is that per capita foodgrain consumption grew a mere 1.86 per cent between 1951 and 1981 despite a 65 per cent growth in NDP per capita (Dandekar, 1986).

The behaviour of food prices and of agricultural *terms of trade* is a matter of some controversy in India (Thamarajakshi, 1977, and Kahlon

---

[18]Whereas a positive and significant time trend is discernible in the case of all other items of consumption including the total, there is no significant trend at all in the case of cereals and cereal substitutes.

and Tyagi, 1980). The controversy relates to the use of wholesale versus farmgate prices; and for the latter, the use of production weights versus shares in marketed surplus. Thamarajakshi found that agriculture's barter terms of trade rose at the compound rate of 1.43 per cent per annum from 1951–2 to 1973–4, while its income terms of trade rose at the rate of 4.53 per cent. Kahlon and Tyagi argue that there was deterioration in the terms for the 1968–74 period. For the 1950/1–1979/80 period, the NDP deflator for the primary sector rose at the annual compound rate of 5.9 per cent compared with 4.9 per cent for total NDP (Rao, 1983, p. 24). The primary sector's relative deflator was seen to rise during the fifties and sixties; for the seventies, it fell. We may conclude that agricultural prices rose at least through the sixties, if not till the mid seventies, and fell thereafter.

The evidence summarized above concerning the behaviour of relative prices and the growth of per capita income and food consumption raises two basic questions. First, what forces prevented the rise of per capita food consumption in conjunction with the rise in income? Second, what accounts for the pattern of change in relative prices? We take up the first question here leaving the second one for consideration in subsection B. The decline in per capita consumption between 1961 and 1977 was sought to be reconciled with the slow but steady rise in income per capita over the same period (Sarma, Roy, and George, 1981). NSS data showed a 10 per cent fall in per capita food consumption between 1964–5 and 1973–4 with no measured deterioration in the distribution of income. The authors accepted the latter finding and hypothesized that the fall in food consumption was explained by the rise in the real price of food over the period. National food balance sheets based on Ministry of Agriculture data showed a 6 per cent decline in apparent per capita consumption between 1970–2 and 1975–7 despite a 3 per cent rise in per capita income and a 5 per cent drop in the relative price of food. If the distribution of income were assumed unchanged during this period, food consumption 'ought' to have been about 10 per cent higher than it apparently was. Even allowing for the rise in the national savings ratio of this period, food consumption was some 7% less than predicted. Finally, Krishnaji (1984) found that, even in the period of high savings growth (1961–81), aggregate real consumption expenditure per capita grew at an annual rate slightly less than one per cent whereas per capita food consumption expenditure was nearly stagnant.

These facts would suggest that food consumption was held down by a shift of incomes against the mass of the population through a rise in food prices or otherwise. The rapid rise in household saving together with the rough constancy of food consumption per capita—which are scarcely disputed and can be viewed as the 'core facts'—suggests either that the terms of trade rose sharply in favour of agriculture or that income distribution became more unequal through factors other than relative price changes or that some combination of the two was operative. The actual mix of these two explanatory factors is difficult to sort out due to conflicting interpretations, or sources, of evidence for them. Space does not permit us to consider the evidence on the distribution of income: we would maintain that the balance of evidence points to a trend of deterioration. Be that as it may, it is quite clear that at least until the sixties, rising prices were an important factor in holding food consumption down.

To sum up, although the government has succeeded in preventing large-scale famines that had been a frequent occurrence during the colonial period, it has failed to provide any sustained increase in per capita food consumption despite rising per capita incomes. Rising food prices help explain the stagnation in food consumption but rising income inequalities may have also been an important factor. Government interventions in the food market have, especially in recent decades, favoured the well-to-do seller (net) of food and worked against the interests of the mass of food buyers (net), both rural and urban. The effect of rising food prices is felt not only by urban consumers but also by the 50 per cent of the rural population who are net purchasers of food. On the other hand, price increases benefit rural (net) sellers in proportion to their share in the marketed surplus. This performance may be characterized fairly as a low-level equilibrium between food demand and supply.

B. Administered Food Markets

The state has intervened in the food market by means of its procurement operations, import policy, public distribution through fair-price shops, public stock operations and, more recently, food-for-work programmes. During the Second and Third Plan periods, the rise in food prices would arguably have been even greater but for the continuing import of PL 480 food. At least till the mid sixties, agricultural price behaviour in India was basically dictated by *market forces*. Thereafter, however, the course of agricultural prices, especially for wheat and rice, became a valued object of government interventions (Mitra, 1977). In the late sixties and the seventies, government repeatedly allowed larger increases in procurement prices than were recommended by the Agricultural Prices Commission (Byres, 1979). Although the latter half of the seventies saw a decline in relative agricultural prices, this was also a period of accumulating food stocks. Quite clearly, prices would have fallen much more sharply but for government support operations.

Empirical simulation of the general equilibrium effects of policy reveal clearly who benefits and who loses from the price policy adopted. Technical improvement under flexible prices serves to benefit the bulk of the rural and urban food-consuming population (including the landless, small farmers, and urban workers), but leaves large and rich farmers with marginal gains or even losses. The latter, however, gain substantially when output prices are not allowed to fall under technical improvement (de Janvry and Subbarao, 1986). From a longer-term perspective, the main beneficiaries of technical progress with price maintenance are the surplus-producing farms of the developed regions and the primary losers (on account of the failure of real purchasing power to rise or even stay constant) are the urban and, particularly, rural poor.

Whereas in the pre-seventies period, import policy was the dominant form of government intervention in the food market, the advent of the New Agricultural Strategy in the sixties saw the growing use of stock and distribution policies. Initially, these policies were justified on the grounds of minimizing price fluctuations for producers and vulnerable consumers. But over time, the price-setting process has come to be heavily politicized so much so that it is proper to regard agricultural prices as being *administered* to a significant degree. As demand has grown slowly, the fear of falling prices coupled with the growing organization and influence of the potential losers has created a strong state presence in the food markets.

Compared to the sixties, the average rate of procurement has been of the order of 15 million tonnes of foodgrains which is about 13–14 per cent of net production (Krishnaji, 1988, p. 50). It appears that government procurement and stock operations have contributed only marginally to lowering fluctuations in aggregate availability relative to fluctuations in aggregate output (the coefficient of variation in the former was 5 per cent, in the latter 6.5 per cent). Notwithstanding the widening spread in per capita foodgrains growth across states, the *variation* in per capita availability for each state has been contained and this must be credited to government procurement operations. However, *average* availability in each state is closely tied to its own level of production which remains a fundamental determinant of grain purchasing power.

The stabilizing role of procurement operations has been bought at a high price, literally. Apart from the fact that procurement prices have not been allowed to fall in years of good harvest (Krishnaji, 1988, p. 62), it is estimated that for wheat, they have been set 25–30 per cent above the ruling market price (Bandyopadhyaya, 1988, p. 31). Since support prices are common for the whole country and apparently set by costs (including imputed labour costs and market-based land rents) in the high-cost states, the implicit subsidy to the more-developed or high-productivity regions is clearly disproportionate. Minimum prices for procurement have also served to eliminate risk to surplus-producing farmers. Because procurement prices have been set high (often leading the market), the disposal of stocks in the market or additions to stocks involve a large subsidy element. The government has chosen, by its own policy, to prevent market adjustment taking place. Had government been willing to allow stock depletion when they grew above a minimum level (governed by the requirements of maintaining stability), it would have been possible to distribute more. But the price would have been lowered.

It is a matter of some irony that while food-for-work programmes and public distribution schemes withdrew a portion of the marketed surplus from the market and thus allowed open-market prices to rise, the *easier* route of raising demand by letting prices drop, in response to increases in production relative to overall demand, has been eschewed. In this context, the argument that prices have been biased against farmers cannot be supported. The weighted price of sales, taking both open-market and controlled prices into account, has not been reduced by government procurement operations.[19] In a comparison of domestic rice and wheat prices with border prices, it was found that (1) nominal protection coefficients for both were less than unity during the eighties but greater than unity for wheat if it is assumed to be an exportable; (2) the implicit tax on rice was greater than on wheat; (3) given nominal protection for tradable inputs, effective protection rates turn out to be less than nominal rates for both rice and wheat; (4) but when the large subsidies to non-tradable inputs are accounted for, the implicit nominal taxation of both falls sharply, particularly so for the states of Punjab and Haryana (Gulati, 1987). The dual pricing system has thus enabled the government to protect some urban consumers while also benefiting surplus producers.

C. Resource Transfers via the Fiscal Mechanism

The growth of Plan investments has been increasingly dependent on government borrowing because the major sources of government revenue remain confined to a host of indirect taxes. Developments during the eighties have brought this issue into sharp focus as a rising interest burden and government deficits have heralded a burgeoning fiscal crisis. The government has failed to shape a fiscal policy consistent with development objectives and with the fiscal potential. A notable area of failure is the continuing low level of resource mobilization from the rural sector. There are several aspects to this lacuna: practically non-existent direct taxation of agricultural surpluses, failure to recover costs on publicly-provided inputs, the growth of production subsidies, substantial output price supports (as noted above), and lack of systematic attempts to mobilize underutilized rural labour to create investments.

The distribution of the total tax burden between the rural and urban sectors remains rather unequal. Although the rural sector is estimated to bear between 44 and 50 per cent of all taxes in the country, it pays only 10–11 per cent of its consumption expenditure by way of taxes compared to 34 to 38 per cent for the urban sector (Gupta, 1986). This difference is explained largely by the differential burden of taxes on the rural and urban elite: while the former pay only 20 to 22 per cent of their consumption expenditures in taxes, the latter are estimated to pay between 71 and 87 per cent of theirs. More glaring is the virtual absence of direct taxes on rural incomes and wealth which have

[19]Hayami, Subbarao, and Otsuka (1982) provide analytical support for these arguments.

actually declined over the four decades of planned development. Thus, the agricultural income tax and land revenue constituted less than 1 per cent of all tax revenues in 1984–5, down from 9 per cent in 1950–1.

The usual explanation for these differences is in terms of the costs of administering rural direct taxes and associated leakages. The proposal for an agricultural holdings tax made by the Raj Committee in 1972 was rejected by the Planning Commission and the states on these grounds. It is readily granted that without a stiff rate of tax and a base elastic with respect to inflation and growth, land taxes may prove to be poor revenue raisers because administrative costs tend to be indivisible and large. But administrative obstacles may well camouflage underlying political hurdles to devising an efficient land tax (with high rates on larger holdings and a high exemption limit). These hurdles to effective taxation are no different from the factors that have scuttled land reforms.

Besides, short of radical land reforms including effective land ceilings, a relatively low-cost alternative to direct taxes on land rents and agricultural profits already exists in the form of the government's procurement system. Although this was devised to feed the public distribution system and to assure stable farm prices, its potential as a *tax* instrument has been largely ignored by planners. By keeping procurement prices low enough, revenues can be raised roughly in proportion to the marketable surplus produced. In practice, far from serving as a means of taxation, it has served as another potent instrument to subsidize the rich.

At constant prices, subsidies for agricultural and rural development rose from Rs 1000 crores in 1974–5 to Rs 2500 crores in 1980–1 (Subbarao, 1984). It is no coincidence that this period witnessed rising food stocks and, to a lesser extent, falling prices and profitability in the better-endowed states. The composition of these subsidies shifted away from irrigation, electricity, and fertilizers (the share of which fell from 75 per cent to 40 per cent) to anti-poverty measures which accounted for 28 per cent of the total in 1980–1. The bulk of these subsidies, together with the effective subsidy from the output side via pricing and stock policies, accrues to the more prosperous states and rich farmers, although anti-poverty expenditures do broadly correspond with the incidence of poverty across states.

Agricultural *input subsidies* (irrigation, credit, electricity, and fertilizers) during the eighties averaged about 17 per cent of agricultural GDP with irrigation accounting for the lion's share (71.6 per cent, credit 11.8 per cent, electricity 8.9 per cent, and fertilizers 7.7 per cent (Gulati, 1989). Most of these subsidies are directly related to the holdings of land and other productive assets so that their impact is as regressive as the wealth distribution is unequal. It is clear that policy decisions sustain these regressive subsidies: low interest rates and rates of recovery characterize much bank lending in agriculture, electricity charges are lower though costs are decidedly higher in rural areas, and fertilizers are subsidized even where their use is not contingent upon the subsidy (Dobbs and Foster, 1972; and Desai, 1982). Water rates are set too low to recover even operational costs, let alone capital expenditures. A lack of decentralization is to be blamed for the low recovery rates.

Failure to mobilize rural resources directly via the fiscal apparatus or indirectly via price policy must ultimately hurt the government's ability to invest in the public goods and infrastructure so critical to agricultural growth. There can be little doubt that infrastructure building-and-maintenance is the crucial motor force in India's rural and agricultural development. Rural electrification, exploitation of water resources, development of transport systems, agricultural research and extension, not to mention the development of rural health and education systems, directly contribute to the growth of production. Many of these also serve to raise living standards directly. Given the framework of private property agriculture and a highly centralized administrative apparatus, their development makes the toughest demands on long-term planning and collective resources. This has been compounded in recent years by a growing threat to the environment. Protecting the environment itself calls for increased investment and difficult choices in the design of rural development.

Recent experience tends to confirm the above-stated expectation. There has been a substantial relative, and even absolute, decline in real agricultural investment in the Sixth and Seventh Plans. The compound annual rate of growth of total (public plus private) gross capital formation in agriculture rose from 3.7 per cent in the fifties to 6.3 per cent in the sixties; it then fell to 5.9 per cent in the seventies. During the eighties, capital formation in agriculture has *declined* at the rate of 2.6 per cent per annum (till 1987–8). Investment relative to the sector's GDP was 6 per cent in the early sixties rising to 8 per cent in the early seventies and peaking at 14 per cent in 1979–80; thereafter, it has fallen persistently reaching a level of about 8 per cent in the 1984–7 period. The recent decline has occurred in both the private and public components. However, public *expenditures* (on revenue and capital accounts) on agriculture relative to its GDP has risen along a trend from 3–4 per cent in the early seventies to over 12 per cent in the 1986–8 triennium: the proportion of maintenance expenditures plus wages and salaries has risen from only 44 per cent of the total to 70 per cent by 1988–9 (Shetty, 1990). Not surprisingly, the growth of irrigation, beyond its exploitation in the favoured regions, has slowed down.

The reasons for the recent trend are not far to seek: (1) the growth of subsidies and expenditures on poverty alleviation programmes has shifted the composition of expenditures away from capital formation; (2) public investment has been hurt by the fiscal squeeze; (3) private investment has been held back on account of the slowing down of complementary public investment; and (4) both public and private investments have responded to the sluggish growth of demand and continuing dim prospects. But the deceleration in investment may well be self-reinforcing as the growth of food demand is itself a function of the growth of agricultural output and employment.

D. Macroeconomics, Politics and Sector Policy

A major link between inequality and growth operates via the *macroeconomic* process—a link we have seen is central to the structuralist vision but entirely absent in the neo-classical approach. Inequality influences the growth rate from both the demand and supply sides: the supply of savings is an increasing function of inequality while the demand for investment depends on profitability (which in turn increases with aggregate demand which is an inverse function of inequality). In a poor country such as India, demand from the rural sectors constitutes a major part of the demand facing non-agricultural sectors (Rangarajan, 1982). Hence, the presumption has been that high rates of agricultural growth and labour absorption will produce rapid overall growth. At the same time, faster output and employment growth in non-agriculture not only raises food demand but also creates the fiscal revenues needed to finance public investment for agricultural growth.

This mutual complementarity between the sectors is stronger the greater is the spread of employment opportunities and income growth (Rao, 1987). Equitable growth also limits the growth of subsidies, whether these are used to shore up the excessive profit expectations of producers in developed regions or to provide ameliorative doles to the groups left behind.

In view of these inter-connections, it is inappropriate to assess agricultural performance in terms of the strength of mutually exclusive conditions of demand and supply. Thus, the sixties saw an especial concern with supply problems while the subsequent growth of food stocks has been taken either to mean that the supply problem has vanished or that a demand problem has taken its place. Theoretically too, the problem of slow growth has beeen viewed in terms *either* of deficient aggregate demand (Nayyar, 1978) *or* of an agricultural supply constraint. A more general understanding of the macro growth process obtains when these constraints are recognized as working jointly and in *mutually reinforcing* ways. A more equitable growth of supply engenders a stronger growth of demand while a high level of demand creates the resources needed for a matching growth of supply. The slow and uneven growth of demand and supply in India reflect, at least in part, the uneven distribution of the gains from growth, across classes and regions, as pointed out earlier.

It appears that there has been a decline in the growth-stimulating effect of agriculture over the years: the elasticity of manufacturing GDP with respect to agricultural GDP has fallen from 2.2 in the fifties to 1.8 during the eighties (Chakravarty, 1987). This may be explained, in the first instance, by the growing input and import intensity of agriculture and by the growing weight in manufacturing output of durables which are more capital and import intensive. But underlying both observations is the role of income distribution and the sources of demand. The weight of agriculture for general economic growth must necessarily appear lesss significant so long as agricultural growth itself fails to spread purchasing power and fuel mass demand. Indicators of the latter include the slow growth of mass consumption, especially real food expenditures. Slow growth has also exacerbated fiscal difficulties, limited infrastructure-investment programmes, and limited the inducement to invest in both industry and agriculture.

Over the past decade, the rise of agrarian protests, organized by the rich peasants and landlords but frequently joined by a wider segment of the rural population, has been a significant new political development. Higher agricultural prices and continued subsidies have been their principal demand. These protests gathered steam, somewhat paradoxically, just when the FCI was rapidly accumulating foodgrain stocks and supporting agricultural prices. There can be no doubt that the principal effect of this action was to ensure a collapse of grain prices from occurring. And the protests must be explained by the fear of surplus producers that without continuing political pressure on the government, the policy would not be sustained. Political scientists may debate the efficacy[20] of the farm lobby in the past and its durability in the future. But it is impossible to ignore the dilemma faced by the government in pursuing long-term policy for agricultural growth. Governments, it should be recognized, are much more under pressure to assure short-term profitability than long-term growth, especially if the latter threatens long-run profitability. Without policies to sustain food demand, it becomes increasingly costly or even impossible to step up the growth rate and, at the same time, placate the farm lobby.

The more general point here is that state policy is severely circumscribed by class interests and the process of uneven development. While possibilities for raising both growth and real wages in a non-inflationary manner exist, their realization requires raising public investment and allowing food prices to fall, policies that may be opposed by rentiers both inside and outside the state apparatus. Policy instruments to promote growth that take the existing fiscal, agrarian, and state structures as given are limited by the political (class) compromises which preserve these structures in the first place. When the compromises become increasingly costly to enforce or are perceived to have been reneged upon, aggrieved groups threaten social and political disruption.

The pressure to maintain profitability in the face of rising capital–output ratios in the advanced regions has been a central factor inhibiting a more progressive price policy. Political imperatives, rather than

[20]While it is true that price/cost margins have not been raised in the face of these protests, this should not be taken to be an index of their failure Rather, the more astonishing fact is that these margins have not fallen as they might have, had government support not been there. On the other hand, the costs of this support are high indeed: mounting food and fertilizer subsidies, substantial losses in stock-holdings, and the embarrassment of mounting stocks despite mass underconsumption.

any compelling concern about maintaining prices as economic incentives underlie this pressure. The concentration of marketed surplus in a few states (Punjab alone contributes about one half of the annual procurement of foodgrains by the government and 80 per cent together with Haryana and Uttar Pradesh) has risen substantially. Whereas in an earlier period, betting on the better-off regions had been rationalized as a way of rapidly raising the marketed surplus and perhaps reinforced by a fear that peasant producers would be unreliable and reluctant suppliers of their output to the market, experience since has shown that the reluctance of capitalist farmers has been no less and the costs (to poorer consumers and producers) far from negligible. Additional Plan funds are diverted to such subsidies in the advanced states while a growing share of funds also has to be earmarked to counter the backwash effects on poverty in the rest of the country. The result is that a smaller amount of funds is available for financing long-term growth investment in the backward areas.

REFERENCES

ADELMAN, I. (1984), Beyond export-led growth, *World Development*, 12, 937–49.

BALE, M.D. and E.L. LUTZ (1981), Price distortions in agriculture: an international comparison, *American Journal of Agricultural Economics*, 63, 8–22.

BANDYOPADHYAYA, N. (1988), The story of land refoms in Indian planning, in A.K. Bagchi, ed., *Economy, Society and Polity: Essays in the Political Economy of Indian Planning*, Oxford University Press, New Delhi.

BINSWANGER, H. and P. SCANDIZZO (1983), Patterns of agricultural protection, World Bank Discussion Paper ARU 15, Washington DC.

BIRD, R.M. (1974), *Taxing Agricultural Land in Developing Countries*, Harvard University Press, Cambridge, Massachusetts.

BYRES, T.J. (1979), Of neo-populist pipe-dreams: Daedalus in the Third World and the myth of urban-bias, *Journal of Peasant Studies*, 6, 210–44.

CHAKRAVARTY, S. (1987), *Development Planning: The Indian Experience*, Clarendon Press, Oxford.

DANDEKAR, V.M. (1986), Agriculture, employment and poverty, Paper presented at the Conference on the Indian Economy, Boston.

DAVID, C.C. (1984), *Economic Policies towards Philippine Agriculture*, Philippine Institute of Development Studies.

DE JANVRY, A. and K. SUBBARAO (1986), *Agricultural Price Policy and Income Distribution in India*, Oxford University Press, New Delhi.

DE JANVRY, A. and E. SADOULET (1987), The conditions for compatibility between aid and trade in agriculture, Unpublished paper, University of California, Berkeley.

DESAI, G.M. (1982), Sustaining rapid growth in India's fertilizer consumption: a perspective based on composition of use, Research Report No. 31, International Food Policy Research Institute, Washington DC.

DOBBS, T. and P. FOSTER (1972), Incentives to invest in new agricultural inputs in northern India, *Economic Development and Cultural Change*, 21, 101–17.

EICHER, C.K. (1982), Facing up to Africa's food crisis, *Foreign Affairs*, Fall, 151–74.

——— (1983), West Africa's agrarian crisis, Paper prepared for the Fifth Bi-Annual Conference of the West African Association of Agricultural Economists, Abidjan, December 7–11.

ELLMAN, M. (1975), Did the agricultural surplus provide the resources for the increase in investment in the USSR during the First Five Year Plan?, *Economic Journal*, 85, 844–64.

Food and Agricultural Organization (1985), *Agricultural Price Policies*, Paper presented to the 23rd FAO Conference, Rome.

GRIFFIN, KEITH (1987), *World Hunger and the World Economy*, Holmes and Meier, New York.

GULATI, A. (1987), Effective protection and subsidies in Indian agriculture—case of wheat and rice, *Indian Journal of Agricultural Economics*, 42, 561–77.

——— (1989), Input subsidies in Indian agriculture: a statewise analysis, *Economic and Political Weekly*, 24, A57–A65.

GUPTA, A. (1986), Taxation and subsidies, in M.L. Dantwala et al., *Indian Agricultural Development Since Independence*, Oxford and IBH, New Delhi.

HAYAMI, Y. and M. KIKUCHI (1978), Inducements to public infrastructure: irrigation in the Philippines, *Australian Journal of Agricultural Economics*.

HAYAMI, Y., K. SUBBARAO, and K. OTSUKA (1982), Efficiency and equity in the producer levy of India, *American Journal of Agricultural Economics*, 64, 655–63.

JABARA, C.L. and R.L. THOMPSON (1980), Agricultural comparative advantage under international price uncertainty: the case of Senegal, *American Journal of Agricultural Economics*, 62, 188–98.

KAHLON, A.S. and D.S. TYAGI (1980), Inter-sectoral terms of trade, *Economic and Political Weekly*, 15.

KRISHNA, RAJ (1982), Some aspects of agricultural growth, price policy and equity in developing countries, *Food Research Institute Studies*, 18, 219–60.

KRISHNAJI, N. (1984), The demand constraint: a note on role of foodgrain prices and income inequality, *Economic and Political Weekly*, 19, 1261–6.

——— (1988), Foodgrain stocks and prices, in A.K. Bagchi, ed., *Economy, Society and Polity: Essays in the Political Economy of Indian Planning*, Oxford University Press, New Delhi.

LEE, R.H. (1979), *Intersectoral Capital Flows in the Economic Development of Taiwan, 1895–1960*, Cornell University Press, Ithaca.

LEWIS, S.R. (1973), Agricultural taxation and inter-sectoral resource transfers, *Food Research Institute Studies*, 12, 93–114.

MELLOR, J. and B. JOHNSTON (1984), The world food equation: interrelations among development, employment and food consumption, *Journal of Economic Literature*, 22, 531–74.

MITRA, A. (1977), *Terms of Trade and Class Relations*, Frank Cass, London.

MODY, A., S. MUNDLE, and K.N. RAJ (1982), Resource flows from agriculture and industrialization: a comparative analysis of Japanese and Indian experiences, International Development Center of Japan, Tokyo.

NAYYAR, D. (1978), Industrial development in India: some reflections on growth and stagnation, *Economic and Political Weekly*, 13, 1265–78.

PETERSON, W.L. (1979), International farm prices and the social cost of cheap food policies, *American Journal of Agricultural Economics*, 59, 12–21.

QUISUMBING, A.R. and L. TAYLOR (1985), Resource transfers from agriculture, unpublished paper, Massachusetts Institute of Technology, Cambridge, Massachusetts.

RANGARAJAN, C. (1982), Agricultural growth and industrial performance in India, International Food Policy Research Institute, Research Report No. 33, Washington DC.

RANIS, S. (1988), Analytics of development: dualism, in H. Chenery and T.N. Srinivasan, eds., *Handbook of Development Economics*, North-Holland, Amsterdam.

RAO, J.M. (1987), Distribution and growth with an infrastructure constraint, unpublished paper, University of Massachusetts, Amherst.

———— (1989), Getting agricultural prices right, *Food Policy*.

RAO, J.M. and J.M. CABALLERO (1990), Agricultural performance and development strategy: retrospect and prospect, *World Development*, 18, 899–913.

RAO, V.K.R.V. (1983), *India's National Income, 1950–1980*, Sage Publications, New Delhi.

SARMA, J.S., S. ROY, and P.S. GEORGE (1979), Two analyses of Indian foodgrain production and consumption data, Research Report 12, International Food Policy Research Institute, Washington DC.

SCHULTZ, T.W. (1978), Introduction, in T.W. Schultz, ed., *Distortions of Agricultural Incentives*, Indiana University Press, Bloomington.

SCRIMSHAW, N.S. and L. TAYLOR (1980), Food, *Scientific American*, September, 78–88.

SHARPLEY, J. (1979), Intersectoral Capital Flows: Evidence from Kenya, *Journal of Development Economics*, 7, 557–71.

SHETTY, S.L. (1990), Investment in agriculture: brief review of recent trends, *Economic and Political Weekly*, 25, 389–98.

SPRAOS, J. (1980), The statistical debate on the net barter terms of trade between primary commodities and manufactures, *Economic Journal*, 90, 107–27.

SUBBARAO, K. (1984), Incentive policies and India's agricultural development: some apects of regional and social equity, Paper prepared for the Institute of Economic Growth Silver Jubilee Seminar, Delhi.

TAYLOR, LANCE (1983), *Structuralist Macroeconomics*, Basic Books, New York.

THAMARAJAKSHI, R. (1977), Price incentives and agricultural production, in D. Ensminger, ed., *Food Enough for Starving Millions*, Tata McGraw-Hill, New Delhi.

TIMMER, C.P. (1988), The agricultural transformation, in H. Chenery and T. N. Srinivasan, eds., *Handbook of Development Economics*, North-Holland, Amsterdam.

WORLD BANK (1982), *World Development Report*, Oxford University Press, New York.

Name Index

Subject Index

absolute ground rent 182, 183, 194
African countries 207, 225
administered
  food markets 230–3
  prices 231
adverse selection models 110–13, 119–22, 125
aggregate demand constraints 225
agrarian
  relations 1, 3, 12–14, 57–60, 160–3
  class differentiations 198–201
  structure, reforms in 1, 38–9, 60, 62
  transformation 206
agriculture
  and industry 204–5
  oriented strategy 221
  policy discrimination against 214
  relative stagnation in 95
  role of 202, 203, 204–5
agricultural
  cooperatives 60–1
  credit 118
  growth 18–19, 93, 220, 235; benefits of 221; constraints on 221; determinants of 26–39; sources of 21–6
  improvement 169–74, variations in 19–20, 28–30, 34–5
  prices 65–8, 209, 222, 223, 231, 232; relative 211, 229
  productivity *see* agricultural yield
  programmes 50–2
  research 31–2, 50–1, 53, 112, 222
  supply constraint 237
  taxation 169, 205, 206, 213, 223, 228, 233
  terms of trade *see* terms of trade, agricultural
  yield 30–9

Agricultural Price Commission 37, 65, 231
area expansion 20, 23, 26–7
Asian countries 94–5, 220; *also see* South Asian countries, East Asian countries
asymmetric information 105–7, 119

balanced growth 205, 206–10, 220–7
bargaining 110–17
barriers-to-investment 184
bandhua mazdoor 159
beej-khad loan 179
biochemical
  inputs 53–6
  technology 20
Bhaduri and Basu (BB) model 141
Bhaduri model 7, 183–4
bonded labour 78, 82, 87, 131–2, as collateral 140
border prices 212, 217
British agriculture 172

capital
  accumulation 202
  classical concept of 171
  formation in agriculture 235
  from agricultural sector 211
capitalism 75–6
capitalist
  farmers 176, 177
  investment 194
  leasing *see* hunger leasing
  production 83–6, 171, 174; efficiency of 181
  tenant 189, 191–3
Chayanov–Cheung framework 166–7
China 226